GIVE US A KING!

GIVE US A KING!

SAMUEL, SAUL, *and* DAVID

A new translation of Samuel I and II
with an introduction and notes by

EVERETT FOX

Paintings, etchings, and drawings by
SCHWEBEL

SCHOCKEN BOOKS
NEW YORK

Dedicated to
Maurice Kleiman (1910-1998)
and
Ada Kleiman
among those most-at-peace, most-trusted in Israel
(II Sam. 20:19)

Library of Congress Cataloging-in-Publication Data

Bible. O.T. Samuel. English. Fox. 1999.
    Give us a king! : Samuel, Saul, and David : a new translation of
Samuel I and II / with an introduction and notes by Everett Fox.
    p.   cm.
Includes bibliographical references.
ISBN 0-8052-4160-4
I. Fox, Everett. II. Title.
BS 1323.F68   1999
222'.405209—dc21   99-23959
                                                                  CIP

Random House Web Address: www.randomhouse.com

Book design by Johanna Roebas

Maps designed by Jeffrey L. Ward

Printed in the United States of America
First Edition
9 8 7 6 5 4 3 2 1

CONTENTS

CONTENTS

$\mathcal{A}$CKNOWLEDGMENTS

I SHOULD LIKE FIRST TO EXPRESS my special thanks to Michelle Kwitkin-Close, whose meticulous reading of I Samuel and several chapters of II Samuel was of inestimable help to me. I have adopted many of her suggestions, and she has both kept me from errors and faithfully reminded me (in detail) of the inner connections of this volume with my earlier one. The final form of the text is, of course, my responsibility alone.

For their ongoing support and much more, I am grateful to my wife, Rabbi Cherie Koller-Fox; my colleague, Professor Ed Greenstein; my editor, Arthur H. Samuelson, and Jennifer Turvey, editorial assistant at Schocken Books.

I am particularly happy to see Schwebel's illustrations accompanying my text. Through his vigorous art and friendship, he has helped me to approach the Samuel material in ways I could not have imagined previously.

As always, I am grateful to my colleagues in the Department of

Foreign Languages and Literatures at Clark University, for providing stimulation in many areas that I have been able to integrate into my work. I have particularly profited from conversations and team teaching with Professors Paul Burke and Michael Spingler. The Allen M. Glick Chair in Judaic and Biblical Studies at Clark was most helpful in defraying computer, book, and other research costs, as well as providing travel to a number of specialized academic conferences.

Finally, I would like to express my gratitude to the many readers of *The Five Books of Moses,* thoughtful in more than one way, who have taken the time to contact me with their reactions. Their patient and often profound engagement with the Hebrew Bible is heartening, especially in an age of watered-down mass culture and the "quick fix." Their encouragement has made it possible for me to continue the work of translation.

TRANSLATOR'S PREFACE

THIS TRANSLATION, like my previous *The Five Books of Moses* (Schocken, 1995), continues in a tradition. It owes its inspiration to the singular German rendition of the Bible undertaken by Martin Buber (1878–1965) and Franz Rosenzweig (1886–1929) beginning in the 1920s. Their work was based on the premise that *hearing* the Hebrew text of the Bible is as important as *reading* it. For although biblical society apparently knew and practiced writing, it seems to have thought of written texts in a fundamentally aural way; writing did not mean the death of the oral storyteller's art, but merely served to expand it. So in the Buber-Rosenzweig mode, the reader of the Bible should ideally recite the text aloud, allowing himself or herself to be led by its sound rather than presupposing what is to be found there. While it will never be possible, for many reasons, to reconstruct the precise impact that the text had upon ancient audiences, we can nevertheless make the effort to echo, more than has often been done by previous translations, the rich means through which the Hebrew Bible speaks.

In practical terms, this requires a translation that encourages the reader/listener to pay particular attention to the text's aural characteristics: its structures, its plays on names and other words, and its use of repetition. Accordingly this volume bears a close resemblance to *The Five Books of Moses*. First, it lays out the book in lines resembling free verse. These are based on my hearing of the text, and often follow the phrase markings of the traditional "Masoretic" Hebrew text. They are designed to move the reader away from the customary paragraph format, and reflect my belief, shared by others, that biblical prose shows some oral influence, as well as lying on the continuum between what we ordinarily call prose and what we designate as poetry.

Second, I have given the Hebrew versions (in modern pronunciation) of proper names—Shemu'el for Samuel, Sha'ul for Saul, Avshalom for Absalom—in the interest of indicating the importance of sound for the text. Most of these names in Samuel contain or generate puns, which in the Bible are generally used not humorously but to underscore a point. Various possibilities are duly noted in the notes and section introductions.

Third, the book makes full use of Buber's concept of "leading words," through which major themes in the text are suggested by repetitions of a word or word-stem throughout a text. This technique, which is so often lost in translators' attempts to be idiomatic, is illustrated in the second part of the Introduction below, and on several occasions in the section introductions. It means that this book can be profitably used in teaching and studying, and not just as a rough guide to what appears in Samuel.

Art and artifice are not the translator's only concerns. A special word needs to be said about the text under consideration. While most translators use as their primary text the Hebrew "Leningrad Codex," an early eleventh century C. E. manuscript in the mainstream (Rabbinic) Jewish Masoretic tradition, they are confronted with a particular challenge in regard to the book of Samuel. The Hebrew text is in very difficult condition. We are forced to rely for help on translations of Samuel in various ancient Greek Septuagint manuscripts, as well as the 10 percent or so of Samuel that survives in the published Qumran (Dead Sea) Hebrew fragments (and the fuller, unpublished Qumran Samuel scroll). In the Masoretic version, there are words missing (cf. I Sam. 13:1, "Sha'ul was _____ years old at his becoming-king . . ."), some incomprehensible constructions, spelling variants, ("Aviner . . . Avner"), and extra words (cf. "the name, the name" in II Sam. 6:2). A frequent occurrence is the problem of haplography, the scribal error through which words or even lines are omitted because of the eye striking similar letter sequences in close proximity.

In the light of these problems, the translator has the unhappy task of deciding what kind of text to present to the reader. One route is to basically accept the Masoretic version as the working one, with notes (the solution of JPS); another, to make some alterations on the basis of ancient readings and manuscripts, while trying to preserve in the main the Masoretic reading; and a third, to make wholesale changes largely on the basis of the Septuagint, trying to restore what may have been a better text (the solution adopted by McCarter). I have tentatively opted for the second approach, on the grounds that full restoration of an "original text" cannot be done with certainty. But ancient readings should not be ignored, and when they can lead the poor reader out of a thorny text they may be helpful—provided that they are restoring what has been lost rather than filling in by conjecture. Often it is difficult to determine which is which.

Why should the text of Samuel in particular be in such poor shape? It is tempting to speculate that scribes in late antiquity may have been put off by the book's ambiguous if not negative portrayal of David, especially if they had hopes (however distant) of an eventual restoration of David's line. More likely is the fact that a revisionist history, the book of Chronicles, had entered the biblical corpus, and that its glorification of David was deemed to have replaced Samuel's more complex view. Chronicles' portrait of David certainly became the dominant one in both classical Judaism and Christianity. Then too, unlike the Five Books of Moses, the "Five Scrolls" (Song of Songs, Ruth, Lamentations, Ecclesiastes, and Esther), and Jonah, which came to play a central role in synagogue reading during the Jewish year, Samuel, except for the use of a few brief excerpts as prophetic readings *(haftarot),* acquired no such role, and hence was not studied as closely over the ages.

The technical apparatus in this volume differs slightly from what I presented in *The Five Books of Moses.* In order to allow the reader to experience the text itself more fully, I have not treated the complicated questions of historicity or the text's development here, but have instead chosen to limit my commentary to short section introductions. Thus I have tried to be suggestive rather than comprehensive. Similarly, in the notes I have concentrated on trying to clarify difficulties in the text, geographic locations, and plays on words, as well as pointing to some literary motifs and interconnections, but have not sought to raise all the pertinent scholarly issues (for instance, tracing the hand of later editors). At the same time, in the interests of greater comprehension, I have included two maps at the beginning of the book, to help place the frequent references in Samuel to sites inside and outside the land of Israel. Israel's varied topography plays an important role in biblical stories and poems, so the reader should consult the maps freely. Then, too, the sections into which the book has been divided are for the sake of convenience only; in manuscripts the text has no such divisions, any more than it has chapter or verse numbers. Finally, the *Suggestions for Further Reading* give only a hint at the immense and stimulating literature on Samuel that exists in English alone. All of this material will be expanded in my forthcoming *The Early Prophets,* which includes the books of Joshua, Judges, and Kings as well as Samuel.

A special feature of this book is the illustrations by the American-Israeli artist Schwebel. Their appearance here is not merely adjunct. I was introduced to Schwebel and his art in the summer of 1996; he was at the time close to finishing his monumental series of paintings and etchings on material in Samuel and Kings, which was published in Israel the following year under the title *David.* It is a unique body of work. Like all great commentaries on the text, it moves back and forth between the past and the present; some pieces appear timeless in background and dress, while many others are set in modern Jerusalem, particularly downtown, in the Judean hills, and even in the

Bronx of Schwebel's youth. The work grew out of the tangled and tragic events of Israel's Lebanon war, but war is not its prominent theme. What makes Schwebel's David series so extraordinary, to my mind, is its emotional power—a power that well matches the impact of the text's own. While it was not the artist's goal to connect with the purely religious dimension of the narrative, he has engaged, in the tradition of classical Western art, with the profound character studies found in Samuel. In his Sha'ul and David, we may find, not "modernizing" portraits, but much of the richness of biblical characters in all their pathos and complexity.

My live encounter with Schwebel's paintings, which in the main are quite large and prominently feature the use of color, had the effect of moving my work on *The Early Prophets* immediately in the direction of Samuel. I was literally compelled to shelve my work on Joshua and Judges to concentrate on this one. For one who had previously received his impetus solely from the aural aspect of the text, this visual development was an unusual one, but it was occasioned by Schwebel's success in underscoring the book of Samuel's intense and deep humanity, and by his engagement with its geographical setting. I am grateful to him for his gift to the text and to me.

Everett Fox
Clark University
Worcester, MA
April 1999
Iyyar 5759

INTRODUCTION

NOT LONG AGO my wife was teaching the book of First Samuel to a thirteen-year-old student. As the two of them read chapter 8, which narrates how the Israelites clamored for a king and how God responded to their request, he looked up at her and said, "I don't see what this has to do with my becoming a computer programmer."

From at least one person's perspective, then, the book of Samuel—for it was a single book in its early written form—is not a book for the turn of the century or the millennium. The balance of the world's people no longer concern themselves with kings or prophets; God is not the determining factor in either foreign or domestic policy in America; and the notion of community, whether cemented by external threat or internal bond, has been reduced considerably from what it once was. In such a world, which seems impossibly distant from eleventh century B.C.E. Palestine, the stories of Samuel, Saul, and David would seem to have lost their currency or their power to grab the imagination.

But the century that has seen the previously unimaginable advances in science and technology that have absorbed our budding computer programmer's attention has also been filled with over-population, exploitation, war, and genocide. It has pushed the great human questions of morality, dignity, and justice to their limits.

The book of Samuel is concerned with what are perhaps the two most important problems arising from these issues: those of personal responsibility and leadership. Samuel's narratives center around the choices made by individuals and collectives, leaders and the communities that select them, and around the consequences of those choices. Embedded in the larger collection of stories that stretch from settlement (the books of Joshua and Judges) through monarchy and eventual collapse several hundred years later (Kings), Samuel reflects a people's struggle with what it means to ask for leadership, how the leaders measure up to the task, and how the ideals of a culture fare in that process.

The stage is dramatically set in I Samuel 8. Throughout the pre-ceding book of Judges, the Israelites, an entity living precariously in the central hill country of Palestine, have relied on a charismatic sys-tem for protection against their enemies. Judges presents a series of rulers, appointed by God and possessed of military skills, who time and time again bail their tribal followers out of situations of foreign domination and oppression. But this system of instant heroes who somehow always show up to rescue the people eventually breaks down. The Israelites are unable to sustain what the Bible sees as the rule of God, a form of governance that depends, in Martin Buber's words, on "pure voluntarism," a community's determined effort to realize the ideal society.

The cause of the people's plight, in the view of the books from

Judges through Samuel and Kings, is that they put their trust in fertility gods like Baal and Astarte and abandon their traditional (or at least ideal) reliance on a God of justice. At the end of the last judge's—Samuel's—career, this is what leads the Israelites to make the fateful move of requesting a king, "to lead us" so "that we may be like all the other nations." In response, God comes to Samuel in a vision, saying "they have rejected me": the people, in the name of security and a desire to fit in with the world's definition of success, have put the old standards of justice and right on the back burner. Samuel, speaking to them in God's name, is quick to point out the dangers of what they are requesting. His speech on "the practice of the king" (8:11–18) tells the Israelites what they can expect of such a system. It is built on the repetition of one key word: *take.* Kings will ultimately act in self-interest; they will seek to accumulate, and in that process the older tribal system, which depends for the ordering of society on families and elders, will be disrupted and violated. Samuel's prophecy turns out to be right on target: kingship, coupled with the abandoning or erosion of time-honored traditions, leads in the book to a fratricidal, unjust, and ultimately defeated society.

This view of power is presented through the careers of three major characters—Samuel, Saul, and David. The narrative emphasizes the forbidding tasks with which they are charged, and the result is not encouraging. Samuel is chosen as a prophet in his childhood and fulfills his mission faithfully, only to fail in the obligation of passing the mantle to the next generation. Saul is chosen as Israel's first king and is granted military success, only to see his leadership dissolve into tentativeness, rejection, and paranoia. And finally, David, chosen to found a dynasty "for the ages," is remarkably successful in his public endeavors, only to come perilously close to losing it all through his private actions. Driven from the throne by his own son, he is saved solely by the disobedience and ruthlessness of his subordinate, Joab.

In these dramatic stories, and the complex way in which they are played out, lies the kernel of a concept of what it means to be human and have leaders. Israel, from Judges through Kings, agonizes over the shortcomings of its leaders, men who are called upon to remain true to an ideal (the "covenant" between God and Israel) and who fail again and again to realize it. These books, to be sure, record the leaders' successes, but they are more interested in their failures, and it is in confronting their failures that the reader is empowered to ponder the meaning of responsibility and leadership for our own time. The narratives in Samuel—unlike later, selective retellings in Jewish and Christian tradition such as the biblical book of Chronicles, which present the major characters in a positive and even idealized light—unfold in a way that cautions human beings about the exercise of power and takes offenders to task.

Nowhere is this as clear as in the case of the book's main focus, David. As the character whose name appears more often in the Bible than that of any other human being, and whose story is "its longest continuous story" (Marcus), he occupies a central place in the biblical compilers' world of ideas and images. In David we encounter a leader whose rise and decline are a match for any modern example. As a youngest son and a shepherd, he rises from powerless beginnings; his youth is marked by unparalleled success as soldier and incipient leader; he is loved by women and by Jonathan, the crown prince (who should be his rival); he miraculously escapes death on numerous occasions in his flight from Saul; his path to the throne is enabled by overzealous subordinates, whose bloody deeds on his behalf somehow do not reach as far as their master; and ultimately he is able to unify a tribal society, secure lasting peace, and create a new order based on a triad of dynasty, royal city, and temple. What a success story! Yet at the very moment that worldly success betokens divine and human approval of David, his own actions topple him from the summit. He commits adultery with Bathsheba and has her husband Uriah murdered in II Sam. 11 and is condemned and punished in chap. 12. Immediately a grave series of events follow, rape and murder perpetrated by and among David's own children, that themselves lead to a terrible and costly revolt.

Thus, in broadest perspective, the portrayal of David in Samuel, far from being an idealized hero account, is predominantly one of struggle. It is not even a full biography (see Smith), but is dominated by what Buber rightly characterizes as "two great stories of flight." That is, the Bible's central human character spends more time in running than he does in victory parades or on the throne. By the end of the book David is back in Jerusalem, restored as king—but just barely, and it comes as no shock to the reader when we encounter, in the opening of Kings, a David who is enfeebled in virtually all the areas that he had previously mastered: military leadership, sexual prowess, and decision-making. Only in political ruthlessness does he retain any of his old flair, and that surely cannot be viewed as a virtue.

David's story in Samuel thus illustrates a wider truth: the fate of the Bible's characters is one means through which it confronts the areas of personal responsibility and of leadership's most problematic aspect, the abuse of power. No one in the Bible gets away with anything—not Jacob, the ancestor of Israel, not Moses, the liberator and lawgiver himself, and not even the charismatic and beloved David, much as he is said to "strengthen himself in YHWH his God" (I Sam. 30:6) and despite the fact that he is credited in biblical tradition with writing some of the world's great religious poetry in the Psalms.

The Bible supplies a second answer to the challenge posed by kingly power: the counter-institution known as prophecy. In the biblical world this transcends the popular conception of "prophesy-ing" (prediction), and becomes the most passionate, trenchant form of social criticism. The paradigm of the prophet who, at great risk to his own life, confronts the king, the nobles, and even his own people in the name of the truth, is central to the biblical mind-set. Prophecy's first great exponent is Moses himself. In standing before Pharaoh, Moses sets the tone for all later prophets, who are charged by God with confronting kings in the halls of power.

These great dissenters figure powerfully in the book of Samuel as well. Samuel, who is portrayed in the book as a prophet from childhood, undoes God's choice of Saul as king (I Sam. 13 and 15), and confirms this act of "rejection" from the grave (chap. 28) in the Hebrew Bible's only presentation of a ghost. David, at the height of his temporal power and success (he does not even feel compelled to lead the troops in battle any more), is confronted by the prophet Nathan's deceptively simple parable of the poor man and his lamb and then by his ringing denunciation of the king's double crime of adultery and murder (II Sam. 12). After these confrontations the book receives the only possible positive resolution, from a third prophet, Gad. He announces God's punishment for a further pre-sumption of power: David's taking of a census, a king's exercising God-like control over the lives of his subjects.

This focus in Samuel, which undoubtedly betrays the hand of later prophetic circles in its composition, reflects above all the Bible's great concern with justice. I Sam. 8 makes it clear that,

unchecked, kings will take and not give, that they will look to
expand their power rather than providing for a just society. And this
is borne out by the stories that begin in Samuel and continue
through Kings. Time and again in these texts the people are ill-
served by their kings. In their rush to be like everyone else, the
Israelites are turned toward idolatry, that is, toward what the Bible
regards as misplaced values; they find themselves oppressed by the
upper classes and their tribal way of life threatened by kings; and
they are forced into wars of rebellion against great empires, whose
might they are in the end unable to withstand. The final editors of
this part of the Bible, sitting in exile in sixth century B.C.E. Babylo-
nia, looked back on the entire history of Israelite monarchy and, as
they mourned their losses, understood that there was something
about that early request for a king that was intimately related to
their present plight.

 This understanding of history is not a conventional one. It is not
a list of kings, their battles and building programs, or a series of
essays on economic cause and effect. The modern historian, to be
sure, will find that kingship was undoubtedly useful and even necessary to the survival of ancient Israel (cf. Meyers). In addition, there
are strong ideological influences in the text; there is much in Samuel
that functions as an apology for David, in order to justify the persis-
tence of his dynasty into later times (Brettler 1995). But Samuel's
understanding of history is, in the main, a judgment of leaders and
events by the standards of the biblical covenant. Despite a solid core
of traditions that chronicled support for a dynasty, praise for a city
and a Temple, and, after their destruction, fervent prayers for their
restoration, ancient Jews somehow understood that what matters to
a community in the long run is not power but right. It was this

vision, born of bitter experience and ultimately powerlessness, that perhaps enabled them to survive the experience of exile and return to create and sustain a culture that spawned Judaism, Christianity, and Islam.

And so, in the end, our young computer programmer's question can only be dealt with if we turn the question back to him. He should be asked: What does computer programming have to do with creating the just society? What will you do to ensure the flourishing of a just society? And what will happen to society if it seeks, and finds, leaders who are not just?

I have suggested that the book of Samuel conveys its prophetic message of social and political criticism through the situations experienced by its characters. But it also does so by means of a second aspect of literature: the allusive quality of language. It is here that translation, if done carefully, has much to contribute. I will present only one set of examples to illustrate what I mean.

Robert Polzin, in his brilliant study of Samuel, draws our attention to the way in which a number of both major and minor characters die. Not only are they assassinated or killed in battle, but they frequently lose their heads. Thus David chops off Goliath's head (I 17), Saul is dismembered after his death by the Philistines (I 31), his son Ish-Boshet's head is brought to David for reward (II 4), the rebel Absalom meets his death as a result of his head becoming stuck in a tree, and the head of the rebel Sheba son of Bichri is thrown off the battlements of Abel, effectively ending the last threat to David's throne (II 20). Polzin (1993) sees these deaths as thematically connected, forming an important symbolic clue to the book as a whole:

However clearly we see this *seizing of the head* as stylized imagery for the grasping of kingship, the semantic fullness of "head" here is scarcely exhausted. For from the beginning of his career to the end, David's character zone is intimately connected with the head as a locus of guilt and death. For one thing, David, wittingly or unwittingly, is constantly associated with the contemplated or actual beheading of his enemies. . . . the head [also] functions as the locus of the guilt and sin of David's enemies. . . . the heady bloodshed surrounding David still remains a significant means by which he rose to become "head of the tribes of Israel (I Sam. 15:17) and "head of nations" (II Sam. 22:44).

But it turns out that the head is not the only body part to have interpretive value in Samuel. The heart, too, comes into play, particularly in the memorable cycle of stories that recounts Absalom's rebellion against his father David (II Sam. 13–20). The tone is set already in the opening story, the rape of Absalom's sister Tamar. Amnon, the crown prince, pretends to be ill and requests that his half sister make *levivot,* usually translated as "cakes," for him. The noun occurs four times, and the root appears twice more in verbal form. But as some interpreters have noticed, the homonym *(levav)* means "heart," and the verbal form of *l-v-v* occurs in the Song of Songs (4:9, "You have captured-my-heart" [JPS]). So a word connected with seduction in love poetry is appropriate enough in the mouth of the lovesick Amnon, and on this and other grounds (see notes below) we are justified in translating *levivot* as "heart-shaped-dumplings."

From this opening salvo we are prepared for permutations of the word throughout the story. Absalom, on hearing that Amnon has raped Tamar, counsels his sister not to "take it to heart" (13:20); when the moment is right—Amnon's "heart is merry with wine" (13:28)—Absalom has his henchmen murder Amnon; King David, misled by the resulting outcry into thinking that all of his sons have been killed, is corrected by Jonadab, who informs him that Amnon alone is dead and tells him not to "take it to heart" (13:33); Joab, David's chief of staff, notices that the king's "heart is toward Absalom" (14:1), and reconciliation is therefore necessary; but eventually, of course, Absalom rebels against David, and meets his end at the hand of Joab, who drives three darts "into Absalom's heart" as he swings in "the heart of the oak" (18:14). There are several more idiomatic uses of the word in the story (14:13, 15:10, 16:3, 19:15); but the significant ones occur in 15:6, where Absalom "steals the hearts" of the men of Israel: in 19:8, where Joab urges David to "speak to the hearts" of those same men; and in 19:15, where the king "inclines the heart of the men of Judah" toward him.

This key word, which is usually translated out for idiomatic reasons (JPS variously renders the above examples as "cakes . . . keep in mind . . . merry . . . think . . . mind . . . chest . . . hearts . . . placate . . . hearts, respectively), is probably a "leading word" in Martin Buber's definition, that is, a word used thematically to point to a major message in the narrative. It seems to me that it functions here to highlight the issue of who will exercise leadership over Israel, David or Absalom. In the language of the text, this comes down to who will command the hearts of the people, the king chosen by God or the upstart who has driven his own father out of Jerusalem, and who in words, at least, has sanctioned his murder. By presenting different uses of the leading word, but retaining the sound links between different passages, the text encourages readers themselves to "take to heart" the painful lessons of this narrative, one that begins with a lovesick prince but whose roots lie in another affair of the heart (the David and Bathsheba incident).

Having begun with heads and hearts, we may make a final, broader observation. Samuel is a book that talks about deep and visceral emotions. Characters' feelings are frequently described as "bitter" and their behavior as "rough," and they express extreme "distress" and "upset." But the text is visceral in another, quite literal way. From head to foot (cf. II Sam. 14:25), the human body absorbs a good deal of the book's energy: We move from Absalom's hair—cause of his pride and perhaps of his death—to failing eyes and broken neck (both Eli's); ears (Saul's) are avoided; hearts weaken and are stirred; some hands slacken, while others are ready to close in on David; ribs are pierced in revenge and assassination; feet (Mephiboshet's) are lame; the blind and the lame seek to bar David's takeover of Jerusalem; and, not least, genitalia, notably David's, become the cause not only of personal but also national disaster. The Bible, like other ancient Semitic literatures, frequently makes reference to parts of the body in both its narratives and its poetry, but Samuel uses them to a remarkable degree.

What could be at work in such a literary onslaught of limbs? Polzin's initial observation, that the text is concerned with the "heads" of society, and that this bodes ill for those who keep their heads as well as for those who lose them, is germane here. One is reminded of a passage from Isaiah (1:5–6), in which the prophet tries to convey the all-pervading corruption of Judean society: "Every head is ailing, / And every heart is sick. / From head to foot / No spot is sound: / All bruises, and welts, / And festering sores— / Not pressed out, not bound up, / Not softened with oil" (JPS). I believe that the same imagery is at work in Samuel. This book, conceding to Israel its heroes and its monarchy, nevertheless wishes to suggest the inherent sickness of the Israelite body politic, and does so literally. The request for a king, and its fulfillment, leads to a communal illness, which in the Bible's view can only be purged away in the purifying fires of exile. The Judean community, ruled over by the House of David, cannot survive as a society that is rotten from top to bottom, presided over by morally ailing heads of state.

After all is said and done, we are still left with Samuel's greatest enigma, the figure of David himself. As recent interpreters have pointed out, he is a man whose feelings are often hidden from us, a man who is acclaimed and loved by others (including his readers) but of whom it is never said that he loved anyone (Steussy). How may we reconcile the book's complex portrait of him with what he came to mean to generations of Jews and Christians? David, after all, was already an extremely important and positive symbolic figure in the Bible. Over time he came to stand as the unshakable symbol of God's eternal promise of a political continuity and a holy city that would never disappear. This conviction, for Jews, remained firm even in the face of destruction and exile, and crystallized in the image of "Messiah son of David," a future God-sent king of David's line who, unlike most of the biblical kings, would not fail, and who would usher in a final age of peace and prosperity for all humanity.

For early Christians as well, David naturally was connected with the figure of the Messiah, both as a foreshadowing of Jesus, in the person of the popular ancient symbol of the "shepherd king," and as his ancestor. It is no accident that the Gospel of Matthew, the opening of the New Testament, begins with the phrase, "An account of the genealogy of Jesus the Messiah, the son of David, the son of Abraham" (NRSV). David thus provides the crucial link between Christianity's literary and biological ancestors, the Hebrew Bible and the Jews, and the new community of believers.

Should we write off this posthumous David, beloved paragon of piety, as simply the product of wishful thinking? Or should we dismiss his at times problematic behavior, as portrayed in Samuel, merely as part of a critical tradition that crept its way into an otherwise unblemished account of a glorious past? To go in either direction is to lose the richness of David. It is more likely that Samuel's morally compromised figure of David has been retained by Jews and Christians precisely because of his depth and suitability as a mediator between the human and the divine.

Like most religions, both Judaism and Christianity came to cultivate the concept of human redemption, the idea that human beings are capable of rising beyond their flaws and, through deeds and/or faith, of helping to perfect the world. David, as a man who is sincere but hardly a saint, has through the ages provided a powerful model for repentance. In the Bathsheba episode he immediately and unflinchingly admits his guilt; in the book's final story, where his exercise of royal power (census-taking) leads to a plague among the Israelites, he accepts responsibility and places his fate in God's hands. He emerges from Samuel as a humble and humbled king, who points the way to the possibilities of genuine change.

Then, too, the choice of David as the forerunner and forefather of the Messiah touches upon a fundamental mystery in the Hebrew Bible, the reason for Israel's becoming the "Chosen People." Throughout Genesis, God favors younger sons—Isaac, Jacob, Joseph—over firstborns without explaining why (see Geller). The reader is left to contemplate the mystery of God's preferences, which seem arbitrary; the constant recurrence of the younger son motif undoubtedly reflects a major anxiety in Israelite culture. But it is precisely through the issue of whether David, the archetypal younger son, is a usurper or the true king, that the most vital question is mediated: Are the people of Israel merely a small, helpless band of latecomers on the ancient Near Eastern scene, or are they God's elect? Like the second-born Jacob, from whose God-given name Israel the people derives its own, David and his struggles become absorbed into the "Children of Israel's" national character. Warrior, ascender to kingship, singer of sacred songs, sinner and repenter, a man whose exploits and tribulations are celebrated by the great bards of ancient Israel, the David portrayed in these pages is the very image of ancient Israel's struggle to understand itself. As such, he is at the core of the rich legacy bequeathed to us by the book of Samuel.

On the name of God
and its translation

THE READER WILL IMMEDIATELY NOTICE that the personal name of the biblical God appears in this volume as "YHWH." That is fairly standard scholarly practice, but it does not indicate how the name should be pronounced. I would recommend the use of traditional "the LORD" in reading aloud, but others may wish to follow their own custom. While the visual effect of "YHWH" may be jarring at first, it has the merit of approximating the situation of the Hebrew text as we now have it, and of leaving open the unsolved question of the pronunciation and meaning of God's name. Some explanation is in order.

The name of God has undergone numerous changes in both its writing and translation throughout the history of the Bible. At an early period the correct pronunciation of the name was either lost or deliberately avoided out of a sense of religious awe. Jewish tradition came to vocalize and pronounce the name as "Adonai," that is, "the/my Lord," a usage that has remained in practice since late antiquity. Another euphemism, regularly used among Orthodox Jews today, is "Ha-Shem," literally, "The Name."

Historically, Jewish and Christian translations of the Bible into English have tended to use "Lord," with some exceptions (notably, Moffatt's "The Eternal"). Both old and new attempts to recover the "correct" pronunciation of the Hebrew name have not succeeded; neither the sometimes-heard "Jehovah" nor the standard scholarly "Yahweh" can be conclusively proven correct.

For their part, Buber and Rosenzweig sought to restore some of what they felt was the name's ancient power; early drafts of their Genesis translation reveal a good deal of experimentation in this regard. They finally settled on a radical solution: representing the name by means of capitalized personal pronouns. The use of YOU, HE, HIM, etc., stemmed from their conviction that God's name is not a proper name in the conventional sense, but rather one which evokes his immediate presence. Buber and Rosenzweig—both of whom wrote a great deal about their interpretation (see Buber and Rosenzweig 1994) based it on their reading of Ex. 3:14, a text in which another verbal form of YHWH appears. They translated it as "I will be-there howsoever I will be-there" (i.e., my name is not a magical handle through which I can be conjured up; I am ever-present). For more on this passage, and the name, see my *Five Books of Moses*.

The B-R rendering has its attractiveness in reading aloud, as is demonstrated by recordings of Buber reading his text, but it is on doubtful grounds etymologically. It also introduces an overly male emphasis through its constant use of "HE," an emphasis which is not quite so pronounced in the Hebrew. For these reasons, and out of a desire to reflect the experience of the Hebrew reader, I have followed the practice of transcribing the name as YHWH.

Readers who are uncomfortable with the maleness of God in these texts may wish to substitute "God" for "he" in appropriate passages. While, as a translator, I am committed to reproducing the text as faithfully as I can, it is also true that the ancient Hebrews viewed God as a divinity beyond sexuality, and modern readers as well may see fit to acknowledge this.

GUIDE TO THE PRONUNCIATION
OF HEBREW NAMES

THE PRECISE PRONUNCIATION of biblical Hebrew cannot be determined with certainty. The following guide uses a standard of pronunciation which is close to that of modern Hebrew, and which will serve for the purpose of reading the text aloud.

a (e.g., Gat, Agag, Naval) as in f*a*ther (never as in b*a*t)
ei (e.g., Eili) as the *a* in c*a*pe
i (e.g., David, Tziva, Uriyya) as *ee*
o (e.g., Yehonatan, Ish-Boshet, Hevron) as in st*o*ne (never as in h*o*t)
u (e.g., Sha'ul, Hanun) as in r*u*ler (never as in s*u*n)

When *e* occurs in both syllables of a name (e.g., Shemesh), it is generally pronounced as the *e* in ten. In such cases the first syllable is the accented one; otherwise, generally speaking, Hebrew accents the last syllable.

When *e* is the second letter of a name (e.g., Shemu'el, Shelomo), it is most often pronounced as the *a* in *ago*.

kh (e.g., Akhish, Mikhal) is to be sounded like the *ch* in Johann Sebastian Ba*ch*.

h (e.g., Hanna, Hanun) most often indicates the Hebrew letter *het*, pronounced less heavily than *kh* but not as an English *h*. I have removed the *h* at the end of names such as Hanna to avoid confusion with *het*.

The system for transcribing Hebrew words used in this volume follows the above model rather than standard scholarly practice (e.g., *shofar* rather than *šopār*), to better serve the general reader. For this reason, I also do not distinguish between the Hebrew letters *alef* and *ayin* in transcription, even though technically speaking their pronunciations differ. I have, however, added an apostrophe when the lack of one might lead the reader to mispronounce the word (e.g., Be'er).

Some well-known names in the text have been transcribed in their traditional English spelling. These include Judah (Heb. *Yehuda*), Egypt *(Mitzrayim)*, Israel *(Yisrael)*, and Jordan *(Yarden)*. Otherwise, I have indicated the familiar English forms of names in the notes, under the rubric "Trad. English. . . ."

KEY TO ABBREVIATIONS

The following abbreviations appear in the notes keyed to the text of the translation.

MT: Masoretic text type, a traditional Hebrew text represented by the so-called *Leningrad Codex* (ca. 1000 C.E.), published in *Biblia Hebraica Stuttgartensia (BHS)* (Stuttgart: Deutsche Bibelstiftung, 1977).

LXX: Septuagint, pre-Christian Greek translation of the Hebrew Bible, existing in several manuscripts.

4QS[a]: Hebrew manuscript of the book of Samuel discovered at Qumran (Cave IV) near the Dead Sea.

JPS: The New Jewish Publication Society Version (1985).

NRSV: The New Revised Standard Version (1989).

B-R: German translation of the Bible by Martin Buber and Franz Rosenzweig, 1925–1962.

McCARTER: The two volumes of the *Anchor Bible* Samuel; the separate publication years are not cited below, but are found in the "Suggestions for Further Reading" at the end of this book.

KIMHI: David Kimhi, twelfth-thirteenth century Bible commentator and grammarian. He lived in Provence.

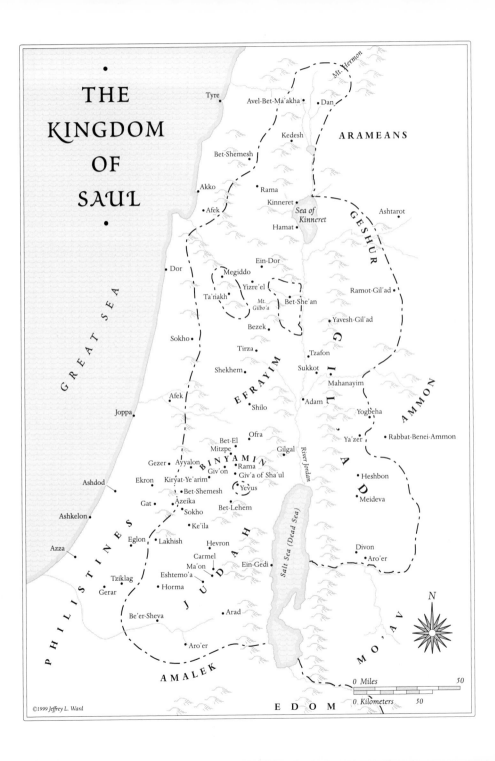

THE
KINGDOM
OF
SAUL

Tyre

Avel-Bet-Ma'akha • Dan

Mt. Hermon

ARAMEANS

Kedesh

Bet-Shemesh

Akko

Rama
Kinneret

Sea of
Kinneret

Ashtarot

GESHUR

Afek

Hamat

Ein-Dor

Dor

Megiddo

Yizre'el

Ramot-Gil'ad

Ta'nakh

Mt.
Gilbo'a

Bet-She'an

Yavesh-Gil'ad

G I L ' A D

Bezek

Sokho

Tirza

Tzafon

Shekhem

Sukkot

Mahanayim

EFRAYIM

Adam

AMMON

Afek

Shilo

Yogbeha

Joppa

Ofra

Ya'zer

Rabbat-Benei-Ammon

Bet-El
Mitzpe

Gilgal

River Jordan

Gezer
Ayyalon

BINYAMIN

Rama

Giv'on

Giv'a of Sha'ul

Heshbon

Ashdod

Ekron

Kiryat-Ye'arim

Yevus

Meideva

Gat

Bet-Shemesh

Azeika

Ashkelon

Sokho

Bet-Lehem

Ke'ila

Azza

Eglon

Lakhish

Hevron

Salt Sea (Dead Sea)

Carmel

Divon

Eshtemo'a

Ma'on

Ein-Gedi

Aro'er

Tziklag

J U D A H

Gerar

Horma

Be'er-Sheva

Arad

P H I L I S T I N E S

Aro'er

M O ' A V

AMALEK

N

EDOM

0 Miles 50

0 Kilometers 50

G R E A T   S E A

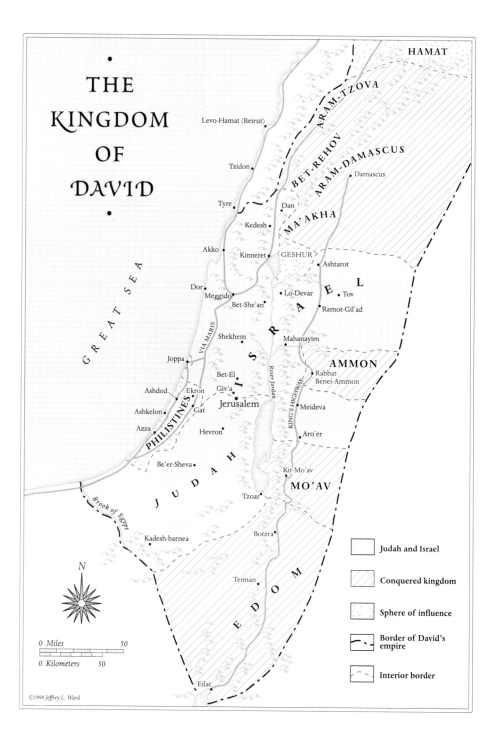

THE KINGDOM OF DAVID

HAMAT

Levo-Hamat (Beirut)

ARAM-TZOVA

BET-REHOV

Tzidon

ARAM-DAMASCUS

Damascus

Tyre

Dan

MA'AKHA

Kedesh

GREAT SEA

Akko

Kinneret

GESHUR

Ashtarot

Dor

Meggido

Lo-Devar

Tov

Bet-She'an

Ramot-Gil'ad

I S R A E L

Shekhem

Mahanayim

VIA MARIS

Joppa

AMMON

Bet-El

Rabbat-
Benei-Ammon

Ashdod

Ekron

Giv'a

Jerusalem

River Jordan

KING'S HIGHWAY

Meideva

Ashkelon

Gat

PHILISTINES

Azza

Hevron

Aro'er

Be'er-Sheva

Kir-Mo'av

J U D A H

Tzoar

MO'AV

Brook of Egypt

Kadesh-barnea

Botzra

N

Teiman

E D O M

0 Miles   50

0 Kilometers   50

Eilat

☐ Judah and Israel

▨ Conquered kingdom

⋮ Sphere of influence

Border of David's
empire

Interior border

©1999 Jeffrey L. Ward

GIVE US A KING!

THE LAST "JUDGES": EILI AND SHEMU'EL (I: 1–7)

The book that introduces the institution of kingship into the Bible begins, appropriately, with a birth. As so often happens in this literature, continuity—here represented by conception—proves to be problematic; but instead of starting with the mere fact of a woman being childless, this book of striking characters presents its first one, Hanna, by imbuing her with considerable depth of feeling and, not surprisingly, a gift for poetry. Women, who throughout both Judges and Samuel provide a profound sounding board for issues of power, here make their voices heard from the very beginning.

It is worth noting, as many (e.g., McCarter, Polzin 1989) have, that Hanna's poem in chapter 2, which is undoubtedly from an independent source, is a prelude to major themes of the book, especially the idea that God, the great Reverser, may choose to exalt the powerless. YHWH, who "brings-low and lifts-up" (v. 7), will be directing the fate of Israel and its early kings, and while he will in the end

3

"give strength to his king" (v. 10), he will also make it clear that "not by might does a man prevail" (v. 9).

The priest-judge Eili, an ineffectual leader, typifies an era that is coming to a close. His first act—mistaking Hanna's deep inner religiosity for drunkenness—sets the tone; he is never talked to directly by God, is incapable of providing the military leadership of his predecessors, and, most tellingly, is unable to control the highly inappropriate behavior of his sons. In this he anticipates his successors, Shemu'el and David. Barely noticeable amid Eili's initial bluster in chapter 1 is a telling detail: that he sits on a "throne" (see Spina). The first part of this section of the book (chaps. 1–4) will end with his death in that very chair, overturned when he hears the disastrous news of the ark's capture. The fall of the House of Eili will be complete, to be superseded by the leadership of his judge-prophet successor.

A central feature of this part of the book, in fact, is the narratives around the ark (here "Coffer"). As the great biblical symbol of the divine presence, its territorial location in these chapters emphasizes the desperate situation in which the Israelites find themselves—or rather, in the eyes of the biblical writer, the situation which they have created. Bereft of God's presence, the people have no chance of either "blessing" or military victory. The Coffer's return, on the other hand, does not provide a full solution as far as they are concerned. That they can envision only in the establishment of a monarchy irrespective of the Coffer. Not until David shows concern about its whereabouts, and brings it to his new capital, Jerusalem, will the kingship be established on a firm footing, with apparent divine approval.

In Shemu'el himself are to be found elements which will characterize some of the central actors of subsequent books, the prophets. Like Jeremiah, he is called by God early in life; like all of the great literary prophets, he is highly critical of monarchy. He functions, as they do, as God's mouthpiece, yet the text eventually finds room for his own emotions, especially in his complex relationship with Sha'ul. This opening section (which covers most of his life!) gives only a passing indication of an inner life; for most of it, the writer seems mainly concerned with establishing Shemu'el's legitimacy. He is the one, in contrast to Eili, who has the vision; he vicariously leads the troops, and it is during his watch that the Coffer returns to Israel; and he functions as the last of the "judges" in his little circuit of central Israelite towns. We will encounter him as a person with deep emotions only in the transitional chapter 8 and what follows.

I *Samuel*

1:1 Now there was a certain man from Ramatayim in Tzofim,
     from the hill-country of Efrayim,
his name was Elkana son of Yeroham son of Elihu son of
     Tohu son of Tzuf, an Efrayimite;

2 now he had two wives
     —the name of the one was Hanna/Grace, and the name of
     the second was Peninna/Pearl,
and Peninna had children, but Hanna had no children.

3 And that man used to go up from his town, from year to year
to prostrate-himself and to slaughter-offer to YHWH of the
     Heavenly-Armies, at Shilo
     —Eili's two sons, Hofni and Pin'has, priests to YHWH, were
     there—.

4 And it was, one day,
     that Elkana was slaughter-offering
     —now he would give to Peninna his wife, and to all her sons
     and daughters, portions,

5 and to Hanna he would give a double portion,

---

1 RAMATAYIM: Possibly Rama (Height), associated with Shemu'el throughout the narratives about him; its location was north of Jerusalem, near the border of what became the Northern Kingdom (Israel).
ELKANA: The name means "God creates."
3 PROSTRATE-HIMSELF: This posture of worship is head to the ground, not merely on the knees.
YHWH OF THE HEAVENLY-ARMIES: This term, occurring well over two hundred times in the Bible, is found for the first time here. Its connection with the Coffer (ark) shows it to be an important name for the biblical God. In this part of the Bible the term has a military ring; *tzeva'ot*, though, can also refer to the "heavenly hosts" (the stars), and so may indicate a wider meaning. This is certainly appropriate for the present passage.
SHILO: Trad. English "Shiloh," one of the important pre-Jerusalem shrines, situated in the hill-country of Efrayim.
EILI: Pronounced "Ay-lee"; trad. English "Eli."

6

for (it was) Hanna (that) he loved,
although Yhwh had closed up her womb.

6 And her rival-wife would vex her with vexation, for the sake of
making-her-complain,
for Yhwh had closed up her womb;

7 and thus was done, year after year:
as often as she would go up to the House of Yhwh, thus would
she vex her.—
. . . and when she wept and would not eat,

8 Elkana her husband said to her:
Hanna, why do you weep? Why don't you eat?
And why is your heart in such ill-humor?
Am I not better to you than ten sons?

9 Hanna arose after eating at Shilo, and after drinking,
—now Eili the priest was sitting on a throne by the doorpost of
the sanctuary of Yhwh—

10 and she was bitter of feelings,
so she prayed to Yhwh, while she began-to-weep, yes, weep.

11 And she vowed a vow, and said:
O Yhwh of the Heavenly-Armies,
if you will see, yes, see the affliction of your maidservant,
and will bear me in mind and not forget your maidservant,
and will give your maidservant seed of men:
then I will give him to Yhwh all the days of his life,
and no razor shall go-up on his head.

---

11 SEE: The preposition used with the verb in Hebrew adds an element of empathy.
I WILL GIVE HIM TO YHWH . . . NO RAZOR: Hanna here makes a commitment similar to the Nazirite laws of Numbers 6, where in fulfillment of a religious vow, a person would not shave (there are other provisions there). Shemu'el thus echoes Shimshon (Samson) before him.

12 Now it was, as she multiplied her praying in the presence of
      Yhwh,
    that Eili was watching her mouth:

13 Hanna was speaking in her heart
    —only her lips were moving, but her voice could not be
      heard—
    so Eili took her for a drunkard.

14 Eili said to her:
    How long will you be intoxicated?
    Put away your wine from off you!

15 But Hanna answered and said:
    No, my lord,
    a woman hardened of spirit am I,
    wine and intoxicant I have not drunk,
    but I have been pouring out my feelings in the presence of
      Yhwh!

16 Don't consider your maidservant as a worthless woman,
    for (it is) out of my great anxiety and vexation (that) I have
      spoken until now.

17 Eili answered and said: Go in peace!
    And may the God of Israel grant your request that you have
      requested of him!

18 She said:
    May your handmaid find favor in your eyes!
    And the woman went on her way, and she ate,
    and her face was no longer (sad).

19 They started-early in the morning:

12 IN THE PRESENCE OF YHWH: The
   phrase usually indicates a sanctuary.
13 TOOK HER FOR A DRUNKARD: Pray-
   ing, as well as reading and writing, was not
   a silent activity in the ancient world, hence
   Eili's error.

they prostrated-themselves in the presence of Y<small>HWH</small>,
then they returned, coming-back to their house in Rama.
And Elkana knew Hanna his wife,
and Y<small>HWH</small> bore her in mind.

20 So it was, at the circuit of days
that Hanna conceived and gave-birth to a son;
she called his name: Shemu'el / The One From God,
meaning: from Y<small>HWH</small> I requested him.

21 Now the man Elkana went up, along with all his household,
to slaughter-offer to Y<small>HWH</small> the yearly slaughter-offering, and
his vow,

22 but Hanna did not go up,
for she said to her husband:
—Until the lad is weaned,
then I will bring him;
once he is seen in the presence of Y<small>HWH</small>,
he is to stay there for the ages.

23 Elkana her husband said to her:
Do whatever is good in your eyes:
stay until you have weaned him,
only: may Y<small>HWH</small> fulfill his word!
So the woman stayed-behind and nursed her son, until she had
weaned him.

24 She brought him up with her, when she had weaned him,

---

20 THE CIRCUIT OF DAYS: Or "of the year,"
namely a year later.
SHEMU'EL: Trad. English "Samuel."
REQUESTED: This verb, *sha'al*, is really
associated with the name of Sha'ul (Saul)
(cf. Verse 28, where "lent-on-request" is
vocalized "*sha'ul*"). While some scholars
are inclined to see a textual confusion here
between two main characters, others
(myself included) find the resulting connection interesting and profound, whatever its
origin. Cf. the discussion in Garsiel 1990.

23 WEANED: At about three years of age or
so.

with a three-year-old bull and an *efa* of flour, and a skin of
    wine,
and brought him to the House of Yhwh at Shilo,
though the lad was (but) a young-lad.

25 They slew the bull,
and then they brought the lad to Eili.

26 She said:
Please, my lord, as you yourself live, my lord:
I am the woman who was standing with you here, to pray to
    Yhwh.

27 (It was) for this lad that I prayed,
and Yhwh has granted my request that I requested of him!

28 So I now lend-him-on-request to Yhwh;
all the days (of his life) he is lent-on-request / *sha'ul* to Yhwh.
And they prostrated-themselves there to Yhwh.

2:1 And Hanna prayed, she said:
My heart swells because of Yhwh,
my horn is raised because of Yhwh;
my mouth is wide-with-boasting over my enemies,
for I rejoice in your deliverance!

2 There is none holy like Yhwh,
indeed, none beside you,
there is no rock like our God!

3 Speak no more so high, so high (and mighty),
letting your mouth run-free,

---

24 *EFA*: A dry measure, perhaps fifteen liters.
THOUGH THE LAD WAS (BUT) A
YOUNG-LAD: The Hebrew is a bit strange;
a LXX version suggests a longer text here
describing the family's pilgrimage.
28 THEY: This is the reading in ancient versions; MT has "he."

for a God all-knowing is YHWH,
by him are actions measured.

4 The bow of the mighty is shattered,
but those-who-stumble are girded with strength.

5 Those once-sated must hire themselves out for bread,
but those once-hungry will endure forever.
The barren-one has given-birth to seven,
while the one (with) many sons is dried-up.

6 YHWH sends-death and sustains-life,
brings-down to She'ol and brings-up.

7 YHWH makes-poor and makes-rich,
brings-low and, yes, lifts-up.

8 He raises the needy from the dust,
he lifts-up the destitute from the dunghill,
to seat (them) with the noble-ones,
and a throne of glory he has them inherit.
For YHWH's are the molten-pillars of the earth,
he has set the world upon them.

9 The feet of his loyal-ones he guards,
but the wicked are silent in darkness—
for not by might does a man prevail.

10 YHWH shatters those-opposing-him,
against (each of) them he thunders from the heavens.
YHWH judges to the limits of the earth;
may he give strength to his king,

---

5 SEVEN: The number of perfection, in the Bible and elsewhere in the ancient Near East.

6 SHE'OL: The biblical underworld. Unlike the later concept of heaven and hell, it appears to be a subdued place where the dead rest (cf. chap. 28 below), similar to the Greek Hades.

10 KING: An anachronism which foreshadows the major concern of the book.

and lift-up the horn of his anointed!

11 And Elkana went to Rama, to his house.

Now the lad began-to-attend upon YHWH, in the presence of
Eili the priest.

12 —Now the sons of Eili were sons of worthlessness,
they did not know YHWH.

13 Now the custom of the priests from the people (was):
When anyone slaughter-offered a slaughter-offering,
the priest's serving-lad would come while the flesh was (still)
boiling
with a fork of three teeth in his hand;

14 he would strike at the pot or the kettle or the cauldron or the
boiler,
(and) everything the fork would bring-up, the priest would
take for himself.
Thus they would do to all Israel who would come there, at
Shilo.

15 (But) even before they would turn the fat into smoke,
the serving-lad of the priest would come and say to the person
doing-the-slaughtering:
Give over (some) flesh for roasting, for the priest,
for he will not take from you boiled flesh, only raw!

16 And (if) the person said to him:
Let them first turn the fat into smoke, yes, smoke,
then take for yourself whatever your appetite craves—
then he would say to him:

---

10 ANOINTED: A synonym for king; the verb
refers to the practice of consecrating someone by pouring oil on his head.
13 FORK: Others, "flesh hook."

No, but give (it) right-now;

if not, I'll take it by force!

17 So the sin of the serving-lads was exceedingly great in the presence of Yhwh,

for the men scorned the gift (intended) for Yhwh.—

18 Now Shemu'el was attending in the presence of Yhwh,

(as) a lad girded with a linen *efod;*

19 his mother used to make him a small cloak

and bring it up from year to year, whenever she went up with her husband to slaughter-offer the yearly slaughter-offering.

20 And Eili would bless Elkana and his wife,

he would say:

May Yhwh give you seed from this woman

in place of the requested-one who was lent-on-request to Yhwh!

And they would go back to their place.

21 And Yhwh took-account of Hanna,

so that she conceived and gave-birth to three sons and two daughters;

but the lad Shemu'el grew up close to Yhwh.

22 Now Eili was exceedingly old,

and when he heard about all that his sons were doing to all Israel,

---

18 *EFOD:* A priestly garment, described in Ex. 28:6ff., which covered the torso.

20 THEIR: So ancient versions; MT has "his."

21 AND: Following 4QS^a; MT has "for."

how they were lying with the women who were acting-as-a-
    workforce at the entrance to the Tent of Appointment,

23 he said to them:
    Why do you act according to these words, which I hear—
    evil accounts of you from all of these people!

24 Don't, my sons!
    Indeed, it is no good, the heard-rumor that I hear YHWH's
      people spreading;

25 if a man sins against (another) man, God will mediate for him,
    but if (it is) against YHWH (that) a man sins, who will intercede
      for him?
    Yet they did not hearken to their father's voice,
    for YHWH desired to have-them-die.

26 Now the lad Shemu'el went on growing greater and more-
      goodly,
    so with YHWH, so with men.

27 A man of God came to Eili and said to him:
    Thus says YHWH:
    Didn't I reveal, yes, reveal myself to your father's house when
      they were in Egypt, (belonging) to Pharaoh's house,

28 and choose them from all the tribes of Israel for myself, to act-
      as-priests:
    to ascend upon my slaughter-site, to send-up smoking-incense,
      to wear the *efod* in my presence?
    And I gave to your father's house all the fire-offerings of the
      Children of Israel.

22 TENT OF APPOINTMENT: A pre-Temple sanctuary, identified here with the one the Israelites carried around in the wilderness after the Exodus.

29 Why have you kicked-away my slaughter-offerings and my
     grain-gifts that I commanded, with a grudging-eye?
   And you have honored your sons (more) than me,
   by letting-them-grow-fat from the premier-part of all the (sac-
     rificial) gifts of Israel, in my presence!

30 Therefore,
   the Utterance of YHWH, God of Israel:
   I had said, yes, said:
   Your house and your father's house will walk in my presence
     for the ages;
   but now, the Utterance of YHWH:
   (Heaven) forbid for me!
   For those who honor me I honor,
   but those who despise me will be cursed!

31 Here, the days are coming
   when I will hew down your arm-strength and the arm-strength
     of your father's house,
   from there being an elder in your house;

32 you will look with a grudging-eye on all the good things (he
     gives) to Israel,
   and there will not be an elder in your house, all the days (to
     come);

33 yet I will not cut off everyone belonging to you from my
     slaughter-offerings,
   (but) to wear out your eyes and exhaust your breath,
   (from) all of the greater-part of your house, men will die.

---

29 THE PREMIER-PART: The part of the sacrifices intended for God.

30 THE UTTERANCE: The usual introduc-
tory formula to a prophetic quotation of
God.

32–33 The text is unclear and difficult to reconstruct.

34 And this is the sign for you that it will happen to your two
   sons, to Hofni and Pin'has:
   on a single day the two of them will die!

35 But I will establish for myself a trusted priest
   who will do (what is) in my heart and in my being;
   I will build him a trustworthy household,
   and he will walk in the presence of my anointed-one all the
   days (to come).

36 And it will be
   that whoever is left in your house:
   he will come to prostrate-himself to him
   for payment of silver and a round-loaf of bread,
   he will say:
   Pray appoint me to one of the priestly-offices,
   in order (for me) to eat a bit of bread!

3:1 Now the lad Shemu'el was attending upon Yhwh in the pres-
    ence of Eili.
    And the word of Yhwh was precious in those days,
    visions were not widespread.

2 And it was on that (particular) day
  that Eili was lying down in his place
  —his eyes had begun to be-dim, so that he was not able to
    see—

3 and the lamp of God had not yet gone-out,

---

35 A TRUSTED PRIEST: Probably referring
   to Tzadok (cf. II Sam. 8:17), whose line
   became the dominant priestly one (cf. the
   discussion in Brettler 1997).

TRUSTWORTHY: Or "secure" (cf. II 7:16)
36 IN ORDER (FOR ME) . . . : Namely, the
   priests will be desperate for food.

16

while Shemu'el was lying down in the sanctuary of YHWH,
    where the Coffer of God was.

4 Now YHWH called to Shemu'el,
and he said:
Here I am.

5 Then he ran to Eili
and said:
Here I am, for you called me.
But he said:
I didn't call you;
return, lie down.
He went and lay down.

6 But YHWH again called Shemu'el,
and Shemu'el arose and went to Eili,
and said:
Here I am, for you called me.
But he said:
I didn't call, my son!
Return, lie down.

7 Now Shemu'el did not yet know YHWH,
not yet had the word of YHWH been revealed to him.

8 And YHWH again called to Shemu'el, a third-time;
he arose and went to Eili
and said:
Here I am, for you called me.
Then Eili understood
that YHWH was calling the lad.

3:3 COFFER: Others, "ark," the chest where the tablets of the Ten Commandments were kept in the center of the Tabernacle, and Israel's most sacred cultic object.

9   Eili said to Shemu'el:

Go, lie down,

and it shall be: if he calls you, you are to say:

Speak, O Yнwн, for your servant hearkens!

So Shemu'el went and lay down in his place.

10   And Yнwн came and took-a-stand

and called as time and time (before): Shemu'el! Shemu'el!

And Shemu'el said: Speak, for your servant hearkens!

11   Yнwн said to Shemu'el:

Here, I am about to do a thing in Israel

such that all who hear of it—their two ears will ring!

12   On that day, I will fulfill upon Eili all that I spoke concerning

his house,

(from) beginning to end!

13   I tell him (now)

that I am passing-judgment on his house, for the ages,

for the iniquity that he has known about,

because his sons were cursing God, yet he did not condemn

them.

14   Therefore I swear concerning the house of Eili:

Should the iniquity of the house of Eili be purged-away

through slaughter-offerings or grain-gifts, for the ages . . . !

15   Shemu'el lay down until daybreak

when they opened the doors of the House of Yнwн,

but Shemu'el was afraid of reporting the seen-vision to Eili.

---

11 RING: The customary "tingle" hardly seems adequate to describe a horrified reaction.

13 CONDEMN: The same Hebrew root in v. 2 (there rendered as "be-dim") refers to Eli's failing eyesight (Fishbane); altogether its use points to Eli's "lack of insight" (Polzin 1989).

14 SHOULD . . . : Namely, the iniquity will *not* be purged-away; the construction implies a curse.

16 And Eili called Shemu'el,
   he said:
   Shemu'el, my son!
   He said:
   Here I am.
17 He said:
   What is the word that he spoke to you?
   Pray don't conceal (it) from me . . .
   Thus may God do to you and thus may he add,
   if you conceal from me (any) word
   from all the words that he spoke to you!
18 So Shemu'el told him all the words, he did not conceal (any-
      thing) from him.
   And he said:
   It is (from) YHWH;
   whatever is good in his eyes, may he do.

19 And Shemu'el grew up, and YHWH was with him
   and did not let any of his words fall to the ground.
20 And all Israel knew, from Dan to Be'er Sheva,
   that Shemu'el was trustworthy as a prophet to YHWH.
21 And YHWH continued to let himself be seen at Shilo,
   for YHWH had revealed himself to Shemu'el at Shilo, according
      to the word of YHWH.
4:1 And the word of Shemu'el was for all Israel. . . .

20 FROM DAN TO BE'ER SHEVA: From north to south. Be'er Sheva is Trad. English "Beersheba."
4:1 The traditional chapter divisions, which are medieval rather than original to the text, do not always fall precisely at the end of a story. In such cases—the present one and nine others (I Sam. 7, 10, 12, 19, 21, and 24, and II Sam. 4, 12, and 19)—I have not skipped a line at the beginning of a new chapter.

Now all Israel went out to meet the Philistines in battle,

they encamped at Even ha-Ezer / The Stone of Help,

while the Philistines encamped at Afek.

2 The Philistines arranged-their-ranks to meet Israel,

and the battle was spread out, so that Israel was smitten before the Philistines—

they struck (them) in ranks in the open-field: about four thousand men.

3 When the people came to the camp, the elders of Israel said:

Why has Yhwh smitten us today before the Philistines?

Let us take for ourselves from Shilo the Coffer of Yhwh's covenant,

that he may come into our midst

and deliver us from the grasp of our enemies!

4 So the people sent to Shilo,

and they carried from there the Coffer of the Covenant of Yhwh of the Heavenly-Armies, (who is) seated (upon) the Winged-Sphinxes

—Eili's two sons were there with the Coffer of God's Covenant, (namely) Hofni and Pin'has.

---

1 PHILISTINES: Israel's great enemy in Judges and Samuel, an eastern Mediterranean people who were part of the late Second Millennium B.C.E. invasion of the "Sea Peoples"; they were repelled by the Egyptians but gained a foothold on the coast of Palestine. Cf. Dotan for a description of relevant archaeological finds. AFEK: Northeast of Joppa, and a customary starting point for Philistine campaigns northward.

3 GRASP: Lit. "palm," often used in Samuel in place of "hand."

4 SEATED (UPON) THE WINGED-SPHINXES: The Coffer serves as a God's footstool, an image found elsewhere in the ancient Near East. The "Winged-Sphinxes" (Heb. *keruvim*), mythical guardians of ancient Near Eastern palaces and temples, are not to be confused with the later image of "cherubim," the chubby little angels of Western art.

5 And it was
when the Coffer of Y<small>HWH</small>'s Covenant came into the camp
that all Israel shouted with a great shout,
so that the land was a-panic.

6 When the Philistines heard the sound of the shouting,
they said:
What is this great sound of shouting in the Hebrews' camp?
Then they knew
that the Coffer of Y<small>HWH</small> had come into the camp.

7 The Philistines were afraid,
for they said (to themselves):
A god has come into the camp!
And they said:
Woe to us,
for it was not like this yesterday and the day-before,

8 woe to us—
who will rescue us from the hand of this mighty god?
This is the (very) god that struck down Egypt with every kind
of striking-down in the wilderness!

9 Strengthen yourselves and act-like-men, O Philistines,
lest you have to serve the Hebrews, as they have served you!
Act-like-men and wage-battle!

10 And the Philistines waged-battle,
and Israel was smitten, so that they fled, each-man to his tent.
The striking-down was exceedingly great:
there fell from Israel thirty thousand foot-soldiers.

11 Now the Coffer of God was taken,

7 YESTERDAY AND THE DAY-BEFORE: A
biblical idiom for "in the past," "recently."

and Eili's two sons died, Hofni and Pin'has.

12 Then there ran a Binyaminite man from the ranks;
    he came to Shilo on that (same) day
    with his uniform torn and earth on his head.

13 When he came, here: Eili was sitting on a throne, beside (the)
        road, waiting-anxiously,
    for his heart was trembling for the Coffer of God.
    Now when the man came to tell about (what had happened),
        in the town,
    the whole town cried out.

14 And when Eili heard the sound of the outcry,
    he said:
    What is this sound of panic?
    And the man hurried, he came and told (the news) to Eili,

15 —Now Eili was ninety-eight years old;
    his eyes were so set that he could not see—

16 the man said to Eili:
    I am the one who comes from the ranks,
    I myself—from the ranks I fled today!
    He said:
    How went the matter, my son?

17 The bringer-of-news answered,
    he said:
    Israel has fled before the Philistines,
    and also there has been a great smiting among the people,

---

12 BINYAMINITE: From the tribe of Bin-
    yamin, trad. English "Benjamin." Their ter-
    ritory was in the center of the country.
    HIS UNIFORM TORN AND EARTH ON
    HIS HEAD: A standard mourning practice
in ancient Israel.
15 NINETY-EIGHT: As with many other bib-
    lical numbers, this one fits a "perfect" pat-
    tern: seven times two-times-seven.

and also your two sons died, Hofni and Pin'has,
while the Coffer of God has been taken!

18 Now it was,
when he made-mention of the Coffer of God,
that he fell from upon the throne backwards, alongside the
gate,
and his neck was broken, so that he died,
for he was an old man, and heavy.
He had led Israel as judge for forty years.

19 Now his daughter-in-law, Pin'has's wife, was pregnant, (about)
to give-birth,
and when she heard the heard-rumor about the taking of the
Coffer of God
and about the death of her father-in-law and her husband,
she crouched and gave-birth,
for her labor-pains had turned upon her.

20 At the time of her dying, those standing over her spoke:
Don't be afraid, for you have given-birth to a son!
But she did not answer, nor did she pay any mind,

21 but she called the lad I-Khavod/Where-is-the-Glory, saying:
Exiled is the glory from Israel!
concerning the taking of the Coffer of God
and concerning her father-in-law and her husband.

22 —She said:
Exiled is the glory from Israel,

18 LED ISRAEL AS JUDGE: As in the Book of Judges, such a person has functions beyond court procedure (especially, and often, military leadership).
FORTY: Another special number, familiar from the Flood and Sinai stories, and used in the previous book, Judges

21 I-KHAVOD: The "I" is pronounced as "ee." Trad. English "Ichabod."

for taken is the Coffer of God!

5:1 Now when the Philistines had taken the Coffer of God,
they had brought it from Even ha-Ezer to Ashdod.

2 and the Philistines took the Coffer of God
and brought it to the House of Dagon,
and set it next to Dagon.

3 When the Ashdodites started-early on the morrow,
here was Dagon, fallen down on his face to the ground
before the Coffer of YHWH!
So they took Dagon and returned him to his place.

4 But when they started-early in the morning, on the morrow,
here was Dagon, fallen down on his face to the ground
before the Coffer of YHWH—
with Dagon's head and the two palms of his hands cut off, on
the threshold;
only (the torso of) Dagon remained on him.

5 —Therefore the priests of Dagon and all who enter the House
of Dagon do not tread on the threshold of Dagon in Ashdod,
until this (very) day.

6 And the hand of YHWH was heavy against the Ashdodites, so
that he devastated them;
he struck them with tumors,

5:1 ASHDOD: One of the five chief Philistine
cities, the others being Ashkelon, Gaza
(Azza), Ekron, and Gath (Gat). All are on
or near the Mediterranean coast.

2 DAGON: A long-worshiped god of the
ancient Near East, here connected with the
Philistines. While no evidence of his worship among them has been found, the

Philistines are known to have adapted
quickly to local cultures.

6 DEVASTATED: Some emend Heb. *sh-m-m*
to *h-m-m*, "panicked," a key word in chapters 4–5.
TUMORS: The written text has "hemor-
rhoids"; scribal tradition has substituted
"tumors" here. These, and the mice-related

Ashdod and its territories.

7 When the men of Ashdod saw that (it was) thus,
   they said:
   The Coffer of the God of Israel must not stay with us,
   for his hand is hard upon us and upon Dagon our god!

8 So they sent and gathered-together all the Philistine overlords
      to them
   and said:
   what are we to do with the Coffer of the God of Israel?
   They said:
   To Gat let the Coffer of the God of Israel be-removed!
   And they had the Coffer of the God of Israel removed (there).

9 But it was, after their removing it,
   that the hand of Yhwh was against the town (in) an exceed-
      ingly great panic,
   he struck the men of the town, from small to great,
   and tumors broke out on them.

10 So they sent off the Coffer of God to Ekron,
   but when the Coffer of God entered Ekron,
   the Ekronites cried out, saying:
   They have removed upon us the Coffer of the God of Israel,
   to cause-our-death and our people's!

11 So they sent and gathered all the Philistine overlords,
   and said:
   Send away the Coffer of the God of Israel, that it may return
      to its place,
   so that it does not cause-our-death and our people's!

---

plague (cf. 6:4), are seen as a further divine curse on the Philistines for their possession of the Coffer.

10–11 TOUR: MT has "my."

11 OVERLORDS: Heb. *seranim,* related to the English word "tyrants" through Greek.

For a death-panic was all throughout the town;
exceedingly heavy was the hand of God there.

12 And the men who did not die were struck with tumors,
and the town's cry-for-help went up to heaven.

6:1 Now the Coffer of YHWH was in the territory of the
Philistines for seven months,

2 and the Philistines called for the priests and for the diviners,
saying:
What are we to do with the Coffer of YHWH?
Let us know how we can send it back to its place!

3 They said:
If you (wish to) send back the Coffer of the God of Israel, do
not send it back empty,
rather, make-restitution, yes, restitution to him (with) a
reparation-offering;
then you will be healed
and it will be made-known to you why his hand has not
turned-aside from you.

4 They said:
What is the reparation-offering by which we are to make-
restitution to him?
They said:
(By) the number of Philistine overlords:
five gold tumors and five gold mice,
for one plague was upon all (of you) and upon your overlords.

6:1 FOR SEVEN MONTHS: LXX adds "and
mice invaded their fields." The text is somewhat difficult in this whole story of the
plague.
3 REPARATION-OFFERING: Heb. *asham*, a
biblical sacrifice, explained in Lev. 5.

5 And you are to make images of your tumors and images of
   your mice that are bringing the land to ruin,
   and you are to give honor to the God of Israel;
   perhaps he will lighten his hand from upon you,
   from upon your gods and from upon your land.

6 Why do you make your heart heavy-with-stubbornness,
   (just) as Egypt and Pharaoh made their heart heavy-with-
      stubborness?
   Was it not when he toyed with them, that they sent-them-free
      and they went off?

7 So-now,
   get and make-ready a new wagon and two milch cows that
      have not yet yielded to a yoke;
   you are to bind the cows to the wagon,
   but you are to turn-back their young behind them, indoors.

8 Then you are to take the Coffer of YHWH
   and are to put it on the wagon;
   and the gold objects with which you are making-restitution to
      him as a reparation-offering
   you are to place in a chest, to its side;
   then you are to send it off, that it may go.

9 And look (well):
   if it goes up by way of its (own) territory, to Bet Shemesh,
   (then it was) he who did to us this great evil;
   but if not,

---

6 HE TOYED: Referring to God, who "toyed" with Egypt in Ex. 10:2.

7 NEW WAGON: New, since it is to be used for sacred purposes.
YET YIELDED . . . YOKE: Heb. *asher lo 'ala 'aleihem 'ol.* The alliteration highlights the importance of the idea: these animals, like others in the Israelite cult system (cf. Num. 19:2), must be perfect, untainted by secular use (like the wagons above).

9 BET SHEMESH: Just east of the Philistine cities.

we will know that his hand did not touch us—
it is an accident (that) happened to us.

10 Then men did thus:
they got two milch cows and bound them to the wagon,
but their young they shut up indoors.

11 And they placed the Coffer of YHWH on the wagon,
along with the chest and the gold mice and the images of their
tumors.

12 And the cows went-straight on the road, on the road to Bet
Shemesh:
on one path they went, going-along (and) lowing,
but they did not turn right or left,
while the Philistine overlords were walking behind them, up to
the territory of Bet Shemesh.

13 Now at Bet Shemesh they were harvesting the wheat harvest,
in the valley;
when they lifted up their eyes, they saw the Coffer,
and they rejoiced seeing (it).

14 Now the wagon came to the field of Yehoshua the Bet
Shimshite, and came-to-a-stop there.
There was a great stone (there).
And they split the wood of the wagon,
while the cows they offered-up as an offering-up to YHWH.

15 Now the Levites had brought-down the Coffer of YHWH
and the chest that was with it, in which the gold objects were,
and had put (them) on the great stone,
while the men of Bet Shemesh had offered-up offerings-up
and slaughter-offered slaughter-offerings on that day to YHWH.

16 Now when the five Philistine overlords saw (it),

they returned to Ekron on that day.

17 And these are the gold tumors by which the Philistines made-
   restitution as a reparation-offering to YHWH:
   for Ashdod, one;
   for ʿAzza, one;
   for Ashkelon, one;
   for Gat, one;
   and for Ekron, one.

18 And the gold mice—
   (by) the number of all the towns of the Philistines, by the five
      overlords,
   from fortified towns to country villages.
   And the great stone on which they deposited the Coffer of
      YHWH
   until this (very) day
   is in the field of Yehoshua the Bet Shimshite.

19 But he struck-down (some) of the men of Bet Shemesh,
   for they had looked at the Coffer of YHWH;
   he struck-down of the people seventy men and fifty thousand
      men.
   So the people mourned,
   for YHWH had struck the people, a great striking-down.

20 The men of Bet Shemesh said:
   Who can stand in the presence of YHWH, this holy God?
   And to whom may (it) be brought-up from off us?

21 They sent messengers to the settled-folk of Kiryat-Yeʾarim,
      saying:
   The Philistines have returned the Coffer of YHWH;
   go-down, bring it up to you!

7:1 So the men of Kiryat-Ye'arim came and brought-up the Coffer
of Yhwh;
they brought it to the house of Avinadav in Giv'a,
and Elazar his son they hallowed to watch over the Coffer of
Yhwh.

2 And it was,
from the time of the Coffer staying in Kiryat-Ye'arim,
—the years multiplied, so that they became twenty years—
that the whole House of Israel sighed after Yhwh.

3 So Shemu'el said to the whole House of Israel, saying:
If it is with all your heart that you are returning to Yhwh,
put-away the foreign gods from your midst, and the Astartes,
and direct your hearts toward Yhwh, and serve him alone;
then he will rescue you from the hand of the Philistines!

4 And the Children of Israel put-away the Baals and the
Astartes,
and they served Yhwh alone.

5 Shemu'el said:
Gather all Israel to Mitzpa/Lookout, so that I may intercede
on your behalf to Yhwh.

6 They were gathered to Mitzpa,
and they drew water and poured it out in the presence of
Yhwh.
And they fasted on that day

---

1 KIRYAT-YE'ARIM . . . GIV'A: Moving
ever closer to the Jerusalem area.
HALLOWED: Or "appointed."
3 ASTARTES: These, and the Baals of v. 4, were
major deities of Canaan, so often referred to
in *The Early Prophets* (Joshua-Kings) as the
objects of the Israelites' religious backsliding.

5 MITZPA: Roughly between Rama and Bet
El—again, a central location in Israel.
6 POURED (WATER) OUT: Perhaps, since it
is accompanied by fasting, this is some kind
of purification ceremony (cf. McCarter).
FASTED: A common ancient response to
national calamity, natural or otherwise.

and declared there:

We have sinned against YHWH!

And Shemu'el acted-as-judge for the Children of Israel at
Mitzpa.

7 The Philistines heard that the Children of Israel had gathered
at Mitzpa,

so the Philistine overlords went-up against Israel;

when the Children of Israel heard, they became-afraid before
the Philistines,

8 and the Children of Israel said to Shemu'el:

Don't be silent from us, from crying out to YHWH our God,

that he may deliver us from the hand of the Philistines!

9 So Shemu'el took a suckling lamb and offered it up as an
offering-up, a whole-offering, to YHWH,

and Shemu'el cried out to YHWH on behalf of Israel,

and YHWH answered him.

10 Now it was that Shemu'el was offering-up the offering-up,
while the Philistines approached for battle against Israel.

And YHWH thundered with a great sound on that day against
the Philistines;

he panicked them, so that they were smitten before Israel.

11 And the men of Israel went out from Mitzpa
and pursued the Philistines;

they struck them as far as below Bet Kar.

12 And Shemu'el took a certain stone and put it between Mitzpa
and Shen/The Rock-Tooth,

and he called its name Even ha-Ezer/The Stone of Help,

---

11 BET KAR: Presumably near Mitzpa.

he said:
Near here, Yhwh helped us.

13 So the Philistines were humbled,
and they did not come any more into the territory of Israel;
and the hand of Yhwh was against the Philistines all the days
of Shemu'el.

14 And the towns that the Philistines had taken away from Israel
(now) returned to Israel,
from Ekron as far as Gat,
and their territory Israel rescued from the hand of the
Philistines.
And there was peace between Israel and the Amorites.

15 Shemu'el led Israel as judge all the days of his life:
16 he would go year after year,
circling about Bet El, Gilgal, and Mitzpa,
and he would act-as-judge over Israel near all these sacred-
places;
17 (then) his return would be to Rama, for there was his house,
and there he would act-as-judge over Israel.
And he built there a slaughter-site to Yhwh.

---

14 AMORITES: A general name for the indige-
nous Canaanite population.
16 GILGAL: Another major Israelite religious
site, associated with important national
events; it lay somewhat northeast of Rama,
possibly near Jericho.

THE REQUESTED KING (I:8–15)

As NOTED IN THE INTRODUCTION above, the memorable chapter 8 not only raises issues about the meaning of kingship in Israel, but gives us a portrait of Shemu'el's own frustrations. The people's request for a king is taken almost more personally by the prophet than by God (the hurt deity has to say in v. 7, "it is not you whom they have rejected . . . from being-king over them [but I]"). His warning about the evils of monarchy is sounded by the oft-noted repetition of "take-away" in this chapter, and he will reiterate this concern in chapter 12 (after the anointing of Sha'ul), stressing how he himself has never "taken" anything from the Israelites. One senses not only Shemu'el's support for the age-old idea of divine rule, but something beyond ideology, something intensely personal. Perhaps he is stung by the same failure as his predecessor, sons who do not "walk in his ways."

Nevertheless, Shemu'el's warning forms an ominous backdrop out of which monarchy is to emerge. Many cultures' traditions tend to stress from the outset a new king's military exploits and charisma, choosing to build kingship on a firm popular foundation; but in the Bible, a note of misgiving needs to be sounded before anything else happens. In this sense, Shemu'el is both the last of the old-time practitioners of theocracy, the rule of God, and the first (excepting Moshe) of the prophetic critics of human kingship.

One of the memorable figures in the Bible, Sha'ul, the "Requested-One," seems doomed from the beginning. Chosen only after Shemu'el's dire warning in chapter 8, and its reiteration and expansion in chapter 12, he must meander about, looking for lost she-asses, until he is "found" (chaps. 9 and 10)—and even then is only anointed after he had "hidden-himself among the gear" (10:22). Such a start is hardly auspicious. On the other hand, he is physically imposing and a great warrior, and even, to the surprise of his people, can at times be seized by the spirit of God "like-a-prophet" (10 and 19). It is this latter endowment, also possessed by several of the judges, that will eventually prove too much for him to handle: God's spirit will depart, leaving an "evil spirit" in its wake (16:14).

Gunn (1980) sees Sha'ul as a scapegoat for God's anger over the Israelites' request for a king. But even if one takes a less fatalistic view of him, it is clear that Sha'ul's kingship is characterized by wrong turns and tragic misperceptions. Once past his initial success against the Ammonites, he runs afoul of both people and prophet. Although God in chapter 8 had conceded the kingship by telling Shemu'el to "hearken to their [the people's] voice," Sha'ul thrice jumps the gun—by inappropriately offering sacrifices (chap. 13), almost killing the heir to the throne (14), and disobeying God's command (15)—by himself "hearkening to [the people's] voice" (15:24) instead of God's. In this disobedience, apparently, lies the reason for his forfeiture of the kingship, similar to the fate of many of the later kings of Israel (although their disobedience almost always involved the practice of idolatry, of which Sha'ul does not seem to be guilty). This rather harsh judgment is perhaps appropriate given Sha'ul's key position as Israel's first king. Other perspectives might stress Shemu'el's (God's) lofty expectations, or the ideology of writers who sought to justify David's claim to the throne.

TROOPS CAME HOME AND
KILLING THE PHILIST
TOWNS OF ISRAEL
DANCING TO GRE
SHOOTING, AND
SANG AS
CHANTED
SAUL H
DAVID, I

SAUL WA
GREATLY
MATI
DAVI
OF T
THEY
AL
KI
DAY
JEA
THE
SPI
SAUL AND
IN THE HOUS
PLAYING TH
DAILY.

*S*ha'ul

8:1 Now it was, when Shemu'el had grown old,
that he made his sons judges for Israel

2 —the name of his firstborn son was Yo'el,
the name of his second, Aviyya—,
judges in Be'er Sheva.

3 But his sons did not walk in his ways:
they turned-aside after profit,
they took bribes and cast-aside cases-for-justice.

4 So all the elders of Israel gathered together
and came to Shemu'el at Rama,

5 they said to him:
Here, you have gown-old,
and your sons do not walk in your ways.
So-now,
make us a king
to lead-us-as-judge, like all the (other) nations!

6 Now the matter was evil in the eyes of Shemu'el, when they
said:
Give us a king, to lead-us-as-judge!
So Shemu'el prayed to YHWH,

7 and YHWH said to Shemu'el:
Hearken to the voice of the people
in all that they say to you;
indeed, it is not you whom they have rejected,
indeed it is I whom they have rejected
from being-king over them,

8 in accordance with all the doings that they have done

2 YO'EL . . . AVIYYA: Trad. English "Joel . . . Abijah." The names are ironically pious ones, meaning "YHWH is God" and "Father [God] is YHWH," respectively.

from the day I brought them up from Egypt until this day:
they have abandoned me,
serving other gods!
Thus they are doing to you as well!

9 So-now, hearken to their voice;
however:
indeed, you are to warn, yes, warn them,
(by) telling them the practice of the king who will reign-as-
king over them.

10 Shemu'el said all the words of YHWH
to the people who were requesting from him a king,

11 he said:
This will be the practice of the king who will reign-as-king
over you:
Your sons he will take-away,
setting him in his chariots and among his riders,
so that they run ahead of his chariot;

12 to make them commanders of thousands and commanders of
fifties,
to plow his plowing and harvest his harvest,
and to make his battle weapons and his chariot weapons;

13 your daughters he will take-away
as ointment-mixers, as cooks, and as bakers;

14 your fields, your vineyards, and your olive-groves, the best-
ones, he will take-away and give to his servants;

15 your sowing-seed and your vine-fruit he will tithe

---

12 COMMANDERS OF THOUSANDS . . .
FIFTIES: Military titles which recur
throughout Samuel and Kings.
15 TITHE: Tax a tenth. I have been careful not

to use the idiomatic English "take a tenth,"
so as not to muddle the key use of "take" in
this passage.

and give to his officers and to his servants;

16 your servants, your maids, and your young-men, the best-ones,
> and your donkeys, he will take-away,
that they may do his work;

17 your flock he will tithe,
and you yourselves will be for him as slaves.

18 And you will cry out on that day
because of your king whom you have chosen for yourselves,
but Y HWH will not answer you on that day!

19 But the people refused to hearken to Shemu'el's voice,
they said:
No!
Rather, let there be a king over us

20 so that we, we too may be like all the (other) nations!
Let our king lead-us-as-judge and go-out before us
and fight our battles!

21 When Shemu'el heard all the people's words,
he spoke them in the ears of Y HWH.

22 And Y HWH said to Shemu'el:
Hearken to their voice:
you are to king them a king!
Shemu'el said to the men of Israel:
Go, each-man to his town!

9:1 Now there was a man of Binyamin,
his name was Kish son of Aviel son of Tzeror son of Bekhorat
> son of Afi'akh, the son of a Binyaminite man,

15 OFFICERS: The term was long translated
"eunuchs," but that does not stand up to
current scholarly scrutiny.

a mighty-man of wealth.

2 He had a son, his name was Sha'ul/Requested-One,
a young-man, and goodly,
there was no man of the Children of Israel more goodly than
he,
from his shoulders and upward, taller than all the people.

3 And some she-asses of Kish the father of Sha'ul strayed,
so Kish said to Sha'ul his son:
Pray take with you one of the serving-lads
and arise, go, seek the she-asses!

4 They crossed the hill-country of Efrayim and crossed the
region of Shalisha, but did not find (them);
then they crossed the region of Sha'alim, but—nothing;
then they crossed the region of (Bin)yamin, but did not find
(them).

5 (When) they came to the region of Tzuf,
Sha'ul said to his serving-lad who was with him:
Come, let us go back,
lest my father stop (being-concerned) about the she-asses and
worry about us!

6 But he said to him:
Now here, there is a man of God in this town;
the man is honored,
all that he speaks comes, yes, comes-to-pass.
So-now, let us go there;

9:1 WEALTH: Heb. *hayil* in these books usually signifies "valor," but here, as with some
other terms for "strength" in the Bible, it
can refer to economic status as well.
2 SHA'UL: Trad. English "Saul."

3 STRAYED: Or "were lost."
4 SHALISHA . . . SHA'ALIM: These locations are unclear.
5 TZUF: Shemu'el's home district.

perhaps he can tell us about our way that we have gone upon.

7 Sha'ul said to his lad:

But here, (if) we go,

what can we bring for the man?

For the food is gone from our vessels,

so that there is no present to bring to the man of God!

What do we have?

8 The lad answered Sha'ul further,

he said:

here, I find in my hand a quarter weight of silver;

I will give (it) to the man of God, so that he may tell us about
  our way.

9 —Formerly in Israel,

thus would a man say on his going to consult God:

Come, let us go to the seer,

for a prophet today was called, formerly, a seer.—

10 Sha'ul said to his lad:

Good are your words;

come, let us go!

So they went to the town where the man of God was.

11 They were going-up the ascent of the town

when they found (some) girls coming-out to draw water;

they said to them:

Is the seer in this place?

12 They answered them and said:

He is, here ahead of you;

hurry now,

for just-now he has come to town,

---

7 WE BRING: Heb. *navi*, homonymous with the word for "prophet."

8 WEIGHT OF SILVER: Coins were not yet in use throughout much of the biblical period.

for (there is to be) a slaughter-offering today for the people, at
the high-place.

13 As soon as you come into the town, then you will find him,
before he goes-up to the high-place to eat
—for the people will not eat until his coming,
for *he* must bless the slaughter-offering (first);
after that, the invited-guests may eat.
So-now, go-up,
and as for him, this very day you will find him.

14 They went-up to the town.
When they were coming into the midst of the town,
here was Shemu'el going-out toward them
to go-up to the high-place.

15 Now Yhwh had revealed (to) Shemu'el's ear
one day before Sha'ul's coming, saying:

16 Around this time tomorrow
I will send to you a man from the region of Binyamin;
you are to anoint him as Prince over my people Israel.
He will deliver my people from the hand of the Philistines—
for I have seen my people,
for their cry has come to me!

17 Now when Shemu'el saw Sha'ul,
Yhwh declared to him:
Here is the man about whom I said to you:
This-one shall restrain my people!

---

16 PRINCE: Or "Designated Leader." The term may have originated as a secular one for "leader"; in any event, it seems to be distinct from "king" (cf. Campbell).
FOR I HAVE SEEN . . . FOR THEIR CRY: Echoing God's redemptive speech at the Burning Bush (Ex. 3:7).

17 RESTRAIN: Others, "govern," but the text could have utilized conventional terms for "rule" or even the much-used "reign-as-king."

18 Sha'ul approached Shemu'el in the gateway
 and said:
 Pray tell me:
 Where is the seer's house?

19 Shemu'el answered Sha'ul,
 he said:
 I am the seer!
 Go-up ahead of me to the high-place;
 you are to eat with me today,
 then I will send you off at daybreak,
 and all that is in your heart I will tell you.

20 And as for the she-asses that were straying from you three days
  (ago),
 do not take them to heart, for they have been found—
 and to whom do all the riches of Israel belong,
 is it not to you and to all your father's house?

21 Sha'ul answered and said:
 Am I not a Binyaminite, from the smallest of the tribes of
  Israel
 —and my clan is the least of all the clans of the tribe of
  Binyamin?
 So why do you speak to me according to these matters?

22 Shemu'el took Sha'ul and his serving-lad, and brought them to
  the dining-hall
 and gave them a place at the head of the invited-guests
 —they were about thirty men.

23 And Shemu'el said to the cook:
 Give-over the portion that I gave you,
 about which I said to you: Set it (aside) with you.

24 The cook lifted the thigh and the fat-tail and offered it up
and set (it) before Sha'ul.
He said:
Here is what-is-reserved;
set (it) before you, eat,
since for this appointed-time it has been kept for you, saying:
I have invited the people.
So Sha'ul ate with Shemu'el on that day.

25 And they went-down from the high-place to the town,
and he spoke with Sha'ul on the roof.

26 . . . they started-early,
and it was, when dawn came-up,
that Shemu'el called Sha'ul to the roof, saying:
Arise, so that I may send you off.
Sha'ul arose, and the two of them went-forth, he and
    Shemu'el, outside.

27 They were going-down, at the edge of the town,
when Shemu'el said to Sha'ul:
Speak to the lad, so that he may cross over ahead of us
—so he crossed over—
but you, stand-still now,
so that I may make you hear the word of God.

10:1 And Shemu'el took a flask of oil and poured it on his head and
    kissed him;

---

24 THIGH . . . FAT-TAIL: Parts of the sacrificial animal that were usually reserved for priestly consumption.
SAYING: I HAVE INVITED THE PEOPLE: Or, with JPS, "when I said I was inviting the people."

25 ROOF . . . : The Hebrew text is difficult here; once again, a chunk of text appears to be missing.

then he said:

Is it not that Yhwh has anointed you over his inheritance as
    Prince?

2 When you go today from me,

you will find two men by Rahel's burial-place in the territory
    of Binyamin, at Tzeltzah;

they will say to you:

They are found, the she-asses that you went to seek.

Here, your father has left-off the matter of the she-asses,

but he is worried about you, saying:

What should I do about my son?

3 So you are to move on from there, and further,

and you will come to the Oak of Tavor;

they will find you, three men going up to (worship) God at
    Bet El—

one carrying three kids,

one carrying three rounds of bread,

and one carrying a skin of wine.

4 They will ask you after (your) well-being,

and they will give you two bread-loaves,

and you are to take (them) from their hand.

5 Afterward, you will come to Giv'at Elohim / The Hill of God,

    where the Philistine garrison is;

10:1 HIS (GOD'S) INHERITANCE: The people of Israel.

2 WHEN YOU GO TODAY: Ancient versions expand here, explaining that the following events will be a "sign" to Sha'ul of his anointing.

RAHEL'S BURIAL-PLACE . . . TZELT-ZAH: The traditional tomb of Rachel in Bethlehem, built in medieval times, has long been felt to be of erroneous location. It most probably stood near Kiryat-Ye'arim, northwest of Jerusalem. *Tzeltzah* may also be related to the "surging" of v. 6.

3 TAVOR: Trad. English "Tabor."

5 GARRISON: Others, "prefect."

it will be, when you come there, to the town,
that you will meet up with a band of prophets coming-down
    from the high-place,
and ahead of them (will be) lyre and timbrel, flute and harp,
and they will be ranting-in-prophecy.

6 Now (it) will surge upon you, the rushing-spirit of Yhwh,
so that you will rant-like-a-prophet with them,
and you will be changed into another man.

7 And it will be,
when these signs come-about for you,
do for yourself whatever your hand finds (to do)!
For God is with you.

8 Then you are to go-down ahead of me, to Gilgal,
and here, I will be going-down to you to offer-up offerings-up
    and to slaughter slaughter-offerings of *shalom;*
for seven days you are to tarry, until I come to you,
then I will make-known to you what you are to do.

9 Now it was,
when he turned his back to go from Shemu'el,
that God changed him another heart,
and all these signs came-about on that day.

10 When they came there, to the Hill,

---

5 PROPHETS . . . RANTING-IN-PROPHECY: The "mantic" form of prophecy referred to here, comprising extreme forms of behavior, is attested throughout the ages (cf. the cult of Dionysus in ancient Greece, and "speaking in tongues" still today). The experiences of "later prophets" such as Isaiah and Jeremiah tend to focus (although not exclusively) on the divine word, usually all too intelligible.

6 RUSHING-SPIRIT: Heb. *ru'ah* can mean either "spirit" or "wind"—so the concept is a spiritual one with physical force.

9 CHANGED HIM ANOTHER HEART: That is, altered his mental/religious state, as if he were another person. This kind of consciousness change is familiar to many cultures and periods down to the present.

here (were) a band of prophets, (coming) to meet him.
There surged upon him the rushing-spirit of God,
and he ranted-like-a-prophet in their midst.

11 It was:
all who knew him from yesterday and the day-before,
when they saw
that here, with the prophets he was ranting-like-a-prophet!—
the people said, each-man to his neighbor:
What is this (that has) happened to the son of Kish?
Is Sha'ul too among the prophets?

12 Now a man from there spoke up and said:
But who is their father?
Therefore (it) became a proverb:
Is Sha'ul too among the prophets?

13 He finished ranting-like-a-prophet, and then he came to the
high-place.

14 Now Sha'ul's uncle said to him and to his serving-lad:
Where did you go?
He said:
To seek the she-asses.
And when we saw that (they were) not (there),
we came to Shemu'el.

15 Sha'ul's uncle said:
Pray tell me:
What did Shemu'el say to you?

16 Sha'ul said to his uncle:
He told, yes, told us
that the she-asses had been found.

---

12 BUT WHO IS THEIR FATHER?: In looking for the prophets' leader, the text perhaps alludes to the larger leadership question of the book.

But (as for) the matter of the kingship,
he did not tell him what Shemu'el had said.

17 Now Shemu'el summoned the people to Yhwh, at Mitzpa.
18 He said to the Children of Israel:
Thus says Yhwh, the God of Israel:
I myself brought-up Israel from Egypt,
I rescued you from the hand of Egypt and from the hand of
the kingdoms that were oppressing you.
19 But you—today—you have rejected your God,
the one delivering you from all your distresses and your disas-
ters!
And you said:
No, rather, a king make over us!
So-now,
station-yourselves in the presence of Yhwh, by your tribes, by
your families.
20 And Shemu'el brought-near each of the tribes of Israel,
and there was taken-by-lot the tribe of Binyamin.
21 Then he brought-near the tribe of Binyamin by its clans,
and there was taken-by-lot the Matrite clan,
and (then) there was taken-by-lot Sha'ul son of Kish.
But when they sought him, he was not to be found.
22 So they inquired further of Yhwh:
Has any other man come here?
And Yhwh said:
Here, he has hidden-himself among the gear!

19 STATION-YOURSELVES: That is, present
yourselves.

23 They ran and took him from there
and he stood amidst the people;
he was taller than all the people, from his shoulders and
upward.

24 Now Shemu'el said to all the people:
Do you see whom YHWH has chosen?
Indeed, there is none like him among all the people!
And all the people shouted,
they proclaimed: (Long) live the king!

25 And Shemu'el spoke to the people
about the practice of kingship, and wrote it in a document,
and put (it) in the presence of YHWH.
Then Shemu'el sent-off all the people, each-one to his house,

26 while Sha'ul too went to his house at Giv'a;
and there went with him the valiant-ones
whose heart God had touched.

27 But some sons of worthlessness said:
How can this-one deliver us?
And they despised him,
they did not bring him a gift.
But he was like a silent-one.

11:1 Now Nahash/Snake the Ammonite went-up
and encamped against Yavesh Gil'ad.
And all the men of Yavesh said to Nahash:
Cut a covenant with us, and we will serve you!

11:1 AMMONITE: The Ammonites occupied the territory well east of the Jordan, between the Dead Sea and the Sea of Galilee (biblical Kinneret).
YAVESH GIL'AD: Trad. English "Jabesh Gilead," on the east bank of the Jordan and hence bordering on Ammonite lands.
CUT A COVENANT: Make a treaty; the "cutting" part may refer to an animal sacrifice (cf. Gen. 15).

49

2 But Nahash the Ammonite said to them:
On this (condition) I will cut a covenant with you—
on (condition) of gouging out every one of your right eyes!
Thus will I lay disgrace upon all Israel!

3 The elders of Yavesh said to him:
Let us tarry for seven days;
we will send messengers throughout all the territory of Israel,
and if there is no deliverer for us,
(then) we will go-out (to surrender) to you.

4 When the messengers came to the Hill of Sha'ul,
they spoke the words in the hearing of the people,
and all the people lifted up their voice and wept.

5 And here, Sha'ul came after the herd, from the open-field,
Sha'ul said:
What is (the matter) with the people, that they are weeping?
They related to him the words of the men of Yavesh.

6 And there surged the rushing-spirit of God upon Sha'ul when
he heard these words, and his anger flared up exceedingly;

7 he took a brace of cattle
and chopped-it-up;
then he sent (it) off throughout all the territory of Israel by the
hand of the messengers, saying:
Whoever does not go out (to war) after Sha'ul and after
Shemu'el—
thus shall be done to his cattle!

---

2 ON THIS (CONDITION): Following Driver.
GOUGING OUT . . . YOUR RIGHT EYES: In the 4QS^a manuscript at Qumran, this chapter opens with a description of Nahash terrorizing the Israelite tribes living east of the Jordan; this prologue, which apparently dropped out of MT, explains the subsequent events of the chapter.

3 (TO SURRENDER): Following Driver.

And a terror of Y<small>HWH</small> fell upon the people,
so that they went out as one man.

8 He counted them (for war) at Bezek:
the Children of Israel totaled three hundred thousand,
while the men of Judah were thirty thousand.

9 And he said to the messengers who came:
Thus you are to say to the men of Yavesh Gil'ad:
Tomorrow there will be deliverance for you, when the sun is
hot!
The messengers came
and told (it) to the men of Yavesh,
and they rejoiced.

10 So the men of Yavesh said:
Tomorrow we will go-out to you,
and you may do with us whatever is good in your eyes.

11 Now it was on the morrow
that Sha'ul put the fighting-people into three divisions,
they entered the midst of the camp at the daybreak watch
and struck Ammon until the day was hot.
And it was that those (who were) left—they were scattered,
so that there were not left among them two together.

12 The people said to Shemu'el:
Who (is it) that said: Shall Sha'ul be-king over us?
Give-over the men, that we may put-them-to-death!

13 But Sha'ul said:
No one is to be put-to-death on this day,

---

8 BEZEK: On the west bank of the Jordan.
THREE HUNDRED THOUSAND: As is
typically the case in ancient accounts, this
number is not to be taken realistically.

for today Yʜwʜ has wrought deliverance in Israel!

14   And Shemu'el said to the people:
Come, let us go to Gilgal,
and let us renew the kingship there!

15   So all the people went to Gilgal
and made Sha'ul king there, in the presence of Yʜwʜ in
     Gilgal.
They slaughtered there slaughter-offerings, of *shalom,* in the
     presence of Yʜwʜ,
and there Sha'ul and all the men of Israel rejoiced exceedingly.

12:1   Shemu'el said to all Israel:
Here, I have hearkened to your voice, in all that you have said
     to me:
I have kinged a king over you.

2   So-now,
here is the king, going-about before you,
but I, I have grown-old, I have grown-hoary,
and as for my sons—here they are with you;
but I, I have gone-about before you from my youth until this
     day.

3   Here I am;
testify against me, before Yʜwʜ and before his anointed:
Whose ox have I taken-away? Whose donkey have I taken-
     away?

---

13 DELIVERANCE: Or "victory."
12:1 KINGED A KING: Heb. *va-amlikh . . .*
melekh.

3 TAKEN-AWAY: The repetition that follows
recalls chap. 8 (Garsiel 1990).

And whom have I defrauded? Whom have I oppressed?

And from whose hand have I taken a ransom, that I might hide
    my eyes in (exchange for) it?

—I will return (them) to you!

4 They said:

You have not defrauded us, you have not oppressed us,

you have not taken-away a thing from anyone's hand!

5 He said to them:

Yhwh is witness before you and his anointed is a witness this
    day,

that you have not found anything in my hand!

They said:

(Yhwh is) Witness!

6 Shemu'el said to the people:

It is Yhwh

who wrought-deeds with Moshe and with Aharon,

and who brought your fathers up from the land of Egypt.

7 So-now,

stand-fast, that I may plead-in-judgment with you in the pres-
    ence of Yhwh

concerning all of Yhwh's acts-of-victory that he has wrought
    with you and with your fathers.

8 When Yaakov came to Egypt,

and your fathers cried out to Yhwh,

Yhwh sent Moshe and Aharon;

they brought your fathers out of Egypt and settled them in
    this place.

---

3 RANSOM: Or "bribe" (cf. Goldman).   "Moses and Aaron."

8 MOSHE AND AHARON: Trad. English

9 But they forgot Yhwh their God,

so he sold them into the hand of Sisera, commander of the
army of Hatzor, and into the hand of the Philistines,

and into the hand of the king of Mo'av,

so that they waged-battle against them.

10 Then they cried out to Yhwh,

they said: We have sinned!

For we abandoned Yhwh and served the Baals and the
Astartes!

So-now, rescue us from the hand of our enemies, and we will
serve you!

11 So Yhwh sent Yerubbaal, and Bedan, and Yiftah, and Shemu'el,

and rescued you from the hand of your enemies round about,

so that you dwelt in security.

12 But when you saw that Nahash king of the Children of
Ammon was coming against you,

you said to me:

No, rather a king must reign-as-king over us—

but Yhwh your God is your king!

13 So-now,

here is the king whom you have chosen, whom you have
requested;

here, Yhwh has given you a king.

14 If you hold Yhwh in awe,

serving him and hearkening to his voice,

and do not rebel against Yhwh's order,

---

9 SISERA . . . HATZOR: Cf. Judges 4–5.
11 YERUBBAAL . . . : Yerubbaal is Gideon
(cf. Judg. 7:1); Yiftah is Trad. English "Jeph-
thah" (Judg. 11); while the identity of

"Bedan" remains a mystery. Kimhi suggests
that it is an abbreviation for *ben Dan,* "son of
Dan," namely Shimshon (Samson).

and both you and the king who reigns-as-king over you (follow) after Y<small>HWH</small> your God . . . !

15 But if you do not hearken to the voice of Y<small>HWH</small>,
and you rebel against Y<small>HWH</small>'s order,
then Y<small>HWH</small>'s hand will be against you (as it was) against your
fathers.

16 So-now, stand-fast and see this great thing
that Y<small>HWH</small> is about to do before your eyes:

17 It is not the wheat cutting today?
I will call out to Y<small>HWH</small>,
so that he gives-forth thunder-sounds and rain—
then learn, then see
that your evil is great that you have done in Y<small>HWH</small>'s eyes,
by requesting for yourselves a king!

18 And Shemu'el called out to Y<small>HWH</small>,
and Y<small>HWH</small> gave-forth thunder-sounds and rain on that day.
And all the people (stood) in exceeding awe of Y<small>HWH</small> and of
Shemu'el.

19 Then all the people said to Shemu'el:
Intercede on behalf of your servants to Y<small>HWH</small> your God, so
that we do not die,
for we have added to all our sins (even more) evil

---

15 ORDER: Literally, "mouth."

16 STAND-FAST AND SEE THIS GREAT
THING / THAT YHWH IS ABOUT TO
DO: Recalling Moses' words at the Reed
Sea, "Stand-fast and see / Y<small>HWH</small>'s deliver-
ance which he will work for you today" (Ex.
14:13).

17 WHEAT CUTTING . . . THUNDER: The
wheat harvest typically occurred in late May
or early June, so there could be no question
of natural rain here, in the dry season.

THEN LEARN, THEN SEE: The use of
these two imperative verbs in sequence is
peculiar to Samuel, Kings, and Jeremiah.
Heb. *yado'a*, here "learn," is elsewhere rendered "know."

by requesting for ourselves a king!

20 Shemu'el said to the people:

Do not be afraid.

You have done all this evil,

but do not turn-aside from Yнwн;

you are to serve Yнwн with all your heart!

21 You are not to turn-aside,

indeed, after the (gods of) confusion who will not avail, who
will not prevail, for they are confusion!

22 For Yнwн will not forsake his people

for the sake of his great name;

for Yнwн has ventured to make you for him into a people.

23 I too—

(Heaven) forbid for me, sinning against Yнwн,

by holding back from interceding on your behalf,

I will instruct you in the good and right way.

24 Only—hold Yнwн in awe:

you are to serve him in truth with all your heart,

for see how he exhibits-greatness with you!

25 But if you do-evil, yes, evil,

both you and your king will be swept-away!

13:1 Sha'ul was _____ years old at his becoming-king,

and for two years he reigned-as-king over Israel.

---

21 CONFUSION: Heb. *tohu*, related to the
chaos at the beginning of Creation in Gen.
1:2 (where Heb. *tohu va-vohu* could be rendered "confusion and chaos"; I chose "wild
and waste").

AVAIL . . . PREVAIL: Heb. *yo'ilu . . .
yatzilu.*

13:1 ___YEARS OLD: The MT is missing the
number here. For some, the "two years"
that immediately follows are suspect as well.

2 Sha'ul chose for himself three thousand (men) from Israel;
there were with Sha'ul two thousand at Mikhmash and at the
hill-country of Bet El
and a thousand were with Yonatan at the Hill of Binyamin;
the rest of the people he sent away, each-one to his tent.

3 And Yonatan struck the garrison of the Philistines that was in
Geva,
and the Philistines heard (about it),
while Sha'ul had the *shofar* sounded throughout all the land,
saying:
Let the Hebrews hear!

4 And all Israel heard, saying:
Sha'ul has struck the garrison of the Philistines,
and also Israel reeks to the Philistines!
And the people were summoned after Sha'ul, to Gilgal.

5 Now the Philistines had gathered to do-battle with Israel,
three thousand chariots and six thousand horsemen,
and fighting-people like the sand that is on the shore of the sea
for multitude;
they came-up and encamped at Mikhmash, east of Bet Aven.

6 Now the men of Israel, seeing that they were in (dire) straits
—for the fighting-people were pressing-hard—
the people hid themselves
in caves, in holes, in boulder-cracks,

---

2 MIKHMASH: Between Mitzpa and Gilgal,
hence north of Rama.
BET EL: Trad. English "Beth El," an important biblical town lying between Shekhem
(today's Nablus) and Jerusalem.
YONATAN: Sha'ul's son and heir, sometimes spelled "Yehonatan" in the text. Trad.

English "Jonathan"; the name means
"YHWH has given (a son)."
HILL OF BINYAMIN: Or "Giv'a [Gibeah]
of Binyamin."

4 REEKS: A biblical expression used to
describe odious behavior and hence reputa-
tion (cf. Also II 10:6, 16:21).

in excavations, and in cisterns,

7 while some Hebrews crossed the Jordan, into the region of
Gad and Gil'ad.

Now Sha'ul was still in Gilgal, when all the people came-
trembling after him.

8 He tarried for seven days,
for the appointed-time that Shemu'el had (set),
but Shemu'el did not come to Gilgal,
and the people began-to-scatter from him.

9 So Sha'ul said:
Bring-close to me the offering-up and the *shalom*-offerings!
And he offered-up the offering-up.

10 But then it was,
when he had (just) finished offering-up the offering-up,
that here: Shemu'el came,
and Sha'ul went out to meet him, to bless him (in greeting).

11 Shemu'el said:
What have you done?
Sha'ul said:
When I saw that the people were scattering from me,
—and as for you, you did not come (within) the appointed
(number of) days—
and the Philistines were gathering at Mikhmash,

12 I said (to myself):
Now the Philistines will go-down against me at Gilgal,
yet YHWH's face I have not soothed!
So I forced myself,
and offered-up the offering-up.

13 Shemu'el said to Sha'ul:
You have acted-foolishly!

If you had kept the command of Yhwh your God which he
   commanded you,

indeed now, Yhwh would have established your kingship over
   Israel for the ages,

14   but now, your kingship will not stand.

Yhwh seeks for himself a man after his (own) heart,

so that Yhwh may commission him as Prince over his people,

for you have not kept what Yhwh commanded you!

15   Shemu'el arose and went-up from Gilgal toward the Hill of
   Binyamin.

And Sha'ul counted-for-war the fighting-people that were
   found with him,

about six hundred men.

16   Now Sha'ul and Yonatan his son, and the people that were
   found with them, were situated on the Hill of Binyamin,

while the Philistines were encamped at Mikhmash.

17   And the ravagers went out of the Philistines' camp in three
   column-heads:

one column facing toward the road to Ofra, toward the Region
   of the Jackal,

18   one column facing the road to Bet Horon,

and one column facing the road of the border which looks out
   over the Ravine of the Hyena, in the wilderness.

19   —Now no metal-worker could be found throughout all the
   land of Israel,

for the Philistines had said (to themselves):

Lest the Hebrews make swords or spears (with them)!

20   And all Israel had to go down to the Philistines, for each-man
   to have-forged his plowshare and his mattock and his axe
   and his sickle,

21 and the sharpening-charge was a *pim* (in price) for plowshares
   and mattocks,
   and for three-pronged (forks) and for axes,
   and for setting the goads.

22 So it was the day of the battle
   that there was not (to be) found a sword or a spear in the hand
   of all the people that were with Sha'ul and Yonatan,
   but they were found for Sha'ul and for Yonatan his son.

23 And the Philistine garrison went-out to the Pass of Mikhmash.

14:1 Now it was on a certain day
   that Yonatan son of Sha'ul said to the serving-lad, his weapons
   bearer:
   Come, let us cross over to the Philistines' garrison,
   (the one) that is across, over there!
   But his father he did not tell.

2 Now Sha'ul was staying at the edge of Geva,
   beneath the Pomegranate (Rock) that is in the Migron;
   and the fighting-people that were with him (were) about six
   hundred men.

3 And Ahiyya son of Ahituv, brother of I-Khavod, son of Pin'has
   son of Eili, priest of YHWH at Shilo, was wearing the *efod*.
   But the people did not know that Yonatan had gone.

4 Now between the crossings that Yonatan sought to cross, to
   (get to) the Philistines' garrison,

21 PIM: Stone weights with the inscription *p-y-m* have been found by archaeologists in Israel (thus the word was probably *payim*). They were two-thirds (lit. "two-mouths") of a silver shekel in value.
AND FOR THREE-PRONGED (FORKS):

Others read as "a third of a shekel."
14:2 THE MIGRON: If related to Heb. *n-g-r*, "gushing," it possibly refers to the Wadi es-Swenit, not too far from Gibeah; the "Pomegranate" would then be the cave referred to in Judges 20:45–47 (Arnold).

(was) a cliff-tooth on one side and a cliff-tooth on the other side:

the name of the one was Botzetz, and the name of the other was Senne.

5 The one tooth was shaped on the north, in front of Mikhmash, while the other was on the south, in front of Geva.

6 Yonatan said to the lad, his weapons bearer:

Come, let us cross over to the garrison of these foreskinned-ones!

Perhaps YHWH will act for us,

for there is no constraint for YHWH from delivering by the many or by the few!

7 His weapons bearer said to him:

Do whatever your heart inclines to—

here I am with you, according to your heart.

8 Yonatan said:

Here, we are crossing over to the men,

and we will be revealing ourselves to them;

9 if they say thus to us:

Halt, until we get-close to you—

we will stand in our place, and will not go-up against them.

10 But if they say thus:

Come-up to us—

we will go-up,

for YHWH will have given them into our hand,

and this (will be) the sign for us.

---

4 BOTZETZ . . . SENNE: Possibly meaning "twinkler" and "thorn."

6 FORESKINNED-ONES: The Israelites' characterization of the Philistines (used already in Judges), who were not circumcised.

7 YOUR HEART INCLINES TO: Following LXX; MT has "your heart. Incline. . . ."
HEART: Often in the Bible with the meaning "mind."

11 The two of them revealed-themselves to the Philistines' garrison,
and the Philistines said:
Here, Hebrews are coming out of the holes where they were hiding-themselves!

12 The men of the garrison yelled out to Yonatan and to his weapons bearer,
they said:
Come-up to us,
and we will show you something!
So Yonatan said to his weapons bearer:
Come-up behind me,
for YHWH has given them into the hand of Israel!

13 Yonatan climbed-up by his arms and by his legs, with his weapons bearer behind him.
And they fell before Yonatan, while his weapons bearer dispatched (them) behind him.

14 And the first striking-down that Yonatan and his weapons bearer struck-down was some twenty men,
(over) about half a furrow (that) a brace (of oxen might plow) in a field.

15 And there was trembling in the camp, out in the open-field,
and among all the fighting-people
—the garrison and the ravagers fell-to-trembling, even they,
and the earth shuddered;
it was a trembling of God.

---

13 DISPATCHED: A slightly different form of the Hebrew root (*m-w-t*) from which "die" and "put to death" are derived.

15 A TREMBLING OF GOD: Others, "a very great panic," "a panic from God."

16 Now Sha'ul's watchmen saw at Geva of Binyamin:
here, the throng was melting-away, going and coming-back.

17 Sha'ul said to the people who were with him:
Pray count and see who has gone-out from us!
They counted, and here: Yonatan and his weapons bearer were
not (there).

18 Sha'ul said to Ahiyya:
Bring-close the Coffer of God
—for the Coffer of God was at that time with the Children of
Israel.

19 And it was,
as Sha'ul was speaking to the priest,
that the panic that was in the Philistines' camp went-on, went-
on (becoming) greater;
and Sha'ul said to the priest:
Withdraw your hand!

20 And Sha'ul cried out, and all the people that were with him,
and they came out to the battle.
And here: every man's sword was against his neighbor,
an exceedingly great panic.

21 Now the Hebrews (that) had been with the Philistines yesterday and the day-before,
in that they had gone-up with them to the camp round-about,
they too (turned) to be with Israel, who were with Sha'ul and
Yonatan,

22 while all the men of Israel, the ones hiding-themselves in the
hill-country of Efrayim, heard that the Philistines had fled,
and they too caught up with them in battle.

23 So YHWH delivered Israel on that day,
and the battle crossed over Bet Aven.

24 Yet the men of Israel were hard-pressed on that day,
for Sha'ul had put an oath-curse on the people, saying:
Damned be the man that eats food until sunset—
I would be-avenged on my enemies!
So all the people tasted no food.

25 Now all the people came into the forest,
and there was honey on the surface of the open-field.

26 And when the people came into the forest,
here: honey was running-out,
but no one reached his hand to his mouth,
for the people were afraid of the sworn-oath.

27 Now Yonatan had not heard when his father had made the
people swear,
so he stretched out the edge of the staff that was in his hand
and dipped it into the honey comb,
then he returned his hand to his mouth, and his eyes brightened.

28 Then a man from the fighting-people spoke up and said:
Your father made the people swear, yes, swear, saying:
Damned be the man who eats food today!
So the people are weary.

29 Yonatan said:
My father has stirred-up-trouble on the land!
Pray see: indeed, my eyes are brightened,
for I tasted this little (bit of) honey;

30 if the people had eaten, yes, eaten today from the enemies'
spoils that they found,

---

27 HIS EYES BRIGHTENED: Focusing on the
life-enhancing properties of honey.

indeed now, wouldn't the strike against the Philistines have
    been greater?

31 They struck-down the Philistines on that day from Mikhmash
    to Ayyalon,
and the people grew exceedingly weary;

32 So people swooped down on the spoil
and took sheep and cattle and young-cattle, slaying them on
    the ground,
and the people ate (them) with the blood.

33 Someone told Sha'ul, saying:
Here, the people are sinning against YHWH, in eating with the
    blood!
He said:
You have (all) dealt-treacherously!
Roll to me a great stone here.

34 And Sha'ul said:
Scatter among the people,
you are to say to them:
Each-man bring-close to me his ox, each-man his lamb;
you are to slay them here and are to eat;
but you are not to sin against YHWH by eating with the blood!
So all the people brought-close, each-man his ox in his hand
    that night, and they slew them there.

35 And Sha'ul built a slaughter-site to YHWH;
it was the first (that he) built (as) a slaughter-site to YHWH.

36 Sha'ul said:

---

34 EATING WITH THE BLOOD: The consumption of blood, which is taken to sym-
bolize life itself, is expressly forbidden in the
Bible, already at the end of the Flood story
(Gen. 9:4).

Let us go down after the Philistines at night, and plunder
  among them till morning light,
and let us not leave a man of them (alive)!
They said:
All (that is) good in your eyes, do!
But the priest said:
Let us (first) draw-near here to God.

37   And Sha'ul inquired of God:
Shall I go down after the Philistines?
Will you give them into the hand of Israel?
But he did not answer him on that day.

38   Then Sha'ul said:
Come-close to here, all (you) "cornerstones" of the people,
and learn, and see
wherein this sin occurred today.

39   For as YHWH lives, who delivers Israel:
indeed, even if it be Yonatan my son,
indeed, he must die, yes, die!
But no one answered him from all the people.

40   He said to all Israel:
You be on one side,
and I and Yonatan my son will be on one side.
And the people said to Sha'ul:
Whatever is good in your eyes, do!

41   Sha'ul said to YHWH the God of Israel:

---

36   DRAW-NEAR: To consult God through an oracle, as in the next verse's "inquired" (which is built on the same verb, *sha'al,* as Sha'ul's name).

38   CORNERSTONES : Nobles; a parallel English idiom might be "pillars [of the community]."

Now give *tammim*!
Yonatan and Sha'ul were taken-by-lot,
and the people escaped.

42 Then Sha'ul said:
Cast (lots) between me and Yonatan my son!
And Yonatan was taken-by-lot.

43 Sha'ul said to Yonatan:
Tell me what you have done!
So Yonatan told him,
he said:
I tasted, yes, tasted with the edge of the staff that was in my
    hand, a little honey.
Here I am; I will die.

44 Sha'ul said:
Thus may God do, and thus may he add,
for you shall die, yes, die, Yonatan!

45 But the people said to Sha'ul:
Shall Yonatan die, who has wrought this great deliverance in
    Israel?
(Heaven) forbid, as YHWH lives,
if a (single) hair of his head should fall to the ground . . . !
For with God he has wrought (victory) this day!
Thus the people redeemed Yonatan, so that he did not die.

46 And Sha'ul went up from (pursuing) after the Philistines,
while the Philistines went to their place.

41 GIVE *TAMMIM:* That is, reveal through the oracle, which apparently made use of the objects known as the *Urim* and *Tummim* (cf. Ex. 28:30). The LXX has a longer text at this point which includes the *Urim.*

43 HERE I AM; I WILL DIE: Following Driver.

67

47 Now Sha'ul had secured the kingship over Israel.
And he waged-battle round-about against all his enemies:
against Mo'av, against the Children of Ammon, against Edom,
against the king of Tzova, and against the Philistines;
and against all whom he faced, he was victorious.

48 He did valiantly: he struck-down Amalek
and rescued Israel from the hand of its pillager.

49 Now the sons of Sha'ul were:
Yonatan, Yishvi, and Malki-Shu'a;
and the name of his two daughters:
the name of the firstborn was Meirav,
and the name of the younger-one was Mikhal;

50 and the name of Sha'ul's wife was Ahino'am daughter of
Ahima'atz;
and the name of the commander of his army was Aviner, son
of Ner, Sha'ul's uncle.

51 Now Kish was the father of Sha'ul, and Ner, the father of
Avner, the son of Aviel.

52 And the battle was strong against the Philistines all the days of
Sha'ul;
whenever Sha'ul would see any man, a mighty-one, or any
valiant-one,

47 MO'AV . . . EDOM: Along with Ammon, traditional enemies understood in Genesis as coming from the same stock as Israel; the Moabites inhabited the region due east of the Dead Sea, with the Edomites occupying the area south of that.
TZOVA: The area north of Damascus.
49 MEIRAV . . . MIKHAL: Trad. English

"Merab . . . Michal."
50 AVINER: Mostly spelled as "Avner"; Trad. English "Abner" (similarly, in II Samuel, "Aminon/Amnon" and "Avishalom/Avshalom"). The name means "Father [God] is a Light/Lamp." He is also, as indicated in the next verse, Sha'ul's cousin.

he would gather him to him.

15:1 Shemu'el said to Sha'ul:
       It was I whom YHWH sent to anoint you as king over his
            people, over Israel;
       so-now, hearken to the voice of YHWH's words:

2   Thus says YHWH of the Heavenly-Armies:
       I have taken-account of what Amalek did to Israel,
       how he set-upon him on the journey, on his going-up from
            Egypt.

3   So-now,
       go and strike-down Amalek;
       you are to devote-to-destruction all that is his
       —you are not to spare him,
       but are to put (everyone) to death,
       from man to woman,
       from child to suckling,
       from ox to sheep,
       from camel to donkey.

4   Sha'ul summoned the fighting-people,
       he counted them in Tela'im:

---

52 GATHER HIM: A term denoting the recruiting of troops.

15:2 WHAT AMALEK DID: In Ex. 17, the Amalekites, who in Sha'ul's day inhabited the Negev, attack the newly freed Israelites in the rear, provoking God to declare a kind of eternal war against them. In the book of Esther, the hero and villain are cast as descendants of Sha'ul and the Amalekite king here, Agag.

3 DEVOTE-TO-DESTRUCTION: Some bib-

lical war accounts speak of the practice of proscribing the spoils of war—"devoting" them to God, which could mean confiscation for the sanctuary or, in the case of persons, death. Cf. the famous case of breaking the ban in Josh. 7.

4 TELA'IM: Perhaps Telem in southern Judah, but the spelling here is identical to that of a word for "lambs" (cf. the language of the previous verse; the word used for lambs in v. 9, however, is different).

two hundred thousand foot-soldiers
along with ten thousand, the men of Judah.

5 And Sha'ul came to the city of Amalek,
and lay-in-ambush in the wadi.

6 Now Sha'ul said to the Kenites:
Come, turn-aside, go-down from amidst the Amalekites,
lest I sweep you away with them!
For you—you dealt-in-loyalty with all the Children of Israel on
    their going-up from Egypt.
So the Kenites turned-aside from amidst Amalek.

7 And Sha'ul struck-down Amalek, from Havila (as far as) where-
    you-come to Shur, which is in front of Egypt.

8 He seized Agag king of Amalek alive,
while all the people he devoted-to-destruction with the mouth
    of the sword.

9 But Sha'ul and the people spared Agag
and the best of the sheep and the cattle, and the second-best,
    the lambs and all that was goodly;
they would not devote-them-to-destruction—
(only) all the property (that was) despised and rejected did they
    devote-to-destruction.

10 Now Yhwh's word came to Shemu'el, saying:

11 I repent
that I kinged Sha'ul as king,
for he has turned from (following) after me,
and my words he has not fulfilled!

---

5 WADI: An often dry riverbed or ravine.
6 KENITES: Another desert tribe, like the Amalekites descended from Moses' father-in-law Jethro. Here the relationship leads to their being spared in the midst of Israel's vengeance.
9 THEY WOULD NOT: Or "They were not willing to."

Shemu'el was upset,
and he cried out to YHWH all night.

12 Then Shemu'el started-early to meet Sha'ul in the morning,
and it was told to Shemu'el, saying:
Sha'ul went to Carmel
—here, he was setting up for himself a monument—
and (then) he turned-about, crossed over and went down to
Gilgal.

13 When Shemu'el came to Sha'ul,
Sha'ul said to him:
Blessed are you of YHWH!
I have fulfilled the word of YHWH.

14 But Shemu'el said:
Then what is this voice of sheep in my ears,
and the voice of oxen that I hear!

15 Sha'ul said:
From the Amalekites they have brought them,
what the people spared as the best of the sheep and the oxen,
in order to slaughter (them) to YHWH your God;
what-was-left we devoted-to-destruction.

16 Shemu'el said to Sha'ul:
Tarry and I will tell you what YHWH spoke to me in the night.
He said to him: Speak!

17 Shemu'el said:
Though you may be too small in your (own) eyes,
aren't you head of the tribes of Israel?
For YHWH has anointed you as king over Israel!

---

12 CARMEL: In southern Judah, just southeast
of Hevron; not to be confused with the high
country in and around present-day Haifa.

18 Now Yhwh sent you on a journey,
    he said:
    Go, devote-to-destruction the sinners, Amalek;
    you are to wage-battle against them until you have finished
        them off.
19 So why didn't you hearken to the voice of Yhwh?
    You swooped down on the spoil
    and did what was evil in Yhwh's eyes.
20 Sha'ul said to Shemu'el:
    I did hearken to the voice of Yhwh!
    I went on the journey on which Yhwh sent me:
    I brought back Agag king of Amalek,
    while Amalek I devoted-to-destruction;
21 but the people took from the spoils
    sheep and oxen, the premier-part of what-was-devoted,
    to slaughter to Yhwh your God at Gilgal!
22 Shemu'el said:
        Is there pleasure for Yhwh in offerings-up and slaughter-
            offerings
        (more) than in hearkening to the voice of Yhwh?
        Here, hearkening is better than slaughter-offering,
        listening than the fat of rams.
23   Indeed, (like) a sin of diviners is rebellion,
        (like) the iniquity of *terafim* a display-of-arrogance.
        Because you have rejected the word of Yhwh,
        he has rejected you from (being) king!
24 Sha'ul said to Shemu'el:
    I have sinned,

23 *TERAFIM*: Household idols (cf. Gen. 31:19,
    33–35).

72

indeed, I have crossed the order of YHWH and your words,
for I was afraid of the people,
and so I hearkened to their voice.

25 But-now,
pray bear-away my sin
and return with me, so that I may prostrate-myself to YHWH.

26 Shemu'el said to Sha'ul:
I will not return with you,
for you have rejected the word of YHWH,
so YHWH has rejected you from being king over Israel!

27 As Shemu'el turned-about to go,
he held-on to the corner of his cloak, and it tore.

28 Shemu'el said to him:
YHWH has torn the kingdom of Israel from off you today
and will give it to your neighbor, the one better than you!

29 And also the Eternal-One of Israel does not speak-falsely and
does not repent—
for he is not a human-being, to repent!

30 He said:
I have sinned—
(but) pray honor me in front of the elders of my people, in
front of Israel:
return with me, so that I may prostrate-myself to YHWH your
God!

31 So Shemu'el returned after Sha'ul,
and Sha'ul prostrated-himself to YHWH.

32 Then Shemu'el said:
Bring-close to me Agag king of Amalek!

---

24 CROSSED: Violated.   27 HE: Sha'ul, in a gesture of entreaty.

Agag went to him (with) faltering (steps),

and Agag said:

Surely the bitterness of death is approaching!

33 Shemu'el said:

As your sword bereaved women,

so will your mother be of women most bereaved!

And Shemu'el hacked Agag (to pieces) in the presence of
YHWH at Gilgal.

34 Then Shemu'el went (back) to Rama,

while Sha'ul went-up to his house (at) the Hill of Sha'ul.

35 And Shemu'el did not again see Sha'ul until the day of his
death,

for Shemu'el was mourning over Sha'ul,

while YHWH had repented that he had made Sha'ul king over
Israel.

32 (WITH) FALTERING (STEPS): Following
LXX and JPS; McCarter, following Kimhi,
reads it as "in fetters."

THE RISE OF DAVID AND
THE FALL OF SHA'UL (I:16–II:1)

AS THE CENTRAL and most vital personality in the books from Joshua through Kings, David will now command three-fourths of the book of Samuel. In the half of I Samuel that remains, we will follow his meteoric rise from the sheepfolds of Bethlehem to the court of Sha'ul, where he will excel as musician and warrior, winning the love (cf. chap. 18) of the people, the heir apparent, and the king's daughter. Although in the story of David's selection as king (16) God constantly admonishes Shemu'el and the reader to ignore what is "seen" (i.e., externals), it does not seem to hurt that David is handsome and talented. Everyone seems to fall at his feet without much exertion on his part: giants, Philistine soldiers, women.

Although these stories have become familiar in the Western world, a rereading will still yield rewards, and occasionally some surprises. A case in point is chapter 17, the Golyat (Goliath) story. Examination of its vocabulary shows that beyond the fairy-tale aspect lies a serious biblical issue: the respect due God. Thus the most-repeated words in the story are "mock" and "ranks [of the Living God]"; Golyat must be killed, not merely to save the Israelites, but to uphold God's honor. Also notable is the fact that David cuts off the giant's head; eventually Sha'ul and his son Ish-Boshet will meet the same fate, which Polzin (1989) sees as emblematic of the leadership issue in this book.

The narratives in these chapters center around several themes: Sha'ul's pursuit of David (18–26); David in exile all over Judah and especially among the Philistine enemy (19–30); his opportunities to kill Sha'ul (24–26); and Sha'ul's last days (28, 31). These are heightened by the powerfully drawn triangle between David, Sha'ul, and Yehonatan, and by the appearance of a number of secondary characters who help to put David's sometimes opaque personality in sharper focus. Thus it takes Golyat (17) to bring out his intense faith, and Avigayil (25) to reveal his not-so-restrained personality (from the looks of that story, he might well have assassinated Sha'ul after all in chapters 24 and 26).

Key words abound and evolve in this section. As previously mentioned, the account of David's anointing centers around "seeing" (cf. Alter 1981). The oft-repeated threat of "death" in chapter 19 will ironically be resolved by that of Sha'ul, not David. The aging king's attempt to catch David in his "hand" (23, 24, 26) will fail, and he knows that in the end, "the kingdom of Israel will be-established in your hand" (24:21). The reader should pay careful attention to these and other repeating words within individual chapters.

As I Samuel closes, David is on the sidelines, and our attention focuses back on Sha'ul, with whom the story of Israel's venture into kingship opened. Despite Sha'ul's failures and his subsequent descent into monomaniacal pursuit of David, there is something that leads many readers to view the first king of Israel not as evil, but as tragically marred. The final stories about him, at Ein Dor (28) and in battle at Mount Gilbo'a (31), naturally elicit sympathy: the medium tenderly feeds him in the former story, while the men of Yavesh Gil'ad care for his body in the latter. As eulogized in David's resonant poem of II Sam. 1, Sha'ul is not a misfit but a "mighty" warrior who has fallen, surely not a cause for rejoicing.

𝒴HWH *said to Shemu'el: / How long*
will you keep-on-mourning for Sha'ul?
I Sam. 16 :1

16:1 YHWH said to Shemu'el:

How long will you keep-on-mourning for Sha'ul,

when I myself have rejected him from being-king over Israel?

Fill your horn with oil and go:

I am sending you to Yishai the Betlehemite,

for I have selected a king for me from among his sons.

2 Shemu'el said:

How can I go?

If Sha'ul hears, he will kill me!

YHWH said:

A she-calf of the herd you are to take in your hand;

you are to say:

It is to slaughter-offer to YHWH (that) I have come.

3 (Then) you are to call Yishai for the slaughter-meal,

and I myself will make-known to you what you are to do;

you are to anoint for me the one that I tell you to.

4 Shemu'el did that which YHWH had spoken,

he came to Bet Lehem,

and the elders of the town trembled to meet him,

they said:

(Is) it in peace, your coming?

5 He said:

In peace—

(it is) to slaughter-offer to YHWH (that) I have come!

Purify-yourselves

16:1 HOW LONG: Lit. "until when."
YISHAI: Trad. English "Jesse."
SELECTED: Another meaning of "see,"
Heb. *ra'iti,* so central in this chapter.
FOR ME: As contrasted with "(for) us"
(Israel) in 8:5 (Goldman, citing Kimhi).

3 SLAUGHTER-MEAL: In the Bible, meat is
rarely eaten outside of a cultic setting—
hence the need to purify the family in v. 5.

so that you may come with me to the slaughter-meal.
So he purified Yishai and his sons
and called them to the slaughter-meal.

6 And it was, when they came,
that he saw Eli'av;
he said (to himself):
Surely, before YHWH is his anointed-one!

7 But YHWH said to Shemu'el:
Do not look at (what you) see of him, or at the tallness of his
    stature,
for I have rejected him!
For not as a human-being sees (does YHWH see)—
indeed, a human-being sees the eyes, but YHWH sees the heart.

8 Then Yishai called Avinadav, and had-him-pass before
    Shemu'el,
but he said:
Also this one, YHWH has not chosen.

9 Then Yishai had Shamma pass by,
but he said:
Also this-one, YHWH has not chosen.

10 So Yishai had his seven sons pass before Shemu'el,
but Shemu'el said to Yishai:
YHWH has not chosen (any) of these!

11 Then Shemu'el said to Yishai:
Are the lads at-an-end?

He said:
There still remains the youngest—
here, he is shepherding the flock.
Shemu'el said to Yishai:
Send and fetch him,
for we will not sit around (the table) until his coming here.
12 He sent and had him come
—now he was ruddy, with fair eyes, and pleasing to see.
Yhwh said:
Arise, anoint him, for this is he!
13 So Shemu'el took the horn of oil and anointed him amid his
    brothers.
And the spirit of Yhwh surged upon David from that day
    onward.
Then Shemu'el arose and went to Rama.

14 Now the spirit of Yhwh departed from Sha'ul,
and tormenting him was an evil spirit from Yhwh.
15 Sha'ul's servants said to him:
Now here, an evil spirit of God is tormenting you;
16 pray let our lord speak—your servants (stand) before you:
let a man be sought,
one-how-knows how to play the lyre,
that it may be, whenever there is upon you an evil spirit of
    God,

---

13 DAVID: Pronounced "dah-*veed*." This is the first occurrence of the name, which means "beloved."

14 AN EVIL SPIRIT: That is, what was previously a gift now becomes a torment. The phrase does not imply a separate creature like a demon.

16 BEFORE YOU: Perhaps connoting "ready" (McCarter).

81

that he may play (it) with his hand, so that it is well with you.

17 Sha'ul said to his servants:
Pray select for me a man who plays well,
and have him come to me!

18 Then spoke up one of the serving-lads and said:
Here, I have seen a son of Yishai the Betlehemite,
one-who-knows how to play;
a mighty-man of valor,
a man of war,
skilled in words,
a man of (pleasing) form—
and Yhwh is with him.

19 So Sha'ul sent messengers to Yishai,
he said:
Pray send me David your son, who is with the flock.

20 Yishai took a donkey (laden with) bread and a skin of wine,
and one goat kid,
and sent (them) by the hand of David his son, to Sha'ul.

21 And David came to Sha'ul, and stood before him;
he grew to love him, exceedingly,
and he became his weapons bearer.

22 Sha'ul sent to Yishai, saying:
Pray let David remain-standing (in attendance) before me,
for he has found favor in my eyes.

23 And (so) it was:
whenever there was a spirit of God upon Sha'ul,
David would take up the lyre and play (it) with his hand,
and Sha'ul would have relief, and it would be-well with him;
the evil spirit would depart from him.

$\mathcal{W}$henever there was a spirit of God upon Sha'ul,
David would take up the lyre and play (it) with his hand

I Sam. 16 : 23

17:1 Now the Philistines gathered their encampments for battle,
they gathered-themselves together at Sokho, which is in Judah,
and encamped between Sokho and Azeika, at Efes-Dammim,

2 while Sha'ul and the men of Israel gathered-together and
encamped in the Valley of the Oak,
and arranged-their-ranks for battle to meet the Philistines.

3 Now the Philistines were stationed on a hill, on this-side,
while Israel was stationed on a hill, on that-side,
with the ravine between them.

4 And there came out the Man of the Space-Between, from the
Philistine ranks—
Golyat was his name, from Gat:
his height was six cubits and a span,

5 a helmet of bronze was upon his head,
(with) armor of scales he was clothed,—the weight of the
armor was five thousand *shekel*-weights of bronze—,

6 greaves of bronze were upon his legs,
and a scimitar of bronze was between his shoulders;

7 now the shaft of his spear was like a weaver's beam,
and the flashing-point of his spear was six hundred *shekel*-
weights of iron.

17:1 SOKHO: West of Bet Lehem, toward
Philistine territory.

4 MAN OF THE SPACE-BETWEEN: A
champion, to fight his opponent in what we
call No-Man's Land. The term takes on
additional resonance in this text; Goylat,
from the narrative's point of view, is the
first great obstacle "between" David and
the fame that paves his way to the throne,
and he is unnaturally tall—a parody of

Sha'ul's most notable physical feature.
GOLYAT . . . GAT: Trad. English
"Goliath . . . Gath."
CUBITS: Biblical units of length based on a
man's forearm; they varied from eighteen
to twenty-two inches. Golyat is thus over
nine feet tall in MT—but LXX and 4QSᵃ
read "four cubits," cutting him down to a
still intimidating six feet nine.

And the shield bearer walked before him.

8 He stood and called out to the ranks of Israel,
he said to them:
Why do you come-out and arrange-your-ranks for battle?
Am I not a Philistine, and you are the servants of Sha'ul?
Choose yourselves a man, that he may come-down to me!

9 If he prevails in doing-battle with me and strikes-me-down,
then we will become your servants,
but if *I* prevail and strike-him-down,
then you will become our servants, and will have to serve us.

10 And the Philistine said:
As for me,
I mock the ranks of Israel this day—
give me a man, so that we may do-battle together!

11 When Sha'ul and all Israel heard those words of the Philistine,
they were shattered and exceedingly afraid.

12 Now David was the son of this Efrayimite man, from Bet
Lehem in Judah,
his name was Yishai;
he had eight sons.
And in the days of Sha'ul the man was old, coming-along
among men.

13 Now they had gone, the three oldest sons of Yishai,
they had gone after Sha'ul, to battle
—the name(s) of his three sons who had gone to battle were:
Eli'av, the firstborn,

the second-to-him, Avinadav,
and the third-one, Shamma.

14 Now David, he was the youngest,
while the three oldest-ones had gone after Sha'ul.

15 Now David would go and return from (attending) upon
Sha'ul,
to shepherd the flock of his father in Bet Lehem.

16 And the Philistine would approach, early and late,
presenting himself for forty days.

17 Yishai said to David his son:
Pray take to your brothers this *efa* of parched-grain, and these
ten bread-loaves,
and run them out to the camp to your brothers,

18 and these ten cuts of milk-cheese, bring to the commander of
a thousand.
As for your brothers—take-account of (their) well-being,
and take-back an assurance from them.

19 For Sha'ul and they and all the fighting-men of Israel in the
Valley of the Oak were doing-battle with the Philistines.

20 David started-early in the morning,
he left the flock with a watchman,
he lifted up (the food) and went, as Yishai had charged him,
and came to the trenches,
as the forces were going-out to the ranks, as they were shouting in battle.

21 And Israel and the Philistines were arranged-in-ranks, rank
opposite rank.

19 THE VALLEY OF THE OAK: Or the Valley
of Eila (Trad. English Elah).

22 And David let down the gear from off him, in the hand of a
      watchman of gear,
    and ran to the ranks;
    when he arrived (there), he asked about his brothers, about
      (their) well-being.

23 While he was speaking with them,
    here, the Man of the Space-Between was coming-up, Golyat
      the Philistine his name, from Gat, from the ranks of the
      Philistines.
    He spoke according to those (former) words, and David heard.

24 And all the fighting-men of Israel, when they saw the man,
    fled before him,
    for they were exceedingly afraid.

25 The men of Israel said:
    Do you see this man who comes-up?
    Indeed, it is to mock Israel that he comes-up!
    It will be (that) the man who strikes-him-down—the king will
      enrich him with great riches,
    his daughter he will give him,
    and his father's house he will make free in Israel!

26 David said to the men who were standing with him, saying:
    What shall be done for the man who strikes-down this Philis-
      tine and removes the mocking from upon Israel?
    For who is this foreskinned Philistine
    that he has mocked the ranks of the Living God?

27 The people told him according to those words, saying:
    Thus shall be done for the man who strikes-him-down.

28 Now Eli'av his oldest brother heard as he spoke to the men,

and Eli'av's anger flared against David,

he said:

Why have you come-down, and with whom have you left that
little flock in the wilderness?

I know (well) your presumption and the evil of your
heart—

indeed, it is in order to see the battle that you have come-down
(here)!

29 David said:

What have I done now? It is only words!

30 And he went-around him, facing another,

and spoke to him according to those (earlier) words,

and the people answered him (with) words according to the
former words.

31 Now the words that David had spoken were heard,

and when they told (them) in the presence of Sha'ul, they had
him fetched.

32 David said to Sha'ul:

Don't let anyone's heart fall within himself!

Your servant will go and do-battle with this Philistine.

33 Sha'ul said to David:

You are not able to go against this Philistine, to do-battle with
him,

for you are (only) a lad,

while he is a man of battle since his youth!

34 David said to Sha'ul:

(Whenever) your servant would shepherd the flock for his
father,

if a lion or a bear came and carried off a lamb from the
flock,

35 I would go out after it and strike-it-down, and rescue (it) from
    its mouth;
    if it rose against me, I would seize it by its beard, and would
        strike it and cause-its-death.

36 Even the lion, even the bear your servant struck-down—
    so this foreskinned Philistine will be like one of them,
    for he has mocked the ranks of the Living God!

37 And David said:
    YHWH,
    who rescued me from the hand of the lion and from the hand
        of the bear,
    he will rescue me from the hand of this Philistine!
    Sha'ul said to David:
    Go, and may YHWH be with you!

38 And Sha'ul clothed David in his uniform:
    he put a helmet of bronze upon his head
    and clothed him in armor.

39 David strapped on his sword, over his uniform,
    and he tried to walk, but he was not used (to them).
    David said to Sha'ul:
    I cannot walk with these, for I am not used (to them).
    So David removed them from himself;

40 he took his stick in his hand
    and chose for himself five smooth stones from the wadi;
    he placed them in the shepherd's bag that he had, that is, in the
        pouch, with his sling in his hand,
    and he approached in Philistine.

41 And the Philistine went-along, going and coming-nearer to
        David,
    with the man, the shield bearer, before him.

42 And when the Philistine looked and saw David, he taunted
him,
for he was (only) a lad,
and ruddy, fair to look at.

43 The Philistine said to David:
Am I a dog,
that you come at me with sticks?
And the Philistine cursed David by his gods.

44 The Philistine said to David:
Come to me,
that I may give your flesh to the fowl of the heavens and to the
beasts of the field!

45 But David said to the Philistine:
You come at me
with a sword and a scimitar and a spear,
but I come at you
with the name of Yhwh of the Heavenly-Armies,
the God of the ranks of Israel, whom you have mocked!

46 This day, Yhwh will turn you over to my hand,
so that I will strike-you-down
and will remove your head from you;
I will give your carcass and the carcass of the Philistine camp
this day
to the fowl of the heavens and to the wildlife of the earth,
so that all the earth may know that Israel has a God,

47 and that all this assembly may know
that it is not with a sword or with a spear that Yhwh delivers—

43 STICKS: Heb. *maklot*, assonant with the immediately following *va-yekallel*, "cursed."
45 WITH THE NAME: A more conventional rendering would be "in the name," but the preposition is the same as the many "withs" earlier in the speech.

for the battle is YHWH's,
and he will give (all of) you into our hand!

48 And it was, when the Philistine arose to come-near to meet
David,
that David hurried-out and ran toward the ranks to meet the
Philistine;

49 and David stretched out his hand to the bag,
he took from there a stone, and slung (it), and he struck the
Philistine on his forehead:
the stone sank into his forehead
and he fell on his face to the ground.

50 So David overcame the Philistine with a sling and a stone,
he struck-down the Philistine and put-him-to-death,
while sword (there was) none in David's hand!

51 David ran and stood over the Philistine,
he took his sword and drew it from its sheath
and he dispatched him,
cutting off his head with it.
And when the Philistines saw that their mighty-man was dead,
they fled,

52 and the men of Israel and Judah arose and shouted,
they pursued after the Philistines as far as where you come to
the ravine, as far as the gates of Ekron,
and the Philistine wounded fell in the road to Shaarayim/
Double-Gate, as far as Gat, as far as Ekron.

53 When the Children of Israel returned from dashing-hotly after
the Philistines, they pillaged their camp.

54 And David took the head of the Philistine and brought it to Jerusalem, and his gear he put in his tent.

55 Now when Sha'ul saw David going out to meet the Philistine,
  he said to Avner, commander of the army
  Whose son is this lad, Avner?
  Avner said:
  As you live, O king, if I know. . . .
56 The king said:
  Make-inquiry yourself:
  Whose son is this youth?
57 So when David returned from striking-down the Philistine,
  Avner took him and brought him before Sha'ul,
  with the head of the Philistine in his hand.
58 Sha'ul said to him:
  Whose son are you, (my) lad?
  David said:
  The son of your servant Yishai the Betlehemite.

18:1 Now it was, when he finished speaking to Sha'ul
  —now Yehonatan's own self had become bound up with
    David's self,
  so that Yehonatan had grown-to-love David like his (own)
    self—
2 that Sha'ul took him (into service) on that day,

---

55 WHOSE SON: Since in the ancient Near East, kings were sometimes referred to as "sons of the gods," Sha'ul's question is not as innocent as it seems, at least to the audience. Cf. II Sam. 7:14. More troubling is why he seems not to know David, although he has met him already in chapter 16. It is apparent that the Golyat story is a separate tradition, a fact which had led to many scholarly analyses. The most helpful approach, I think, is the one expressed by Alter (1981, quoting Gros Louis, 1977), in which both theological and folkloric perspectives are found in the story, reflecting David as private person and David as public person. These two aspects will become crucial in all the stories about David.

18:1 SELF: Heb. *nefesh*, a person's life-essence or emotions, often translated anachronistically as "soul."

and did not give him (leave) to return to his father's house.

3 And Yehonatan and David cut a covenant,
because of his love for him, like his (own) self;

4 Yehonatan stripped off the cloak that he had on and gave it to
David,
along with his uniform, including his sword, his bow, and his
belt.

5 And David went out,
(and) everywhere that Sha'ul sent him, he prospered.
Sha'ul placed him over the men of war,
and it was good in the eyes of all the people, and also in the
eyes of Sha'ul's servants.

6 And it was in their coming-back, at David's return from striking the Philistine,
that women went out from all the towns in Israel, for singing
and dances,
to meet King Sha'ul with timbrels, with joyful-sounds and
with triangles.

7 And the dancing women chanted and said:
Sha'ul has struck-down his thousands,
but David—his myriads!

8 Sha'ul became exceedingly upset,
this matter was evil in his eyes,
he said (to himself):
They give-credit to David (for) myriads,
but to me they give-credit for thousands!
There yet (remains) for him only the kingdom!

---

7 MYRIADS: Units of ten thousand.

9 And Sha'ul was keeping-an-eye on David from that day on.

10 Now it was on the morrow,
that an evil spirit of God surged upon Sha'ul, and he ranted-
like-a-prophet in the midst of the house,
while David was playing (the lyre) with his hand, as (he had)
day after day,
and (there was) a spear in Sha'ul's hand;

11 and Sha'ul hurled the spear, he said (to himself):
I will strike David and the wall (together)!
But David evaded him twice.

12 And Sha'ul was afraid before David,
for YHWH was with him,
while from Sha'ul he had turned-away.

13 So Sha'ul kept-him-away from his (presence),
he made him a commander of a thousand,
and he went-out and came-back before the people.

14 So it was: David was prospering in all his ways,
and YHWH was with him.

15 And when Sha'ul saw that he was prospering exceedingly, he
was-in-dread before him,

16 but all Israel and Judah loved David,
for he was going-out and coming-back before them.

17 So Sha'ul said to David:
Here is my oldest daughter, Meirav,
her I will give you as a wife;
only: be for me a son of valor,
and fight the battles of YHWH!

11 DAVID AND THE WALL (TOGETHER):   13 WENT-OUT   AND   CAME-BACK: An
He seeks to pin David to the wall.   idiom denoting military leadership.

—for Sha'ul said (to himself):

Let not my (own) hand be against him,

but let there be against him the Philistines' hand!

18 David said to Sha'ul:

Who am I and who are my living-relatives, my father's clan in
Israel,

that I should become son-in-law to the king?

19 But it was

at the time for giving Meirav daughter of Sha'ul to David,

that she was given to Adriel the Maholatite as a wife.

20 Yet Mikhal daughter of Sha'ul had fallen-in-love with David,

and when it was told to Sha'ul, the matter was right in his eyes,

21 Sha'ul said (to himself):

I will give her to him,

that she may become a snare to him,

that against him may be the Philistines' hand!

So Sha'ul said to David a second (time):

You are to become-a-son-in-law to me today!

22 And Sha'ul charged his servants:

Speak to David secretly, saying:

Here, the king is pleased with you,

and all his servants love you;

so-now, become-a-son-in-law to the king!

23 And Sha'ul's servants spoke these words in David's hearing.

But David said:

Is it a light-thing in your eyes, becoming-a-son-in-law to the
king

—and I am but a man poor and of light-worth!?

---

21 SNARE: Driver understands this as "the
trigger of a trap."

24 Sha'ul's servants told him, saying:
   According to these words did David speak.
25 Sha'ul said:
   Say thus to David:
   The king takes no pleasure in any bride-price except for a hun-
      dred Philistines' foreskins
   to be avenged on the king's enemies
   —for Sha'ul planned to cause David's fall by the Philistines'
      hand.
26 So his servants told David all these words,
   and the matter was right in David's eyes to become-son-in-law
      to the king.
   Not (many) days were fulfilled
27 when David arose and went, he and his men,
   and he struck-down of the Philistines two hundred men.
   And David brought their foreskins and paid-them-in-full to the
      king,
   (for him) to become-son-in-law to the king;
   and Sha'ul gave him Mikhal his daughter as a wife.
28 And Sha'ul saw and knew that YHWH was with David,
   while Mikhal daughter of Sha'ul loved him.
29 And Sha'ul continued to be afraid of David, (even) more,
   Sha'ul was bearing-enmity to David all the days.
30 And the Philistine commanders went out (to battle),
   but it was, as often as they went-out, that David prospered
      more than all of Sha'ul's (other) servants,
   so that his name became exceedingly esteemed.

26 WERE FULFILLED: Passed.

19:1 So Sha'ul spoke to Yonatan his son and to all his servants
    about causing David's death.
    But Yehonatan son of Sha'ul took exceeding pleasure in David,

2 and Yehonatan told David, saying:
    Sha'ul my father is seeking to cause-your-death.
    So-now, pray take-care in the morning
    that you stay in a secret-place and hide-yourself.

3 As for me, I will go-out and stand next to my father in the field
      where you are;
    I myself will speak about you to my father,
    and whatever I see, I will tell to you.

4 So Yehonatan spoke of David (for) good to Sha'ul his father,
    he said to him:
    Let not the king sin against his servant, against David,
    for he has not sinned against you,
    for his deeds have been to your good, exceedingly!

5 He took his life in his hands and struck-down the Philistine,
    and YHWH wrought a great deliverance for all Israel
    —you saw (it) and rejoiced.
    So why would you sin against innocent blood
    by causing David's death for nothing?

6 And Sha'ul hearkened to Yehonatan's voice,
    Sha'ul swore:
    As YHWH lives, if he should be put-to-death . . . !

7 So Yehonatan called David,
    and Yehonatan told him all these words.
    And Yehonatan brought David to Sha'ul,

19:1 TOOK EXCEEDING PLEASURE IN: Or   5 THE PHILISTINE: Golyat.
"was exceedingly fond of."

and he was in his presence as yesterday and the day-before.

8   The battles continued;
David went out to do-battle against the Philistines,
and he struck them down, a great striking-down,
so that they fled before him.

9   And an evil spirit of Yhwh came upon Sha'ul:
he was sitting in his house, (with) his spear in his hand,
while David was playing (the lyre) with (his) hand.

10 And Sha'ul sought to strike, with his spear, David and the wall
(together),
but he slipped-away from Sha'ul,
so that he struck (only) the wall with his spear.
And David fled, escaping on that night.

11 And Sha'ul sent messengers to David's house, to watch out for
him and to put-him-to-death at daybreak,
but Mikhal his wife told David, saying:
If you don't escape with your life tonight,
tomorrow you will be put-to-death!

12 So Mikhal let David down through the window;
he went off, he got-away and escaped.

13 And Mikhal took *terafim* and put (it) in the bed,
and some twined goats'-hair she put at its head,
and covered (it) with a garment;

14 when Sha'ul sent messengers to fetch David,
she said:
He is sick.

15 So Sha'ul sent the messengers to see David, saying:

13 *ERAFIM:* See note to 15:23.

Bring him up in the bed to me, to put-him-to-death!

16 When the messengers arrived,
now here: *terafim* were in the bed, with some twined goats'-
hair at its head!

17 Sha'ul said to Mikhal:
Why have you deceived me thus?
You have sent-free my enemy, so that he has escaped!
Mikhal said to Sha'ul:
He said to me: Send me free—
why should I put-you-to-death?

18 Now David had gotten-away and escaped, coming to Shemu'el
at Rama,
and he told him all that Sha'ul had done to him.
And he went, he and Shemu'el, and they stayed in Nayot.

19 It was told to Sha'ul, saying:
Here, David is in Nayot, in Rama!

20 So Sha'ul sent messengers to take David,
and they saw a group of prophets ranting-in-prophecy,
with Shemu'el standing (there), stationed over them.
And there came upon Sha'ul's messengers the spirit of God,
so that they ranted-like-prophets, they too.

21 They told Sha'ul,
and he sent other messengers,
and they ranted-like-prophets, they too.
And Sha'ul again sent, a third (group of) messengers,
but they ranted-like-prophets, they too.

22 So he went, he too, toward Rama;

18 NAYOT: Either a place-name or possibly
"pasture-settlement" where prophets lived
(McCarter).

99

when he arrived at the great cistern that is in Sekhu,
he made-inquiry, he said:
Where are Shemu'el and David?
They said:
Here, in Nayot in Rama.

23 So he went there, to Nayot in Rama,
and there came upon him, him too, the spirit of God;
he went, going-along and ranting-like-a-prophet, until he
    arrived at Nayot in Rama.

24 And he stripped off, he too, his garments,
and he ranted-like-a-prophet, he too, before Shemu'el:
he fell down naked all that day and all night.
Therefore they say:
Is Sha'ul too among the prophets?

20:1 Now David fled from Nayot in Rama;
when he arrived (there), he said before Yehonatan:
What have I done?
What is my iniquity, what is my sin before your father
that he is seeking my life?

2 He said to him:
(Heaven) forbid!
You will not die—
(for) here, my father does not do anything great or small with-
    out revealing (it to) my ear.
Why should my father hide this matter from me? This cannot
    (be)!

3 David swore and said:
Your father knows, yes, knows
that I have found favor in your eyes,

so he has said (to himself):

Yehonatan is not to know about this, lest he be pained;

but: as Y<small>HWH</small> lives, and as you yourself live,

indeed, there is only the like of a footstep between me and
death!

4 Yehonatan said to David:

Whatever you yourself say, I will do for you.

5 David said to Yehonatan:

Here, the New-Moon is tomorrow,

when I must sit, yes, sit beside the king to eat;

send-me-free, and I will hide in the open-field, until the third
evening.

6 If your father takes-account, yes, account of my (absence)

and you say: David requested, requested-leave for himself
from me to run back to Bet Lehem his town

—for the yearly slaughter-meal is (happening) there for the
entire clan—:

7 if he says thus: Good!

(then) it is well for your servant.

But if he is upset, yes, upset,

know that he has concluded (to do) evil.

8 So act with loyalty toward your servant—

for you brought your servant into Y<small>HWH</small>'s covenant with you.

Now if there were in me any iniquity,

you would put-me-to-death,

but to your father, why would you bring me?

20:3 THE LIKE OF A FOOTSTEP: Following
Driver.
5 NEW-MOON: A major festival in biblical

times. This particular story is still read by
Jews in synagogue on the Sabbaths when
the new moon falls on the next day.

9 Yehonatan said:
(Heaven) forbid for you!
If I were to know, yes, know that my father has concluded evil
  to come against you,
would I not tell *that* to you?

10 David said to Yehonatan:
Who will tell me if your father answers you roughly?

11 Yehonatan said to David:
Come, let us go-out to the open-field.
So the two of them went-out to the open-field.

12 And Yehonatan said to David:
By Yhwh, the God of Israel,
when I have sounded out my father at this time tomorrow (or)
  the third (day),
and here: there is good (determined) toward David,
shall I not then send (word) to you and reveal (it to) your ear?

13 Thus may Yhwh do to Yehonatan, and thus may he add:
if it seems-good to my father, the evil (determined) against you,
I will reveal (it to) your ear
and will send you away, that you may go in peace.
And may Yhwh be with you, as he was with my father!

14 Will you not, while I am still alive,
will you not deal with me in the loyalty of Yhwh,
so that I do not die?

15 And you must not cut off your loyalty from my house, for the
  ages,
not even when Yhwh cuts off David's enemies, each-one from
  the face of the earth!

16 If Yehonatan be cut off from the House of David,
   may Yhwh seek (it) from the hand of "David's enemies!"

17 And Yehonatan swore to David again, by his love for him,
   for he loved him with a love (he had) for his very self.
   Then Yehonatan said to him:

18 Tomorrow is the New-Moon;
   you will be accounted-missing, for your seat will be accounted-
      empty.

19 (Once) you are three-days gone, go-down exceedingly
      (quickly);
   when you arrive at the place where you were hiding at the
      time of the (earlier) doings,
   you are to sit near that stone.

20 As for me, I will shoot three arrows to the side, to send-it-
      flying from me at a target.

21 Now here, I will send the serving-lad (saying):
   Go, find the arrows!
   If I say, yes, say to the lad:
   Here, the arrows are to-the-side-of-you, over there—
   fetch him and come-back, for it is well for you,
   there is no problem, as Yhwh lives.

22 But if I say thus to the boy:
   Here, the arrows are to-the-side-of-you, farther on—
   (then) go,
   for Yhwh will have sent you away.

16 IF YEHONATAN BE CUT OFF . . . MAY
   YHWH SEEK (IT): Following LXX and
   McCarter. "Seek" means "seek retribu-
   tion," "hold responsible."
   "DAVID'S ENEMIES": As in II Sam. 12:14,
   later scribes have added the word "enemies,"
   in order to avoid placing a curse on David (in
   the other passage, God is the object).

17 WITH A LOVE (HE HAD) . . . : Following Waltke and O'Connor.

19 THAT STONE: Heb. Unclear; MT "the
   Ezel Stone."

23 And as for the promise that we have spoken, I and you,
here: YHWH will be between me and you, for the ages!

24 So David hid in the open-field,
and it was at the New-Moon, when the king sat by the food to
eat,

25 that the king sat in his seat as time and time (before),
at the seat (next to) the wall.
Yehonatan was at-the-front, and Avner sat at Sha'ul's side,
but David's place was counted-empty.

26 Now Sha'ul did not say anything on that day,
for he said (to himself):
It is an accident,
he is not ritually-pure, for he has not been purified.

27 But it was on the morrow of the New-Moon, (on) the second
(day),
that David's place was counted-empty.
So Sha'ul said to Yehonatan his son:
Why hasn't the son of Yishai come, even yesterday, even today,
to the food?

28 Yehonatan answered Sha'ul:
David requested, yes, requested-leave for himself from me, to
(go to) Bet Lehem;

29 he said: Pray send me off,
for (it is) the slaughter-meal of the clan for us in the town,
and my brother commanded me (to come).
So-now, if I have found favor in your eyes,

---

25 AT-THE-FRONT: Following LXX (reflecting *vykdm*); MT has *vykm,* "arose."

26 ACCIDENT . . . NOT RITUALLY-PURE:
The New-Moon festival required ritual

purity of its participants; if one had a bodily
discharge of the "polluting" kind (cf. Lev.
11–15), for instance, one was temporarily
excluded.

pray let me escape, that I may see my brothers.
Therefore he has not come to the king's table.

30 Sha'ul's anger flared up against Yehonatan,
he said to him:
Son of a rebellious girl!
Don't I know that you have chosen the son of Yishai,
to your shame and to the shame of your mother's nakedness?

31 Indeed: all the days that the son of Yishai is alive on the earth,
you will not be established, you or your kingdom!
So-now,
send and fetch him to me,
for he is a son of death!

32 Yehonatan answered Sha'ul his father,
he said to him:
Why should he be put-to-death? What has he done?

33 But Sha'ul hurled the spear at him, to strike him down,
and (so) Yehonatan knew
that his father had concluded to put David to death.

34 Yehonatan arose from the table in flaming anger;
he did not eat food on the second day of the New-Moon,
for he was pained about David,
for his father had humiliated him.

35 So it was at daybreak,
that Yehonatan went out to the open-field to (his) appointment
(with) David,
a young serving-lad with him.

36 He said to his lad: Run, pray find the arrows that I shoot.
As the lad ran, he shot an arrow past him,

---

30 SON OF A REBELLIOUS GIRL!: JPS: 31 A SON OF DEATH: Or "a dead man."
"son of a perverse, rebellious woman!"

37 and when the lad came to the place of the arrow that
 Yehonatan had shot,
 Yehonatan called after the lad, he said:
 Isn't the arrow to-the-side-of-you, farther on?
38 And Yehonatan called after the lad:
 Hurry! Be-quick! Don't stand-still!
 So Yehonatan's serving-lad collected the arrow and brought it
 to his lord.
39 Now the lad knew nothing;
 only Yehonatan and David knew (about) the matter.
40 And Yehonatan gave his weapons to the lad that he had,
 he said to him:
 Go, bring (these) to the town.
41 When the lad went off,
 David arose from the Negev direction,
 he flung-himself on his brow to the ground, and prostrated-
 himself three times
 and each-man kissed his fellow,
 and each-man wept with his fellow, until David (had wept) a
 great-deal.
42 Yehonatan said to David:
 Go in peace,
 (seeing) that the two-of-us, (even) we have sworn in the name
 of Yhwh, saying:
 May Yhwh be between me and you, between my seed and
 your seed, for the ages!
21:1 He arose and went away,
 while Yehonatan came (back) to the town.

41 NEGEV DIRECTION: South.

2 And David came to Nov, to Ahimelekh the priest,
   and Ahimelekh trembled (coming) to meet David,
   he said to him:
   Why are you alone, with no (other) man with you?

3 David said to Ahimelekh the priest:
   The king has charged me with a matter,
   he said to me:
   No-man is to know anything about the matter that I am send-
       ing you on, that I have charged you with—
   and (to) the serving-lads I have made-known (about only) such
       and so a place.

4 So-now,
   what do you have on hand?
   Five (rounds of) bread give into my hand, or whatever (can be)
       found.

5 The priest answered David and said:
   There is no ordinary bread on hand,
   only consecrated bread is there—
   provided that the lads have kept themselves away, of course,
       from women.

6 David answered the priest,
   he said to him:
   Certainly women have been held-back from us, so yesterday
       and the day-before;
   whenever I went out, the lad's vessels were holy, even (if it
       was) an ordinary journey,
   how much more so today—the vessels are consecrated!

7 So the priest gave him consecrated (bread),

21:2 NOV: Trad. English "Nob," just northeast   4 ON HAND: Lit., "under your hand"; simi-
(and within sight) of Jerusalem.   larly in verses 5 and 9.

for there was no bread there except for the Bread of the Presence that was removed from the presence of YHWH,
for (them) to put warm bread (there) at the time of its being
   taken away.

8   Now a man was there from the servants of Sha'ul that day,
held (in custody) in the presence of YHWH,
his name was Do'eg the Edomite,
chief of the shepherds that Sha'ul had.

9   And David said to Ahimelekh:
Don't you have on hand here a spear or a sword?
For neither my sword nor my weapons did I take along in my
   hand,
for the matter (from) the king was urgent!

10   The priest said:
The sword of Golyat the Philistine, whom you struck down in
   the Valley of the Oak—
here it is, wrapped up in a garment, behind the *efod*.
If it is what you (want to) take for yourself, take (it),
for there is no other-one besides it in-this-place!
David said: There is none like it—give it to me!

11   David arose,
he got-away on that day from the presence of Sha'ul,
and came to Akhish king of Gat.

12   Now the servants of Akhish said to him:
Isn't this David, the king of the land?

---

7 BREAD OF THE PRESENCE: Cf. Ex.
25:30, where this bread is placed in the
"Dwelling" (Tabernacle); it corresponds to
food set out for the gods in pagan sanctuar-
ies. In the Bible its use is merely symbolic.
8 HELD: The reason for his detention is not
clear.
DO'EG: The name derives from (or at least
sounds like) the verb "worry"; he becomes
cause for more than worry in the next chapter (cf. David's words in 22:22).

Isn't it about this-one that they chant in (their) dances, saying:
Sha'ul has struck-down his thousands,
but David—his myriads!?

13 David took these words to heart, and was exceedingly afraid in
the presence of Akhish king of Gat;

14 so he altered his demeanor in their eyes
and feigned-madness (while he was) in their hands:
he drummed on the doors of the gate
and let his spittle run-down his beard.

15 Akhish said to his servants:
Here, look at the man acting-crazy!
Why do you bring him to me?

16 Do I lack crazy-people
that you have brought this-one to act-crazy around me?
Should this-one come into my house?

22:1 David went from there and escaped to the Cave of Adullam.
When his brothers and his father's entire house heard, they
went-down to him there.

2 And there gathered to him every man (in) straits, every man
that had a creditor, and every man of bitter feelings—
he became commander over them.
And there were with him about four hundred men.

3 David went from there to Mitzpe/Lookout of Mo'av;
he said to the king of Mo'av:
Pray let my father and my mother stay with you
until I know what God intends-to-do with me.

---

14 DRUMMED: Following LXX.
22:1 ADULLAM: A town in the foothills between Bethlehem (south of Jerusalem) and
Gath (cf. Gen. 38).

4 So he led them into the presence of the king of Mo'av, and
   they stayed with him, all the days of David's being at the
   stronghold.

5 But the prophet Gad said to David:
   You are not to stay at the stronghold;
   go, come-you-forth to the land of Judah.
   So David went and came to the Forest of Heret.

6 And Sha'ul heard that David's (whereabouts) were known, and
   (those of) the men that were with him.
   Now Sha'ul was staying at Giv'a, under the tamarisk at Rama,
   with his spear in his hand,
   and all his servants were standing-in-attendance around him.

7 Sha'ul said to his servants who were standing around him:
   Pray hearken, O Binyaminites:
   Is it really to all-of-you that the son of Yishai will give fields and
   vineyards?
   Will he make all-of-you commanders of thousands and com-
   manders of hundreds,

8 that all-of-you have banded-together against me?
   And no one reveals (it to) my ear when my son cuts (a covenant) with the son of Yishai;
   none of you is concerned about me or reveals (it to) my ear
   that my son has raised up my servant against me as an
   ambusher, as is this day!

9 Then Do'eg the Edomite spoke up
   —he was standing near the servants of Sha'ul—
   and said:

---

3 MO'AV: Trad. English "Moab," the territory due east of the Dead Sea (in today's
Jordan).

5 GAD: A prophet not previously mentioned;
cf. II Sam. 24:11 ff.

8 BANDED-TOGETHER: Others, "conspired."

I saw the son of Yishai come to Nov, to Ahimelekh son of
    Ahituv;

10 he inquired for him of YHWH, and provisions he gave him,
    and the sword of Golyat the Philistine he gave him!

11 The king sent to call Ahimelekh son of Ahituv the priest
    along with all of his father's house, the priests that were at
      Nov,
    and all-of-them came to the king.

12 Sha'ul said:
    Pray hearken, son of Ahituv!
    He said:
    Here I am, my lord.

13 Sha'ul said to him:
    Why have you (all) banded-together against me, you and the
      son of Yishai,
    by your giving him food and a sword
    and inquiring for him of God,
    to rise up against me as an ambusher, as is this day?

14 Ahimelekh answered the king, he said:
    But who among all your servants is like David—trustworthy,
    the king's son-in-law, commander over your obedient-
      bodyguard, and honored in your house?

15 (Only) today I first inquired for him of God—(Heaven) forbid
      for me:
    don't let the king place a word (of accusation) against his ser-
      vant (or) against all my father's house,
    for your servant did not know about all this, anything small or
      great!

14 OBEDIENT-BODYGUARD: From Heb.
shamo'a, "hearken, obey."

16 But the king said:
　　You shall die, yes, die, Ahimelekh,
　　you and all your father's house!

17 So the king said to the outrunners who were standing near
　　　　him:
　　Turn-about and put-to-death the priests of YHWH,
　　because their hand too is with David,
　　and because they knew that he was getting-away and did not
　　　　reveal (it to) my ear!
　　But the king's servants would not stretch out their hand
　　to smite the priests of YHWH.

18 So the king said to Do'eg:
　　You turn-about and smite the priests!
　　So Do'eg the Edomite turned-about, and *he* smote the priests:
　　he put-to-death on that day eighty-five men who wore a linen
　　　　efod;

19 and as for Nov, the town of the priests, he struck it with the
　　　　mouth of the sword,
　　from man to woman and from child to suckling,
　　and ox and donkey and sheep,
　　with the mouth of the sword.

20 But there escaped one son of Ahimelekh son of Ahituv,
　　his name was Evyatar,
　　he got-away after David.

21 And Evyatar told David
　　that Sha'ul had killed the priests of YHWH.

22 Then David said to Evyatar:

17 OUTRUNNERS: Goldman notes their
function as executioners (cf. II Kings 10:25).

I knew that day, when Do'eg the Edomite was there,
that he would tell, yes, tell Sha'ul.
I myself am responsible for every life in your father's house!

23 Stay with me, do not be afraid,
for they must (first) seek my life who seek your life;
indeed, you (will be) under guard with me.

23:1 They told David, saying:
Here, (the) Philistines are waging-battle against Ke'ila,
they are plundering the threshing-floors!

2 David inquired of YHWH, saying:
Shall I go and strike these Philistines?
YHWH said to David:
Go and strike the Philistines, and deliver Ke'ila.

3 Now David's men said to him:
Look, we are here in Judah, afraid;
shall we really go to Ke'ila, against the Philistine ranks?

4 So David once again inquired of YHWH,
and YHWH answered him, he said:
Arise, go-down to Ke'ila,
for I give (the) Philistines into your hand!

5 So David went, along with his men, to Ke'ila,
he waged-battle against the Philistines:
he led-away their livestock and struck them down, a great
striking-down;
thus David delivered the settled-folk of Ke'ila.

---

20 EVYATAR: Trad. English "Abiathar." The name appropriately suggests the verb *yatar*, "to remain" (Garsiel 1991).

22 RESPONSIBLE: Following LXX; MT has "turned-about," recalling its use in v. 18.

23:1 KE'ILA: South of Adullam, where David had fled from Gat.

6 —Now it was, when Evyatar son of Ahimelekh had gotten-
away to David, to Ke'ila,
that an *efod* had gone-down in his hand.—

7 When it was told to Sha'ul that David had come to Ke'ila,
Sha'ul said (to himself):
God has alienated him into my hand,
for he has turned-himself-over by entering a town (with)
double-doors and bars!

8 Sha'ul summoned all the fighting-people for battle,
to go-down to Ke'ila, to besiege David and his men.

9 When David realized that Sha'ul was concocting evil against
him,
he said to Evyatar the priest: Bring-close the *efod*!

10 And David said:
O Yhwh, God of Israel,
your servant has heard, yes, heard
that Sha'ul is seeking to come to Ke'ila to bring-ruin to the
town on my account!

11 Will the inhabitants of Ke'ila turn-me-over to his hand?
Will Sha'ul go-down as your servant has heard?
O Yhwh, God of Israel,
Pray tell your servant . . .
Yhwh said:
He-will-go-down.

12 David said:
Will the inhabitants of Ke'ila turn-me-over, along with my

---

6 AN *EFOD* HAD GONE-DOWN: In typical biblical fashion, what seems like an intrusion here will make sense later (v. 9).

7 ALIENATED: Transferred, as in "alienating property" (Edward Greenstein, written communication).
TURNED-HIMSELF-OVER: Lit., "closed himself up"; others, "delivered."

men, to the hand of Sha'ul?

YHWH said:

They-will-turn-(you)-over.

13 So David and his men arose, about six hundred men,

they moved-out from Ke'ila, and went-about wherever they
could go-about.

Now when it was told to Sha'ul that David had escaped from
Ke'ila,

he held (himself) back from moving-out.

14 And David stayed in the wilderness, in the strongholds,

he stayed in the hill-country, in the Wilderness of Zif,

and Sha'ul sought him all the days,

but God did not give him into his hand.

15 And David saw that Sha'ul was going-forth to seek his life

—David was in the Wilderness of Zif, in the woods.

16 But Yehonatan son of Sha'ul arose and went to David in the
woods,

he strengthened his hand in God

17 and said to him:

Do not be afraid,

for the hand of Sha'ul my father will not find you;

you yourself will reign-as-king over Israel,

and I will be your second-in-command.

Even Sha'ul my father knows this!

---

14 WILDERNESS OF ZIF: Southeast of Hevron, flanking the Judean desert.

15 IN THE WOODS: Or perhaps a place-name,
"Horeish." In fact much of biblical Israel

seems to have been wooded, a situation
which began to change already in antiquity.

16 STRENGTHENED HIS HAND: Encour-
aged. For the reverse image, cf. II 4:1.

18   So the two of them cut a covenant in the presence of Yhwh.
   And David stayed in the woods, while Yehonatan went-back to
      his house.

19   Some Zifites went up to Sha'ul at Giv'a, saying:
   Isn't David hiding-himself among us in the strongholds in the
      woods,
   at the Hill of Hakhila which is south of the wasteland?
20   So then, according to all your craving, O king, to come-
      down—come-down,
   and (it will be) our (task), turning him over to the king's hand.
21   Sha'ul said:
   Blessed are you of Yhwh,
   that you have taken-pity on me!
22   Pray go, ascertain once-again,
   learn and see his place where his foot (treads and) who has
      seen him there,
   for they have said to me that that he acts-shrewdly, yes,
      shrewdly.
23   So see and learn in which of all the hiding-places he hides-
      himself,
   and return to me when (it is) certain,
   then I will go with you,
   and it will be: if he is in the region,
   I will search for him among all the thousands of Judah.
24   They arose and went to Zif, ahead of Sha'ul,
   while David and his men were in the Wilderness of

19 HILL OF HAKHILA: Exact location unknown.

Ma'on/Abode, in the plain south of the wasteland.

25 Then Sha'ul and his men went to seek (for him);

when it was told to David,

he went down to a certain crag and stayed in the Wilderness of Ma'on.

When Sha'ul heard, he pursued after David, in the Wilderness of Ma'on.

26 And Sha'ul went on (one) side of a hill, over-here,

with David and his men on the (other) side of the hill, over-there.

And David was in haste to get-away from Sha'ul,

while Sha'ul and his men were closing in on David and his men, to capture them.

27 But messenger came to Sha'ul, saying:

Hurry! Come,

for the Philistines are raiding the region!

28 So Sha'ul had-to-turn-back from pursuing after David,

he went to meet the Philistines.

Therefore that place was called: Crag of the Parting.

24:1 And David went up from there

and stayed in the strongholds of Ein Gedi.

2 Now it was, when Sha'ul returned from (pursuing) after the Philistines,

that it was told to him, saying:

Here, David is in the Wilderness of Ein Gedi!

---

24 MA'ON: Northwest of Masada and hence west of the Dead Sea.

24:1 EIN GEDI: The name means "Spring of the Goat-Kid." It is the famous oasis just west of the Dead Sea.

3   So Sha'ul took three thousand men, hand-picked from all
      Israel,
   and went to seek out David and his men, in front of the Wild-
      Goat Rocks.

4   He came to (some) sheep pens along the way, and (there) was a
      cave there;
   and Sha'ul went in to "cover his feet,"
   while David and his men were staying in the recesses of the
      cave.

5   David's men said to him:
   Here is the day about which Yhwh said to you:
   Here, I give your enemy into your hand!
   You may do with him whatever seems-good in your eyes!
   So David arose and cut off the corner of the cloak that
      belonged to Sha'ul, stealthily.

6   But it was after that,
   that David's heart struck him (with remorse),
   because he had cut off the corner that belonged to Sha'ul,

7   He said to his men:
   (Heaven) forbid for me from Yhwh
   if I should do this thing to my lord, to Yhwh's anointed,
   to stretch out my hand against him,
   for he is Yhwh's anointed!

8   And David rebuked his men with these words,
   and did not give-them-leave to rise up against Sha'ul,

---

4 COVER HIS FEET : A euphemism for
defecating; "feet" can refer to "genitals" in
other biblical expressions (cf. II Sam. 11:8).

5 CORNER OF THE CLOAK: In ancient
Near Eastern practice, the hem of a cloak

or robe was a personal sign, used for identi-
fication.

7 FOR HE IS YHWH'S ANOINTED!: This
passage has at times served in European
history as an argument against regicide.

while Sha'ul arose from the cave, and went on his way.

9 But David arose after that
and came-out of the cave, and he called out after Sha'ul, say-
ing:
My lord king!
When Sha'ul looked behind him,
David bowed, brow to the ground, and prostrated-himself,

10 and David said to Sha'ul:
Why do you hearken to people's words (who are) saying:
Here, David is seeking evil-against-you?

11 Here, this day your (own) eyes have seen
how Yhwh gave you today into my hand, in (this) cave;
I intended to kill you,
but I had-compassion on you:
I said (to myself):
I will not stretch out my hand against my lord,
for he is Yhwh's anointed!

12 And Father, see too:
see the corner of your cloak in my hand—
for when I cut off the corner of your cloak,
I did not kill you!
(So) learn and see that there is no evil or rebellion in my hand,
nor have I sinned against you—
yet you are stalking my life, to take it!

13 May Yhwh see-justice-done between me and you,
and may Yhwh take-vengeance for me upon you—
but my hand shall not be against you!

14 As the ancient proverb says: From wicked-ones comes
wickedness!

But my hand shall not be against you!

15 After whom has the king of Israel gone out?
After whom are you pursuing?
After a dead dog?
After a single flea?

16 May YHWH be decider, and may he judge between me and you:
when he sees, may be uphold my cause
and exact-justice from your hand!

17 Now it was, when David had finished speaking these words to
   Sha'ul,
that Sha'ul said:
Is that your voice, my son David?
And Sha'ul lifted up his voice and wept,

18 he said to David:
You are in-the-right, more than I,
for you have dealt with me (for) good, while I have dealt with
   you (for) evil!

19 And you yourself have told me today
how you have done good with me:
how YHWH turned me over to your hand, yet you did not kill
   me.

20 If a man comes-upon his enemy,
does he send him off on the road in good-condition?
May YHWH pay you back in-good-measure for this day,
(given) what you have done with me!

21 So-now, here: I know

that you will reign-as-king, yes, king,
and that the kingdom of Israel will be-established in your
    hand;
22 so now, swear to me by Yʜᴡʜ:
should you cut off my seed after me,
should you destroy my name from my father's house . . . !
23 And David swore (thus) to Sha'ul.
Then Sha'ul went (back) to his house,
while David and his men went up to the stronghold.

25:1 And Shemu'el died;
all Israel gathered and beat (the breast) for him,
then they buried him at his house in Rama.
And David arose and went-down to the Wilderness of Ma'on.

2 Now (there was) a man in Ma'on, with his doings in Carmel,
and the man was exceedingly great (in wealth):
he had sheep, three thousand, and a thousand goats,
and he was (occupied in) shearing his sheep in Carmel.
3 The man's name was Naval/Vile-One,
and his wife's name was Avigayil;
now the woman was of good sense, and fair of form,
but the man was rough and evil in deeds,

---

22 SEED: Descendants.
23 THE STRONGHOLD: Probably Masada, just west of the Dead Sea.
25 BEAT (THE BREAST): My thanks to Edward Greenstein for this renderin
25:2 MA'ON: MT has 'Par'an''; the present reading follows ancient versions.

3 NAVAL/VILE-ONE: Trad. English "Nabal." In some other contexts it means "fool, foolish-one." A more colloquial translation might use contemporary "jerk" or "idiot." Naval is also the anagram of another biblical villain, Jacob's uncle Lavan (Laban) in Genesis.

and he was a Calevite.

4   And David heard in the wilderness that Naval was shearing his
    sheep,

5   so David sent ten lads,
    David said to the lads:
    Go-up to Carmel;
    when you come to Naval, you are to inquire of him in my
        name for peace,

6   and you are to say thus: To Life!
    May you be (in) peace, your house be (in) peace,
    and all that is yours be (in) peace!

7   So-now, I have heard that you have shearers,
    now: the shepherds that you have were with us,
    we did not hurt them,
    and nothing has been unaccounted-for by them
    all the time of our being in Carmel—

8   inquire of your lads and they will tell you.
    So may (my) lads find favor in your eyes,
    for upon a good day we have come—
    pray give whatever you can find in your hand to your servant,
        to your son David!

9   So David's lads came
    and spoke to Naval according to all these words, in David's
        name,
    and then they stood-at-ease.

10 And Naval answered David's servants, he said:

---

3 CALEVITE: Descended from Calev (Caleb),
with Yehoshua (Joshua) one of the "good
spies" in Num. 13. More to the point here is
the play on *kelev*, "dog," a negative image

that recurs a number of times in Samuel.
6 TO LIFE!: The Hebrew is obscure; some
read "my brother," but that does not seem
appropriate.

Who is David? Who is the son of Yishai?

Nowadays (there are) many servants who break away, each-
one from his lord!

11 So should I take-away my bread, my water and my butchered-
meat that I butchered for my shearers,

and give (it) to men who come from I don't know where?

12 David's lads turned-about, back on their way,

when they returned, they came and told him according to all
these words.

13 Then David said to his men:

Each-man gird-on his sword!

Each-man girded-on his sword,

and also David girded-on his sword;

they went-up after David, about four hundred men,

while two hundred stayed with the gear.

14 Now Avigayil wife of Naval

was told (by) a lad from among the serving-lads, saying:

Here, David sent messengers from the wilderness to give-
blessing-of-greeting to our lord,

but he shrieked at them.

15 Now the men were exceedingly good to us,

we were not hurt (by them), we did not (find) anything unaccounted for the entire time we went-about with them,
during our being in the field;

16 they were a wall about us,

even by day, even by night,

the entire time we were beside them, pasturing the sheep.

---

14 SHRIEKED: A rare verb related to the
noun for "bird of prey," i.e., "shrieker."

17 So-now,
 learn and see what you should do,
 for evil is concluded against our lord and against his entire
  house!
 But he is (too much of a) son of worthlessness to speak to!
18 Avigayil hurried and took two hundred loaves-of-bread and
  two skins of wine
 and five sheep made-ready and five *seahs* of parched-grain
 and a hundred raisin-cakes and two hundred pressed-figs,
 and she put them on (some) donkeys.
19 Then she said to her lads:
 Cross-on ahead of me,
 here, I'll be coming behind you—
 but her husband Naval she did not tell.
20 And it was,
 as she was riding on the donkey, going-down a covert in a hill:
 here (were) David and his men, going-down to meet her,
 and she encountered them.
21 Now David had said (to himself):
 Surely (it was) in vain that I kept-safe all that belongs to this-
  one in the wilderness,
 and that nothing from all that belongs to him was
  unaccounted for—
 he has returned to me evil in place of good!
22 Thus may God do to "the enemies of" David, and thus may he
  add,
 if I leave from all that belongs to him, by the light of daybreak,
  (even) one peeing against the wall!

18 FIVE *SEAHS*: About a bushel.   THE LIGHT OF: Missing in MT but found
22 "THE ENEMIES OF": Cf. note to 20:16. in some manuscripts.

23 When Avigayil saw David,
    she hurried and got-down from the donkey
    and flung-herself before David, on her face,
    and prostrated-herself to the ground.
24 Having-flung-herself at his feet, she said:
    (On) me myself, my lord, be the iniquity!
    Pray let your maidservant speak (a word) in your hearing,
    and hearken to the words of your maidservant:
25 Pray let not my lord pay (any) mind to this worthless man, to
      Naval,
    for as his name is, so is he:
    Naval/Vile-One is his name, and vileness is with him!
    But as for me, your maidservant,
    I did not see my lord's lads whom you sent.
26 So-now, my lord,
    as YHWH lives and as you yourself live,
    (given) that YHWH has prevented you from coming into blood-
      guilt
    or delivering yourself by your hand (alone)—
    so-now,
    may your enemies be like Naval,
    (yes,) those who seek evil against my lord!
27 And now,
    this token-of-blessing that your handmaid has brought to my
      lord,
    let it be given to the lads who go-about in my lord's footsteps.

PEEING AGAINST THE WALL: Others, euphemistically, "a single male," but the imagery is doglike again. Unlike most modern translations, the King James Version got it right: "one that pisseth by the wall."
26 MY LORD: David.

28 Pray bear-in-forgiveness the rebellion of your maidservant,
    for when Yhwh makes, yes, makes of my lord a secure house
    —for the battles of Yhwh does my lord fight,
    and no evil may be found in you (all) your days—

29 should anyone arise to pursue you, to seek your life,
    may my lord's life be bound up in the bond of life with Yhwh
        your God,
    but may the life of your enemies be slung-away in the hollow
        of a sling!

30 And may it be,
    when Yhwh does for my lord according to all that he has
        promised—the good-things (come) upon you,
    and he commissions you as Prince over Israel:

31 then do not let this be for you an obstacle or a stumbling-block
        of heart (to) my lord, to shed blood for nothing,
    and for my lord to find-deliverance by himself (alone)!
    And when Yhwh does-good to my lord,
    then call-to-mind your maidservant!

32 David said to Avigayil:
    Blessed is Yhwh, the God of Israel,
    who has sent you this day to meet me!

33 And blessed is your discernment, and blessed are you,
    who has restrained me this day from coming into blood-guilt
        and delivering myself by my hand (alone).

34 For: as Yhwh, the God of Israel, lives, who has prevented me
        from doing evil to you—
    indeed, had you not hurried and come to meet me,

---

29 BOUND UP IN THE BOND OF LIFE: "Bond" here may mean a "bundle," i.e., a written document, as in the ancient idea of a "Book of Life." The phrase is still used by Jews in memorial prayers.

there wouldn't have been left to Naval by the light of daybreak
(even) one peeing against the wall!

35 David took from her hand what she had brought him,
and to her he said:
Go-up in peace to your house;
see,
I have hearkened to your voice, and have lifted up your face!

36 So Avigayil went back to Naval,
and here: he was having a drinking-meal in his house, like a
king's drinking-meal.
Now Naval's heart was in good-humor upon him—he was
intoxicated to excess—
so she did not tell him a thing, small or great, until the light of
daybreak.

37 But it was at daybreak,
when the wine was going out of Naval,
that his wife reported those things to him,
and his heart died within him, and he himself became (like a)
stone.

38 And it was about ten days (later)
that YHWH smote Naval, so that he died.

39 When David heard that Naval was dead,
he said:
Blessed is YHWH,
who has upheld my cause at having-been-mocked at the hand
of Naval,

---

37 THE WINE WAS GOING OUT OF
NAVAL: A play on another meaning of
n-v-l, "wineskin." The translator regrets not
being able to use "vial" in this context.
(LIKE A) STONE: Heb. le-aven, yet
another play on n-v-l.

and his servant he has held-back from (doing) evil!

And as for the evildoing of Naval, Yʜwʜ has returned (it) on
his head.

David sent and spoke for Avigayil, to take her for him as a wife;

40 David's servants came to Avigayil, to Carmel,

and spoke to her, saying:

David sent us to you, to take you as a wife for him.

41 She arose and prostrated-herself, brow to the ground,

and said:

Here, your maidservant is a handmaid to wash the feet of my
lord's servants!

42 Avigayil hurried and arose, mounting a donkey, with five of
her girls who went in her footsteps,

and went, (following) after David's messengers,

and she became for him a wife.

43 Now Ahino'am (too) David had taken, from Yizre'el,

and the two of them alike became wives for him;

44 for Sha'ul had given Mikhal his daughter, David's wife,

to Palti son of Layish, who was from Gallim.

26:1 Some Zifites came to Sha'ul at Giv'a, saying:

Isn't David hiding-himself at the Hill of Hakhila, facing the
wasteland?

2 So Sha'ul arose and went down to the Wilderness of Zif,

and with him were three thousand men, hand-picked (ones) of
Israel,

---

43 AHINO'AM: Levenson (1978) makes the
case that this is the wife of Sha'ul (cf. 14:50),
thus explaining Natan's words in II 12:7–8. A
son or successor stealing away his predecessor's wife or concubine thus established his
new power base; in this passage, the
process is muted but there.

to seek out David in the Wilderness of Zif.

3   And Sha'ul encamped at the Hill of Hakhila, which faces the
       wasteland, along the road,
     while David was staying in the wilderness;
     and when he saw that Sha'ul had come after him into the
       wilderness,

4   David sent spies, that he might know that Sha'ul had come for
       certain.

5   Then David arose and came to the place where Sha'ul was
       encamped;
     David saw the place where Sha'ul was lying, along with Avner
       son of Ner, the commander of his army,
     with Sha'ul lying in the trench, and all the fighting-people
       encamped round-about him.

6   And David spoke up, he said to Ahimelekh the Hittite and to
       Avishai son of Tzeruya, Yo'av's brother, saying:
     Who will go-down with me to Sha'ul, to the camp?
     Avishai said:
     I will go-down with you!

7   So David went, and Avishai, to the fighting-people at night-
       time,
     and here: Sha'ul was lying asleep in the trench,
     with his spear stuck into the ground at his head
     and with Avner and the fighting-people lying round-about
       him.

8   Avishai said to David:

6 YO'AV: Trad. English "Joab," David's
future commander in chief, who is also his
cousin (as Avner is to Sha'ul).

God has turned over your enemy today to your hand!
So-now, pray let me strike him with a spear into the ground
    (just) one time;
I will not (have to do) it twice to him!

9 But David said to Avishai:
You are not to bring him to ruin!
For who could stretch out his hand against Yhwh's anointed
    and be cleared?

10 And David said:
As Yhwh lives,
rather, Yhwh will smite him:
either his day will come, and he will die,
or into battle he will go-down and be swept away!

11 (Heaven) forbid for me, by Yhwh,
from stretching out my hand against Yhwh's anointed!
So-now,
pray take the spear that is at his head, and the cruse of water,
and let us go on our (way).

12 So David took the spear and the cruse of water at Sha'ul's
    head, and they went on their (way);
no one saw, no one knew, and no one awoke,
for all of them were sleeping,
for a deep-slumber (from) Yhwh had fallen upon them.

13 When David had crossed over the crossing,
he took-a-stand on the top of the hill, afar off,
—great was the space between them—

9 CLEARED: Of punishment.
12 DEEP-SLUMBER: A God-induced sleep (cf.
Gen. 2:21).

14 and David called out to the fighting-people and to Avner son of
Ner, saying:
Won't you answer, Avner?
Avner answered and said:
Who are you, (that) you call to the king!

15 David said to Avner:
Aren't you a man?
And who is like you in Israel?
So why haven't you kept-watch over your lord the king?
For one of the fighting-people came to bring-ruin to the king,
your lord!

16 No good is this thing that you have done!
As Yhwh lives,
indeed, you are (all) sons of death,
(given) that you did not keep-watch over your lord, over
Yhwh's anointed!
So now, see:
where are the king's spear and the cruse of water that (were) at
his head?

17 Sha'ul recognized David's voice,
he said:
Is that your voice, my son David?
David said:
(It is) my voice, my lord king!

18 And he said:
Why does my lord pursue after his servant?
Indeed, what have I done?

And what evil is there in my hand?

19 So-now,

pray let my lord the king hearken to the words of his servant:

if (it is) Yhwh (who) incited you against me, let him smell a
gift-offering;

but if (it was) by humans,

(then) let them be damned before Yhwh,

for they have driven me away today from being-attached to
Yhwh's inheritance, saying:

Go, serve other gods!

20 So now,

let not my blood fall to the earth, away from the presence of
Yhwh!

For the king of Israel has come out to seek a single flea,

as one pursues a partridge in the hills!

21 Sha'ul said:

I have sinned; return, my son David!

I will do no more evil to you,

since my life was precious in your eyes this day.

Here, I have acted-foolishly and have erred, exceedingly
greatly!

22 David answered and said:

Here is the king's spear;

let one of the serving-lads cross over and fetch it,

23 and may Yhwh return upon each-man his righteousness and
his trustworthiness

(seeing) that Yhwh gave you into my hand

---

19 LET HIM SMELL A GIFT-OFFERING:
The smell of the offering was understood

to be pleasing to God (cf. Gen. 8:21).

20 PARTRIDGE: Homonymous with "caller."

but I would not stretch out my hand against Y<small>HWH</small>'s anointed.

24 Here, as your life has been deemed-great this day in my eyes,
so may my life grow-great in Y<small>HWH</small>'s eyes,
may he rescue me from every trouble!

25 Sha'ul said to David:
Blessed are you, my son David;
you will do, yes, do (well),
you will prevail, yes, prevail!
David went on his way, and Sha'ul returned to his place.

27:1 And David said in his heart:
(Here) now,
I will be swept away one day by the hand of Sha'ul;
there is nothing better for me than that I should escape, yes,
escape to the land of the Philistines,
then Sha'ul will despair of me, of continuing to seek me
throughout all the territory of Israel, and I will escape from
his hand.

2 So David arose and crossed-over, he and the six hundred men
that were with him, to Akhish son of Ma'okh, king of Gat.

3 And David stayed with Akhish in Gat, he and his men,
each-man and his household,
David and his two wives,
Ahino'am the Yizre'elite-woman and Avigayil wife of Naval,
the Carmelite-woman.

4 And it was told to Sha'ul that David had fled to Gat,
but he did not continue to seek him again.

5 David said to Akhish:
Pray if I have found favor in your eyes,

let there be given to me a place in one of the outlying towns,
    and let me settle there;
why should your servant settle in the king's town with you?

6 So Akhish gave him Tziklag on that day,
therefore Tziklag came-to-belong to the kings of Judah, until
    this (very) day.

7 And the number of days that David stayed in the Philistine
    country was a year and four months.

8 Now David would go up, along with his men,
they would raid the Geshurites, the Gezerites, and the
    Amalekites
—for they were the settled-folk of the land that were from
    (former) ages—
as you come to Shur, as far as the land of Egypt.

9 And David would strike the land,
he would not leave-alive man or woman;
he would take sheep and oxen, donkeys and camels and gar-
    ments,
then he would return and come back to Akhish.

10 And when Akhish would say:
Where did you raid today?
David would say:
Against the Negev of Judah,
or: against the Negev of the Yerahme'elites,
or: against the Negev of the Kenites.

27:5 KING'S TOWN: Royal city.
6 TZIKLAG: Trad. English "Ziklag," a town on the edge of Philistine territory, between Gaza and Beersheba.
8 SHUR: "The Wall," the eastern boundary of Egypt.
10 THE NEGEV OF . . . : These were sub-regions of the large area of southern Israel, inhabited by various raiding tribes.

134

11 But no man or woman would David leave-alive to bring to Gat,
    saying (to himself):
  Lest they report concerning us, saying:
  Thus did David do
  and thus was his practice,
  all the days that he stayed in the country of the Philistines.
12 And Akhish came-to-trust David, saying (to himself):
  He has made himself reek, yes, reek so to his (own) people, to
    Israel,
  so he will be servant to me for the ages!

28:1 Now it was in those days
  that the Philistines gathered their encampments into an army,
    to wage-battle against Israel.
  Akhish said to David:
  You know, yes, know that you must go out with me in the
    camp, you and your men.
2 David said to Akhish:
  Then you yourself will know what your servant can do!
  So Akhish said to David:
  Then I will make you my chief bodyguard for all the days (to
    come)!
3 Now Shemu'el had died;
  all Israel had beaten (the breast) for him and buried him in
    Rama, in his town.

---

2 MY CHIEF BODYGUARD: Lit., "guardian
of my head."

Now Sha'ul had removed the ghosts and the favorable-spirits
    from the land.

4 And the Philistines gathered and came, encamping at Shunem,
    and Sha'ul gathered all Israel, encamping at Gilbo'a.

5 When Sha'ul saw the Philistines' camp,
    he became-afraid, and his heart trembled exceedingly.

6 So Sha'ul made-request of Yhwh,
    but Yhwh did not answer him,
    either through dreams, or through *Urim,* or through prophets.

7 So Sha'ul said to his servants:
    Seek for me a woman, a possessor of ghosts,
    that I may go to her, that I may consult (the dead) through her.
    His servants said to him:
    Here, (there is) a woman, a possessor of ghosts, at Ein Dor.

8 Sha'ul disguised himself, clothing himself in other garments,
    and then he went, he and two men with him,
    and came to the woman at night.
    He said:
    Pray divine for me by a ghost,
    bring-up for me the one that I will say to you!

9 The woman said to him:
    Here, you know what Sha'ul has done,
    how he has cut off ghosts and favorable-spirits from the land.
    So why do you want to ensnare my life, to cause-my-death?

---

3 GHOSTS . . . FAVORABLE-SPIRITS: The calling up of the dead was illegal in biblical literature (cf. Deut. 18:11), but obviously not regarded as ineffective.

4 SHUNEM . . . GILBO'A: These hills controlled the towns of the Jezreel Valley on the way to Bet She'an (Beth Shean), where there seems to have been a historical Philistine presence.

7 POSSESSOR: Following Waltke and O'Connor.

10 So Sha'ul swore to her by YHWH, saying:
   As YHWH lives, should any guilt befall you through this
      matter . . . !
11 The woman said:
   Whom shall I bring-up for you?
   He said:
   Bring-up Shemu'el for me.
12 Now when the woman saw Shemu'el,
   she cried out in a loud voice,
   the woman said to Sha'ul, saying:
   Why have you deceived me?
   You are Sha'ul!
13 The king said to her:
   Don't be afraid;
   rather, what do you see?
   The woman said to Sha'ul:
   I see a godlike-being coming-up from the ground.
14 He said to her:
   What is its form?
   She said:
   An old man is coming-up,
   and he is wrapped in a cloak.
   Then Sha'ul knew that it was Shemu'el,
   and he bowed, brow to the ground, and prostrated-himself.
15 Shemu'el said to Sha'ul:
   Why have you disturbed me, (by) bringing me up?
   Sha'ul said:
   I am exceedingly distressed—
   the Philistines are waging-battle against me,
   and God has turned-away from me:

he no longer answers me,

either by the hand of the prophets or by dreams.

So I have called you to make-known to me what I should do!

16 Shemu'el said:

Why do you make-request of me?

For YHWH has turned away from you and has gone-over to
   your fellow!

17 YHWH has done to you as he promised by my hand:

YHWH has torn away the kingdom from your hand

and has given it to your fellow, to David

18 —as you did not hearken to YHWH's voice,

and did not carry-out his flaming anger against Amalek.

Therefore this thing has YHWH done to you this day!

19 And YHWH will also give Israel with you into the hand of the
   Philistines;

tomorrow you and your sons (will be) with me,

(and) also the camp of Israel YHWH will give into the hand of
   the Philistines!

20 Sha'ul hurried and fell his full stature to the ground

(for) he was exceedingly afraid at Shemu'el's words,

also there was no strength (left) in him,

for he had not eaten food all day and all night.

21 When the woman came to Sha'ul,

she saw that he was exceedingly disturbed,

so she said to him:

Here, your handmaid hearkened to your voice,

and I put my life in your hand,

---

16 MAKE-REQUEST: Alluding to Sha'ul's
name again: (*Ve-lamma*) *tish'aleini* (Exum).

17 TO YOU: So LXX and manuscripts; MT has
"to him."

I hearkened to your words which you spoke to me.

22 So then,

pray hearken, you also, to your handmaid's voice:

I will put before you a bit of food—eat,

so that there may be strength in you, when you go on your way.

23 He refused, and said: I will not eat!

But his servants pressed him, and also the woman,

so he hearkened to their voice;

he arose from the ground and sat-down on a bed.

24 Now the woman had a stall-fed calf in the house,

she hurried and slaughtered it,

she took meal and kneaded (it), and baked it (into) unleavened-cakes;

25 and she brought (it) close, before Sha'ul and before his servants, and they ate.

Then they arose and went away, that (very) night.

29:1 The Philistines gathered all their encampments at Afek,

while Israel was encamped at the spring that is in Yizre'el.

2 The Philistine overlords were crossing-over by (divisions of) hundreds and by (divisions of) thousands,

with David and his men crossing-over in the rear, beside Akhish.

3 And the Philistine commanders said:

What about these Hebrews?

Akhish said to the Philistine commanders:

1 AFEK: Cf. note to 4:1 above.
YIZRE'EL: The fertile Jezreel Valley of northern Israel.

Isn't this David, servant of Sha'ul king of Israel,

who has been with me (all) these days, these years?

Yet I have found nothing (wrong) in him, from the day of his
    falling-in (with us) until this day!

4 The Philistine commanders became-furious with him,

the Philistine commanders said to him:

Return the man, and let him return to his place where you
    assigned him,

but don't let him go-down with us into battle,

so that he won't be an adversary to us in battle!

By what will this-one make himself acceptable (again) to his
    lord—

isn't it with the heads of those men?

5 Isn't this David,

about whom they chanted with dancing, saying:

    Sha'ul has struck-down his thousands,

    but David—his myriads!?

6 So Akhish had David called

and said to him:

As Yhwh lives,

indeed, you are upright,

and good in my eyes is your going-out and your coming-in
    with me in the camp,

for I have not found in you (any) evil from the day of your
    coming to me until this day—

but in the eyes of the Philistine overlords, you are not good!

7 So now,

turn back, and go in peace,

so that you don't do evil in the eyes of the Philistine overlords.

8 David said to Akhish:

Indeed, what have I done,
what (wrong) have you found in your servant
from the day that I (first stood) before you, until this day,
that I may not come and wage-battle against the enemies of
    my lord the king?

9 Akhish answered and said to David:
I acknowledge that you are as good in my eyes as a messenger
    of God;
however, the Philistine commanders say:
He may not go-up beside us into battle!

10 So now, start-early in the morning,
and as for your lord's servants who came with you,
you are (all) to start-early in the morning;
when (there is) light for you, go!

11 So David started-early, he and his men, to go in the morning,
    to return to the land of the Philistines,
while the Philistines went-up to Yizre'el.

30:1 And it was, when David and his men came to Tziklag, on the
    third day
—now Amalekites had made-a-raid on the Negev, on Tziklag,
they had struck Tziklag, burning it with fire,

2 and they had taken-captive the women that were in it, from
    young to old,
they had not killed any (of them),
but had led (them) away and gone on their way—

3 that when David and his men came to the town,
and here: (it was) burned with fire,
with their women and their sons and their daughters taken-
    captive!

4   And David and the fighting-people that were with him lifted
      up their voice and wept
    until there was no strength (left) in them to weep.

5   Now David's two wives had been taken-captive,
    Ahino'am the Yizre'elite-woman and Avigayil wife of Naval
      the Carmelite.

6   David was exceedingly distressed,
    for the people intended to stone him,
    for bitter were all the people's feelings,
    each-man over his sons and over his daughters—
    but David strengthened-himself in YHWH his God.

7   David said to Evyatar the priest, son of Ahimelekh:
    Pray bring-close to me the *efod*!
    Evyatar brought-close the *efod* to David.

8   And David inquired of YHWH, saying:
    Shall I pursue after this robber-band?
    Will I overtake them?
    He said to him:
    Pursue,
    for you will overtake, yes, overtake (them), and will rescue,
      yes, rescue (them)!

9   So David went, he and the six hundred men that were with
      him,
    they came to Wadi Besor / News, while those (that were) left
      stayed-behind.

10 And David gave-pursuit, he and four hundred men,

9 WADI BESOR: South of Tziklag and running eastward to Bet Lehem and beyond.

and two hundred men stayed-behind, who were (too)
 exhausted to cross Wadi Besor.

11 And they found an Egyptian man in the open-field, and took
 him to David,

they gave him food and he ate, and they gave him water to
 drink,

12 and they gave him a slice of pressed-figs and two (bunches of)
 raisins, and he ate;

then his spirit returned to him

—for he had not eaten food and had not drunk water for three
 days and three nights.

13 Then David said to him:

To whom do you (belong)?

And where are you from?

He said:

I am an Egyptian serving-lad, servant of an Amalekite man,

and my lord abandoned me, since I became-sick three days
 ago.

14 We were making-a-raid on the Negev of the Kereitites,

against what belongs to Judah,

and against the Negev of Calev,

and Tziklag we burned with fire.

15 David said to him:

Will you bring me down to this troop?

He said:

Swear to me by God:

if you should put-me-to-death, if you should turn-me-over to
 the hand of my (former) lord . . . !

So I will bring you down to this troop.

16 He brought him down,

and here: they were sprawled out all over the surface of the
ground,

eating and drinking and celebrating, among all the great spoils
that they had taken from the land of the Philistines and
from the land of Judah.

17 And David struck them from the (dawn) breeze until the sunset of the morrow,

and not a man of them escaped except for four hundred
serving-lads who mounted camels and fled.

18 So David rescued everything that Amalek had taken,

and his two wives David rescued (as well);

19 nothing was lacking of theirs, from small to great, to sons and
daughters, or from the spoils,

to all that they took for themselves—

everything David returned.

20 David took all the flocks and all the herds,

they drove them before that (other) livestock, and they said:

These are David's spoils!

21 Now David came-back to the two hundred men who had been
(too) exhausted to go after David

—they had had them stay at Wadi Besor—,

they went out to meet David and to meet the fighting-people
that were with him.

When David came-close to the people, he inquired of them for
peace;

22 but there spoke-up every evil and worthless man of the men
who had gone with David,

they said:

Because they did not go with me,
we will not give them (any) of the spoils that we rescued
except (to) each-man his wife and his children;
let them drive (them) away and go!

23 David said:
You mustn't do thus, my brothers,
with what YHWH has given us!
—He guarded us and gave the troop that came against us into
our hand.

24 For who would hearken to you in this matter?
Indeed, like the share of the one going-down to battle
(shall be) the share of the one staying by the gear:
together they shall divide-shares.

25 So it was from that day and forward
that they made (it) a prescribed-law and practice in Israel,
until this (very) day.

26 When David came back to Tziklag, he sent off (some) of the
spoils to the elders of Judah, to his fellows, saying:
Here, it is a gift-of-blessing for you, from the spoils of YHWH's
enemies:

27 for those in Bet El, for those in Ramot-Negev, for those in Yat-
tir,

28 for those in Aro'er, for those in Sifmot, for those in Eshtemo'a,

29 for those in Rakhal, for those in the Yerahme'elite towns, for
those in the Kenite towns,

22 DRIVE (THEM) AWAY: The verb is often
used of animals, hence it may have a
derogatory flavor here.

27 FOR THOSE IN . . . : The towns mentioned are in the Negev region.

29 RAKHAL: LXX has "Carmel."

30 for those in Horma, for those in Bor-Ashan, for those in Atakh,
31 for those in Hevron,
   and for all the places that David went-around in, he and his
      men.

31:1 Now the Philistines were waging-battle against Israel,
   and the men of Israel fled before the Philistines;
   the slain fell on Mount Gilbo'a.
2 And the Philistines pressed Sha'ul and his sons hard,
   the Philistines struck-down Yehonatan and Avinadav and
      Malki-Shu'a, Sha'ul's sons.
3 And the battle was heavy around Sha'ul,
   the shooters, men at the bow, found him,
   and he was seriously wound by the shooters.
4 And Sha'ul said to his weapons bearer:
   Draw your sword and run-me-through with it,
   lest these these foreskinned-ones come and run-me-through
      and toy with me!
   But the weapons bearer would not, because he was exceed-
      ingly afraid, so Sha'ul took (his) sword and fell on it.
5 And when his weapons bearer saw that Sha'ul was dead,
   he too fell on his sword, and died with him.
6 So Sha'ul died, and his three sons and his weapons bearer,
   and also all his men, on that day together.
7 And when the men of Israel saw, those across the Valley and
      those across the Jordan,
   that the (other) men of Israel had fled,

31 HEVRON: Trad. English "Hebron."

and that Sha'ul and his sons were dead,
they abandoned the towns and fled,
and the Philistines came and settled in them.

8 Now it was on the morrow,
when the Philistines came to strip the slain,
that they found Sha'ul and his three sons, fallen on Mount
Gilbo'a.

9 They cut off his head and stripped off his armor,
and they sent (word) throughout the land of the Philistines,
round-about,
to bring-the-news into the house of their carved-idols and
among the people.

10 They placed his armor in the House of Astarte,
and his body they impaled on the wall of Bet She'an.

11 When the settled-folk of Yavesh Gil'ad heard about it,
what the Philistines had done to Sha'ul,

12 all the men of valor arose and went all night,
they took-down Sha'ul's corpse and the corpses of his sons
from the wall of Bet She'an,
they brought (them) to Yavesh, and burned them there;

13 then they took their bones and buried (them) under the
tamarisk in Yavesh,
and they fasted for seven days.

31:7 THE TOWNS: Ancient versions read "their
towns."
11 THE SETTLED-FOLK OF YAVESH

GIL'AD: Whom Sha'ul had rescued in his
first great victory, in chapter 11.

II *Samuel*

1:1 It was after the death of Sha'ul
—when David had returned from striking the Amalek(ites)—
that David stayed in Tziklag for two days.

2 And it was on the third day,
that here: a man was coming from the camp, from Sha'ul,
with his clothes torn and earth on his head;
and it was, when he came to David, that he flung-himself on
the ground and prostrated-himself.

3 David said to him:
Where are you coming from?
He said to him:
From the camp of Israel have I escaped!

4 David said to him:
How went the matter? Pray tell me!
He said:
(It was) that the fighting-people fled from the battle,
and also many of the people fell, and they died;
and also Sha'ul and Yehonatan his son died.

5 David said to the lad, the one telling him:
How do you know that Sha'ul and Yehonatan his son are dead?

6 The fighting-lad, the one telling him, said:
I encountered, yes, encountered (them) on Mount Gilbo'a,
and here: Sha'ul was leaning on his spear,

1:1 THE AMALEK(ITES): MT appears to be missing a letter here.

4 HOW WENT THE MATTER?: Exactly Eili's question, in parallel circumstances, in I 4:16.

and here: the charioteers and the horsemen were pressing-
   him-hard.
7 When he faced-about behind him and saw me,
   he called out to me,
   and I said: Here I am.
8 He said to me:
   Who are you?
   I said to him:
   I am an Amalekite.
9 He said to me:
   Pray stand over me and dispatch me,
   for dizziness has taken-hold of me,
   though (there is) still life in me!
10 So I stood over him and dispatched him,
   since I knew that he could not live after his fall;
   I took the diadem that was on his head
   and the bracelet that was on his arm,
   and have brought them to my lord here.
11 David took-hold-of his clothes and tore them,
   and likewise all the men that were with him;
12 they beat (the breast) and they wept
   and they fasted until sunset
   over Sha'ul and over Yehonatan his son,
   over the fighting-people of YHWH and over the House of Israel,
   since they had fallen by the sword.

---

9 STAND OVER ME: Goldman understands
this as "rise up against me."
THOUGH . . . LIFE IN ME! following NRSV.
10 DIADEM . . . BRACELET: These consti-

tute Sha'ul's "royal insignia" (McCarter),
and hence would have served as proof that
the Amalekite had encountered the king.
12 YHWH: LXX reads "Judah" (Heb. *yehuda*).

13 Then David said to the lad, the one telling him:
Where are you from?
He said:
I am the son of a sojourner man, an Amalekite.

14 David said to him:
How (is it that) you were not afraid
to stretch out your hand to bring-to-ruin Yнwн's anointed-
one?

15 And David called to one of the serving-lads
and said:
Approach, smite him!
He struck him down, so that he died.

16 And David said to him:
Your blood be on your head!
For your (own) mouth bore-witness against you, saying:
I myself dispatched Yнwн's anointed-one!

17 Now David sang-dirge (with) this dirge
over Sha'ul and over Yehonatan his son,

18 he said:
To teach the Children of Judah the Bow,
here, it is written in the Book of the Upright:

19   O beauty of Israel, on your heights are the slain;
how have the mighty fallen!

13 SOJOURNER: A resident alien; a foreigner.
18 TO TEACH . . . THE BOW: The Hebrew
phrase may simply mean that "The Bow" is
the title of the poem (see JPS).
THE BOOK OF THE UPRIGHT: An
ancient collection of poems or songs, to
which Josh. 10:13 also refers. Along with the
"Book of the Wars of Yнwн (Num. 21) and
the "Book of the Annals of the Kings of
Judah," cited frequently in Kings, it is an indication that the Bible is but a selection of
the literature that existed in ancient Israel.
19 BEAUTY: Or "gazelle."

20 Tell it not in Gat,
spread not the news in Ashkelon's streets,
lest they rejoice, the daughters of the Philistines,
lest they exult, the daughters of the foreskinned-ones!

21 O hills of Gilbo'a, let there be no dew, no rain upon you,
or surging of the (watery) deeps,
for there lies-soiled the shield of the mighty, the shield of
Sha'ul,
no more anointed with oil.

22 From the blood of the slain, from the sword of the mighty,
Yehonatan's bow never turned back, Sha'ul's sword never
returned empty.

23 Sha'ul and Yehonatan, those beloved and delightful ones—
in their lives, in their deaths they were not parted;
they were swifter than eagles, they were mightier than
lions!

24 O daughters of Israel, weep over Sha'ul,
who-clothed-you in scarlet together with luxuries,
who with golden ornaments decked your clothing!

25 How have the mighty fallen, in the midst of battle,
Yehonatan slain on your heights—

26 I am distraught over you, my brother Yehonatan,
you were exceedingly delightful to me;
more wonderful was your love to me
than the love of women!

27 How have the mighty fallen,
(yes,) perished the weapons of battle!

---

21 SURGING OF THE DEEPS: Suggested by
Edward Greenstein, following an emenda-
tion by H.L. Ginsberg (*shera' tehomot* for

sedei terumot.
22 SWORD OF THE MIGHTY: Reading, with
ancient versions, *herev* for *helev,* "fat."

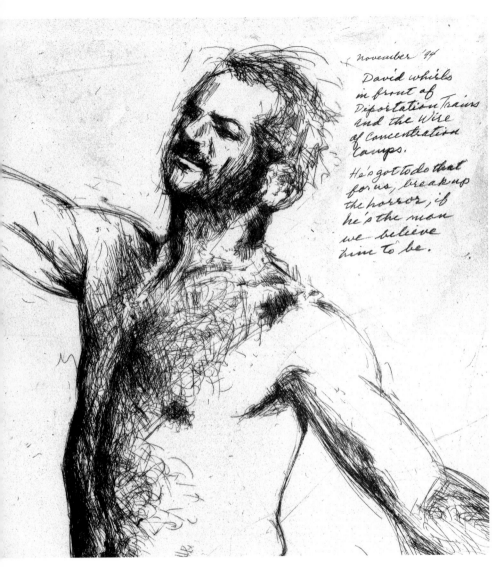

november '94

David whirls in front of Deportation Trains and the Wire of Concentration Camps.

He's got to do that for us, break up the horror, if he's the man we believe him to be.

*K*ing David leaping and whirling in the
presence of Yʜᴡʜ
II Sam. 6 : 16

*D*AVID'S RULE CONSOLIDATED (II:2–8)

T<small>HREE STAGES CHARACTERIZE</small> the solidification of David's ascension to power as Israel's second king: the elimination of rivals, principally from the house of Sha'ul, the establishment of a capital, and the subduing of external enemies. The accomplishment of the first is marred by three violent deaths: one in battle (David's nephew Asa'el), one standing by a gate (Sha'ul's general Avner), and one in bed (Sha'ul's son Ish-Boshet). All three are stabbed in the heart. While David absolves himself of these events, and we are inclined to believe him, the conclusion is inescapable: that, as Polzin (1993) points out, kingship in Israel is "a major cause of frequent fratricide on a tribal or national level." It is a pattern that will be repeated in the second half of the book, within the royal house itself.

The second part of this section relates the capture of Jerusalem, a previously unconquered and hence politically neutral site which had the advantages of central location and natural defenses. In a small existing town, whose entirety would today be enveloped by the Arab village of Silwan, directly south of the Old City, David establishes his capital, builds a palace, and brings the Coffer to its final and fitting resting place. At the last, his great moment of triumph and a remarkable blend of the political, the religious, and the personal, we see David in all his complexity: a conqueror who can bring the ancient tablets of God to the seat of royal power; a believer uninhibitedly religious enough to leap and whirl before God; and a man allied to Sha'ul's house by marriage, who can nevertheless act on his own instincts. And it is to the term "house" (as many have noted) that the text turns in the long climax of chapter 7, with its emphasis on the seeming permanence of Temple and dynasty. It is punctuated by God's use of the adjectives "secure" and "firm," with David's use of the root "great/greatness" in reply, and the refrain "for the ages" in both speeches. The David who emerges from this section is king of a dominant and unified nation, centered around a royal city and a dynasty that enjoy the blessing of God.

Finally there is the matter of defeating the surrounding nations. The Bible sees David as militarily the most successful of Israel's leaders to this point. He at long last subdues the Philistines, who had plagued the Israelites for generations, and he establishes for his son Shelomo a territorial sphere of influence (see map on p. xxxvii) which, if historically accurate, far exceeds that of any previous or succeeding Israelite ruler. The latter might be explained by the relative weakness of the traditionally powerful empires of Egypt and Mesopotamia/Assyria in the eleventh-tenth centuries B.C.E. In that context, Israel's Golden Age—or a memory of something approximate—is the calm before the storm, for subsequent centuries were to witness Israel's complete domination and, ultimately, its incorporation, by ancient Near Eastern imperial powers.

The section ends with a list of David's court officials, as does chapter 20. Brettler (1995) points out that I Samuel 14 ends similarly, thus bracketing a possible ancient unit which he terms "David as Proper King." This yet another indication that biblical books such as Samuel probably reflect a complex history of composition, with the resulting texts (the books as we have them) giving evidence of overlapping structures.

2:1 It was (some time) after this
that David inquired of YHWH, saying:
Shall I go-up into one of the towns of Judah?
YHWH said to him:
Go-up!
David said:
To where shall I go-up?
He said:
To Hevron.

2 So David went-up there,
and also his two wives,
Ahino'am the Yizre'elite-woman, and Avigayil the wife of
Naval the Carmelite.

3 As for his men who were with him, David brought (them) up,
each-man and his household,
and they settled in the towns of (the) Hevron (area).

4 And the men of Judah came and anointed David there as king
over the House of Judah . . .

And they told David, saying:
The men of Yavesh Gil'ad have buried Sha'ul.

5 So David sent messengers to the men of Yavesh Gil'ad,
he said to them:
Blessed are you of YHWH,
in that you did this act-of-loyalty to your lord, to Sha'ul,
by burying him!

6 So-now,
may God do to you loyalty and trust,
and I too will do good to you,

in exchange for your having-done this thing!

7　And now,

let your hands be strengthened,

and be sons of valor,

for your lord Sha'ul is dead,

and already (it is) I (whom) the House of Judah has anointed as
king over them.

8　But Avner, the son of Ner, commander of the army that
belonged to Sha'ul,

had taken Ish-Boshet son of Sha'ul, and had him cross over to
Mahanayim;

9　he had made-him-king over Gil'ad, over the Geshurites, and
over Yizre'el,

over Efrayim and over Binyamin—over Israel, all-of-it.

10　Forty years old was Ish-Boshet son of Sha'ul

when he (began to) reign-as-king over Israel,

and for two years he reigned-as-king.

But the House of Judah were (following) after David.

11　And the number of days that David was king in Hevron, over
the House of Judah,

was seven years and six months.

8　ISH-BOSHET: The original name was "Ish-Baal," "Man of Baal"; scribal tradition, uncomfortable with the pagan overtones, has changed it (and similar names—cf. 11:21, which originally read "Yerubbaal") to "Man of Shame" (boshet).

MAHANAYIM: On the east bank of the Jordan, east of Shechem.

9　GIL'AD: Trad. English "Gilead," the region in which Mahanayim is located (east of the Jordan, between the Dead Sea and the Sea of Galilee).

GESHURITES: MT has "Ashurites," but Geshur, east of the Sea of Galilee, fits the geography here.

11　NUMBER OF DAYS: Or "number of years," "amount of time."

12 And Avner son of Ner went-out, along with the servants of
 Ish-Boshet son of Sha'ul, from Mahanayim to Giv'on,

13 while Yo'av son of Tzeruya and David's servants went-out (as
 well).
 They met them by the Pool of Giv'on together,
 and they sat down, these by the pool on one-side,
 and those by the pool on one-side.

14 And Avner said to Yo'av:
 Pray let the fighting-lads arise and do-a-war-dance before us!
 Yo'av said:
 Let them arise!

15 So they arose and crossed-over by number:
 twelve for Binyamin and for Ish-Boshet son of Sha'ul,
 and twelve of David's servants.

16 And each-man took-hold of his neighbor's head,
 while his sword (he thrust) into his neighbor's side,
 and they fell together.
 So that place was called: Helkat ha-Tzurim / Field of the
 Sword-Edges, which is in Giv'on.

17 Now the battle was rough—exceedingly so—on that day,
 and Avner and the men of Israel were smitten-hard before
 David's servants.

18 Now there were three of the sons of Tzeruya there:
 Yo'av, Avishai, and Asa'el;

---

12 GIV'ON: Trad. English "Gibeon," northwest of Jerusalem.
13 YO'AV: Trad. English "Joab," David's
nephew (through his sister Tzeruya) and
commander in chief.
14 DO-A-WAR-DANCE: Following B-R; it
seems to indicate a winner-take-all contest

(McCarter).
16 SWORD-EDGES: Or "flints." The entire
scene here is emblematic of the conflict
within Israelite society.
18 ASA'EL: Trad. English "Asahel"; the name
means "God does / acts."

and Asa'el was swift of feet, like one of the gazelles that is in
the open-field.

19 And Asa'el pursued after Avner,

not swerving to go to the right or to the left from after Avner.

20 And Avner faced-about after him,

and he said:

Is this you, Asa'el?

He said:

(It is) I.

21 Avner said to him:

Swerve-you to your right or to your left,

and take-hold for yourself (instead) one of our fighting-lads,
and take for yourself his armor!

But Asa'el would not turn-aside from (going) after him.

22 Once again Avner said to Asa'el:

Turn-yourself-aside from (going) after me;

why should I strike you to the ground—

how (then) could I lift my face to Yo'av your brother?

23 But he refused to turn-aside,

so Avner struck him with the after-part of the spear in the
fifth (rib),

so that the spear came out after him;

he fell there and died on the spot.

And it was: all who came to the place where Asa'el had fallen
and died, stopped;

---

19 AFTER: Polzin (1993) notes that the frequent
use of this word vv. 19–30 is emblematic of
pursuit, both of kings and of brothers.

21 TAKE-HOLD . . . TAKE: Two different
verbs in Hebrew.

23 AFTER-PART: The butt of the spear, often
sharpened for sticking into the ground.

FIFTH (RIB): Modern translations generally use "belly" here. But the King James
version may be right; if a person is stabbed
on the left side at the fifth rib, the blade will
pierce the heart (my thanks to Dr. Harold
Kozinn for clarifying this problem).

AFTER HIM: Through his back..

24   but Yo'av and Avishai pursued after Avner.
Now when the sun had come-in,
they came to the Hill of Amma, that faces Gi'ah,
on the way to the Wilderness of Giv'on.

25   And the Children of Binyamin gathered-themselves (to follow)
     after Avner,
they became a single band
and stopped at the top of a hill.

26   And Avner called-out to Yo'av,
he said:
Is it forever that the sword must devour?
Don't you know
that it will be bitter afterwards?
How long won't you bid the fighting-people to turn-back from
     (going) after their brothers?

27   Yo'av said:
As God lives,
indeed, had you not spoken,
indeed, then (only) in the morning would the people have
     gone-up, each-man from after his brother!

28   Then Yo'av gave-a-blast on the *shofar*, and all the people
     stopped,
they no longer pursued after Israel,
they no longer continued to do-battle,

29   while Avner and his men went through the Plain all that night;
they crossed the Jordan
and went through the whole canyon, and came to Mahanayim.

---

26 AFTERWARDS: Others, "in the end."
28 *SHOFAR:* The ram's horn, often used in
the Bible for signaling.

29 THE PLAIN: The Aravah, or Jordan valley.
THE WHOLE CANYON: Others, "all
morning."

30 Now when Yo'av returned from (going) after Avner,
   he gathered all the people,
   and there were counted (missing) of David's servants nineteen
       men along with Asa'el,
31 while David's servants struck-down (some) of Binyamin,
       among Avner's men:
   three hundred and sixty men died.
32 They carried-away Asa'el and buried him in the burial-place of
       his father, which is in Bet Lehem.
   Then they went all night, Yo'av and his men,
   with light-breaking upon them in Hevron.

3:1 And the war was long-lasting between the House of Sha'ul
       and the House of David;
   David went-on becoming-stronger, while the House of Sha'ul
       went-on becoming-weaker.
2 Now sons were born to David in Hevron:
   his firstborn was Amnon, by Ahino'am the Yizre'elite-woman,
3 second-to-him was Kil'av, by Avigayil wife of Naval the
       Carmelite,
   the third was Avshalom son of Ma'akha, daughter of Talmai,
       king of Geshur,
4 the fourth was Adoniyya son of Haggit,
   the fifth was Shefatya son of Avital,
5 the sixth was Yitre'am, by Egla wife of David.

3:2–4 AMNON . . . AVSHALOM . . .
ADONIYYA: Trad. English "Amnon . . .
Absalom . . . Adonijah," the three sons who
will struggle for succession to David from II

Sam. 13 to I Kings 2. None will become
king; that will fall to Shelomo (Solomon).
3 TALMAI: Avshalom will to flee to this
maternal grandfather in chapter 13.

These were born to David in Hevron.

6 Now it was,
   when there was war between the House of Sha'ul and the
      House of David:
   Avner was gaining-strength in the House of Sha'ul.
7 Now Sha'ul had a concubine, her name was Ritzpa the daugh-
      ter of Ayya.
   And (Ish-Boshet) said to Avner:
   Why did you come in to my father's concubine?
8 Avner became exceedingly upset over the words of Ish-Boshet,
      he said:
   Am I the head of a dog belonging to Judah?
   Today I do an act-of-loyalty to the House of Sha'ul your father,
   for his brothers and for his friends,
   and haven't let you come into David's hand—
   yet a fault concerning a woman is accounted to me today!
9 Thus may God do to Avner, and thus may he add to him,
   indeed, as YHWH swore to David, indeed, thus I will do to
      him—
10 to transfer the kingship from the House of Sha'ul,
   to establish the throne of David over Israel and over Judah,
   from Dan to Be'er Sheva!
11 He was not able to answer Avner another word, out of his fear
      of him.
12 And Avner sent messengers to David on his behalf, saying:
   Whose is (the) land?
   Cut your covenant with me,
   and here: my hand is with you, to bring all Israel around to
      you!

13 He said:
Good,
I myself will cut a covenant with you;
but one thing I will require of you, namely:
you are not to see my face
unless you first bring Mikhal daughter of Sha'ul, when you
come to see my face.

14 So David sent messengers to Ish-Boshet son of Sha'ul, saying:
Give over my wife, Mikhal,
whom I betrothed to myself for a hundred Philistine foreskins!

15 Ish-Boshet sent and took her from (her) husband, from Palti'el
son of Layish.

16 And her husband went with her, going-along and weeping
after her, as far as Bahurim.
Avner said to him:
Go, turn-back! And he turned-back.

17 Now the word of Avner was with the elders of Israel, saying:
Even yesterday, even the day-before, you have been seeking (to
set) David as king over you.

18 So-now, do (it)!
For Yhwh has said of David, saying:
By the hand of David my servant
I will deliver my people Israel from the hand of the Philistines
and from the hand of all their enemies.

19 And likewise Avner spoke in the ears of Binyamin,

---

13 REQUIRE: The same verb, *sha'al,* as "request" or "inquire" elsewhere.
16 BAHURIM: Just south of Jerusalem.
17 EVEN YESTERDAY, EVEN THE DAY-

BEFORE: Cf. Note to I 4:7.
18 I WILL: From manuscript readings; MT has "he will."

and likewise Avner went to speak in the ears of David in
    Hevron
all that was good in the eyes of Israel and in the eyes of all the
    House of Binyamin.

20   Avner came to David in Hevron,
    —with him were twenty men—
    and David made a drinking-feast for Avner and for the men
        that were with him.

21   Then Avner said to David:
    Let me arise, let me go,
    and let me gather to my lord king all Israel,
    so that they may cut a covenant with you
    and you may become-king according to all that your appetite
        craves.
    So David sent Avner away,
    and he went off in peace.

22   Now here, David's servants and Yo'av came-back from raiding,
        and abundant spoils they brought with them—
    but Avner was not with David in Hevron,
    for he had sent him away, and he had gone-off in peace.

23   When Yo'av and all the army that was with him came,
    (someone) told Yo'av, saying:
    Avner the son of Ner came to the king,
    but he sent him away and he went-off in peace!

24   So Yo'av came to the king, and he said:
    What have you done?
    Here, Avner came to you—

why did you send him off,
so that he has gone, yes, gone?

25 You know Avner the son of Ner:
indeed, it was to dupe you (that) he came,
to gain-knowledge of your going-out and your coming-in,
and to gain-knowledge of all that you are doing!

26 When Yo'av went out from David,
he sent messengers after Avner;
they returned him from the Cistern of Sira,
but David did not know (about it).

27 And when Avner returned to Hevron, Yo'av took him to the
middle-part of the gate, to speak with him quietly,
and he struck him (in) the fifth (rib) there, so that he died,
(in exchange) for the blood of Asa'el his brother.

28 When David heard after this,
he said:
Cleared-of-blame am I and my kingdom by YHWH, for the
ages,
from the blood of Avner son of Ner,

29 (but) may it alight on the head of Yo'av and on all his father's
house;
may there never be cut-off from the House of Yo'av (anyone)
with a flow, or with *tzara'at*, or one taking-hold of the spindle, or one falling by the sword, or one lacking food!

26 THE CISTERN OF SIRA: North of Hevron.
27 QUIETLY: Others, "in private."
29 (ANYONE) WITH A FLOW: A bodily
excretion rendering a person ritually pol-
luted; cf. Lev. 15.
TZARA'AT: A skin disease, not leprosy,
which in the Bible usually indicates some
wrongdoing on the part of the victim. Cf.
Lev. 13.
ONE TAKING-HOLD OF THE SPINDLE:
That is, doing what was considered
women's work.

30 —for Yo'av and Avishai his brother had killed Avner
on account that he had brought-death to Asa'el their brother at
    Giv'on, in battle.

31 David said to Yo'av and to all the people that were with him:
Tear your garments and gird-yourselves with sackcloth,
and beat (the breast) before Avner!
Now King David (himself) walked after the bier.

32 They buried Avner in Hevron,
and the king lifted up his voice and wept upon the burial-place
    of Avner,
and all the people wept.

33 And the king intoned-a-dirge over Avner, he said:
    Like the death of a vile-one, should Avner have died?

34   Your hands were not bound,
        your feet were not put in double-bronze;
        like one falling before sons of corruption you fell!
And all the fighting-people continued to weep over him.

35 Then all the people came to feed David with bread while it was
    (still) daylight,
but David swore, saying:
Thus may God do to me, and thus may he add,
if before the coming-in of the sun I taste bread or anything
    (else)!

36 All the people took-note, and it was good in their eyes;
like all that the king did, in the eyes of the people (it was)
    good.

37 And all the people and all Israel knew on that day

---

31 SACKCLOTH: Another standard biblical
sign of mourning.

that it had not been (intended) by the king to cause-the-death
of Avner son of Ner.

38 The king said to his servants:

Don't you know

that a commander and a great (man) has fallen in Israel this
day?

39 As for me, today I am soft-hearted, though anointed as king,
while these men, the sons of Tzeruya, are too rough for me.
May YHWH pay-back the doer of evil according to his evil-deed!

4:1 When_____the son of Sha'ul heard that Avner was dead in
Hevron,

his hands grew-slack,

while all Israel were terrified.

2 Now two men, commanders of raiding-bands, belonged to
the son of Sha'ul;

the name of the one was Baana, and the name of the second
was Rekhav,

sons of Rimmon the Be'erotite, of the Children of Binyamin.

—For Be'erot too was reckoned to Binyamin:

3 the Be'erotites got-away to Gittayim,

and they have continued sojourning there, until this day. —

4 Now Yehonatan son of Sha'ul had a son, stricken (in the) feet;

he had been five years old when the tidings had come of Sha'ul

---

4:1 _____THE SON OF SHA'UL: As in v. 2,
the name is missing in MT.
HIS HANDS GREW-SLACK: Others,
"he/his heart lost courage."

2 BE'EROTITE: Be'erot was northwest of Jerusalem.

3 GITTAYIM: Further west of Be'erot. The

name means "Double-Winepress."

4 A SON . . .: This interruption in the text
establishes that, despite the impending
assassination, someone from Sha'ul's line
survives (McCarter).
STRICKEN: Crippled.

and Yehonatan, from Yizre'el,

and when his caretaker had lifted him up and fled,

it was in her haste to flee that he had fallen and been made-
lame.

And his name was Mefiboshet.—

5 The sons of Rimmon the Be'erotite, Rekhav and Baana, went

and they came, at the heat of the day, to the house of Ish-
Boshet

while he was lying down for the noonday nap.

6 And here, they came into the midst of the house, (as) fetchers
of wheat,

and struck him in the fifth (rib),

while Rekhav and Baana his brother escaped.

7 —They had come into the house

while he was lying on his bed, in his sleeping-room,

and had struck him down, causing his death,

and had removed his head. —

And they took his head

and went off, by way of the Plain, all night.

8 They brought the head of Ish-Boshet to David at Hevron,

and said to the king:

Here is the head of Ish-Boshet son of Sha'ul your enemy, who
sought your life—

Yhwh has granted to my lord king vengeance this day

on Sha'ul and on his seed!

9 David answered Rekhav and Baana his brother, the sons of

MEFIBOSHET: Trad. English "Mephibo-sheth," meaning "from the Mouth of Baal/Boshet."

6–7 AND HERE. . . : The Hebrew text is confusing here. I follow B-R, but other possibil-ities exist (such as LXX's addition of a sleeping guard).

6 (AS) FETCHERS OF WHEAT: Pretending to be farmhands, and thus with access to the house.

Rimmon the Be'erotite,
he said to them:
As Yhwh lives,
who saved my life from every trouble:

10 indeed, the one telling me, saying: Here, Sha'ul is dead!,
though he was like a bearer-of-(good)-news in his eyes,
I took-hold of him and I killed him in Tziklag,
(one) to whom I might-have-given (something for his) news!

11 How-much-more-so, when guilty men have killed an innocent
man in his (own) house, on his couch!
So-now,
should I not seek (satisfaction) for his blood at your hand,
and so burn you out from the land?

12 So David commanded the fighting-lads,
and they killed them and hewed off their hands and their feet
and hung them up by the pool in Hevron,
while the head of Ish-Boshet they took
and buried in the burial-place of Avner in Hevron.

5:1 And all the tribes of Israel came to David in Hevron;
they said, saying:
Here we are—your bone and your flesh are we!

2 Even yesterday, even the day-before, when Sha'ul was king
over us,
(it was) you who took-out and brought-back Israel (in battle),

---

11 SEEK (SATISFACTION): Premeditated murder is punishable in the Bible by death. Cf. the classic statement in Gen. 9:5.
BURN YOU OUT: JPS "rid the earth of you." In Deuteronomy (e.g., 13:6, 17:7) this phrase appears often as a refrain referring to serious offenses.

and Y<small>HWH</small> said to you:

You will shepherd my people Israel,

you will be Prince over Israel!

3 And all the elders of Israel came to the king at Hevron;

King David cut with them a covenant at Hevron, in the presence of Y<small>HWH</small>,

and they anointed David as king over Israel.

4 Thirty years old was David when he became-king,

for forty years he reigned-as-king:

5 in Hevron he reigned-as-king over Judah for seven years and six months,

and in Jerusalem he reigned-as-king for thirty-three years, over all Israel and Judah.

6 And the king and his men went to Jerusalem, to the Yevusites, the settled-folk of the region,

but they said to David:

You are not to enter here!

—For the blind and the lame had incited (them), saying:

David is not to enter here! —

7 But David conquered the Fortress of Zion—that is (now) the City of David.

8 And David said on that day:

Whoever strikes-down a Yevusite

4 THIRTY YEARS . . . FORTY YEARS: Patterned numbers, which in the Bible tend to signify perfection or rounded-out periods, rather than exact totals.

6 THE BLIND AND THE LAME: Perhaps used here as a taunt, i.e., even those not fit to fight could turn away enemies, because of Jerusalem's impregnability.

HAD INCITED THEM: In this difficult passage, read (with McCarter, following 4QS^a) *hesit* for *hesir* (removed).

7 ZION: Later understood as the hill just north of David's city which became the "Temple Mount," not the present Mount Zion.

should attack at the windpipe,
since the lame and the blind are hated by David's very being;
therefore they say:
The blind and the lame are not to enter the Temple-House!

9   And David settled in the fortress,
he called it: The City of David;
and David built round-about, from the *Millo* and inward.

10   David went-on, going-on becoming-great;
YHWH God of the Heavenly-Armies was with him.

11   And Hiram king of Tyre sent messengers to David,
along with cedar wood and wood carvers and stone wall
carvers;
they built a palace-house for David.

12   And David knew that YHWH had established him as king over
Israel,
and that he had exalted his kingdom for the sake of his people
Israel.

13   And David took further concubines and wives in Jerusalem,
after his coming-back from Hevron;
there were born further to David, sons and daughters.

14   And these are the names of those-born to him in Jerusalem:
Shammua and Shovav,

---

8 AT THE WINDPIPE: Namely, a fatal blow. So B-R and McCarter (1984); it has also been understood architecturally, as "water-pipe." In any event the passage is difficult.

9 MILLO: From the verb "fill," possibly a landfill structure which was there previously, or a filled-in casemate wall (Edward Greenstein, written communication); some identify it with the "stone stepped structure" just south of the present Old City of Jerusalem.

10 GOD: Lacking in some ancient versions.

11 HIRAM KING OF TYRE: He provides both David and his son Shelomo with building materials, principally cedar wood. The name is pronounced "Hee-rahm."

Natan and Shelomo,

15 Yivhar and Elishua, Nefeg and Yafia,

16 Elishama, Elyada and Elifelet.

17 When the Philistines heard that they had anointed David as
     king over Israel,
   all the Philistines went up to seek out David.
   When David heard, he went down to the fortress.

18 Now the Philistines had come,
   spreading out in the Valley of the Shades.

19 So David inquired of Yhwh, saying:
   Shall I go-up against the Philistines?
   Will you give them into my hand?
   Yhwh said to David:
   Go-up,
   for I will give, yes, give the Philistines into your hand.

20 David came to Baal-Peratzim / Master of Bursting-Forth,
   and David struck them there.
   He said:
   Yhwh has burst my enemies before me like a bursting-forth of
     water!
   Therefore they called the name of that place Baal-
     Peratzim / Master of Bursting-Forth.

21 They abandoned their idols there,
   and David and his men carried them off.

22 But the Philistines went-up again,

14 NATAN: Not the important court prophet of chapter 7 ff.
18 VALLEY OF THE SHADES: "Shades" refers to the *Refa'im,* primeval giants. The location is today within the municipal boundaries of Jerusalem.
20 BAAL-PERATZIM: Southwest of Jerusalem.

spreading out in the Valley of the Shades.

23 So David inquired of YHWH,

and he said:

You are not to go-up;

lead (your men) around, behind them,

come at them in front of the balsam-trees.

24 Let it be:

when you hear the sound of marching on the tops of the
balsam-trees, then you are to act-decisively,

for then YHWH will go-out before you, to strike-down the camp
of the Philistines.

25 David did thus, as YHWH had commanded him;

he struck the Philistines from Geva until where-you-come to
Gezer.

6:1 And David continued (gathering) every chosen-fighter in Israel, thirty thousand.

2 And David arose and went, along with all the fighting-people
who were with him, from Baala in Judah,

to bring-up from there the Coffer of God, over which was
called there

the Name of YHWH of the Heavenly-Armies, (who is) Seated
(upon) the Winged-Sphinxes.

3 They mounted the Coffer of God on a new wagon

---

23 BALSAM-TREES: Others take Heb. *bekha'im* as a place-name.

25 GEZER: David drives the Philistines well to the west.

6:1 THIRTY THOUSAND: Some understand Heb. *elef* as units or divisions, thus making for more realistic numbers (thirty divisions).

2 THERE / THE NAME: The text is jumbled; MT reads "the Name, the Name."
(WHO IS) SEATED (UPON) THE WINGED-SPHINXES: A title of YHWH, enthroned as king. Cf. I Sam. 4:4.

3 NEW WAGON: Cf. note to I 6:7, above.

and transported it from the house of Avinadav, that is in Giv'a,

while Uzza and Ahyo, the sons of Avinadav, were driving the
    new wagon.

4 They transported it from the house of Avinadav that is in
    Giv'a, with the Coffer of God,

with Ahyo walking in front of the Coffer.

5 Now David and the whole house of Israel were dancing in the
    presence of Yhwh,

with all the fir-wood-instruments,

with lyres and lutes and timbrels,

with rattles and with cymbals.

6 But when they came to the threshing-floor of Nakhon,

Uzza stretched out (his hand) to the Coffer of God and held-it-
    steady,

for the oxen had let (it) slip.

7 And Yhwh's anger flared-up at Uzza,

God struck-him-down there because of his carelessness, so
    that he died there,

beside the Coffer of God.

8 And David was upset over (the fact) that Yhwh had burst-forth,
    a bursting-out against Uzza,

so he called that place: Peretz Uzza / Bursting-Out (at) Uzza,

until this (very) day.

9 And David was fearful of Yhwh on that day,

he said:

3–4 TRANSPORTED . . . GIV'A: The repetition and resulting confusion here are probably the result of scribal error.

5 WITH ALL THE FIR-WOOD INSTRU-
MENTS: I Chron. 13:8 reads "with all their

might and with songs."

6 NAKHON: 4QS^a reads "Nadon."

7 BECAUSE OF HIS CARELESSNESS: Following some ancient witnesses; others indicate a longer text.

$\mathcal{N}$ow David was whirling with all (his) might in
the presence of Yʜᴡʜ

II Sam. 6 : 14

How will the Coffer of Yhwh (ever) come to me?

10 And David would not remove the Coffer of Yhwh from him to
the City of David,

so David turned it aside to the house of Oved-Edom the Gittite.

11 The Coffer stayed at the house of Oved-Edom the Gittite for
three months,

and Yhwh blessed Oved-Edom and all his household.

12 And it was told to King David, saying:

Yhwh has blessed the house of Oved-Edom and all that is his,
on account of the Coffer of God;

so David went and brought-up the Coffer of God from the
house of Oved-Edom to the City of David, with rejoicing.

13 And it was,

when those transporting the Coffer of Yhwh had stepped-
forward six steps,

he offered-up an ox and a fatling.

14 Now David was whirling with all (his) might in the presence of
Yhwh;

David was girded with an *efod* of linen.

15 Now David and all the House of Israel were bringing-up the
Coffer of Yhwh with shouting and with the sound of the
shofar.

16 And it was, (as) the Coffer of Yhwh was coming into the City
of David:

---

10 OVED-EDOM THE GITTITE: Interest-
ingly, it is a foreigner's house that is blessed.
His name means "Servant of Edom, native
of Gat."

13 AN OX AND A FATLING: McCarter takes
this as a hendiadys, "a fatted bull."

Mikhal daughter of Sha'ul was looking out through the window;

when she saw King David leaping and whirling in the presence of Yhwh,

she despised him in her heart.

17 They brought the Coffer of Yhwh

and set it in its place, in the midst of the tent that David had spread-out for it.

And David offered-up offerings-up in the presence of Yhwh, and *shalom*-offerings.

18 When David had finished offering-up the offering-up and *shalom*-offerings,

he blessed the people in the name of Yhwh of the Heavenly-Armies,

19 and he divided up (food) for the whole people, for the whole throng of Israel, from man to woman,

—for each-one: one cake of bread, one roll, and one raisin-cake.

then all the people went off, each-one to his house.

20 When David returned to bless his household,

Mikhal daughter of Sha'ul went out to meet David

and said:

How he has gotten-honor today, the king of Israel,

who has exposed himself today before the eyes of his servants' (own) maids—

like one of (those) empty-men exposes-himself!

21 David said to Mikhal:

---

19 ROLL: Others, "date cake."

20 EMPTY-MEN: LXX, adding a letter, reads "dancers" here.

In the presence of YHWH, who chose me over your father and
    over all his house, to commission me as Prince over the
    people of YHWH, over Israel:
I'll dance in the presence of YHWH,

22 and will hold-myself-lightly (even) more than this;
I'll be lowly in my (own) eyes—
with the (very) maids of whom you spoke,
with them I'll get honor!

23 And Mikhal daughter of Sha'ul had no child
until the day of her death.

7:1 Now it was
when the king sat in his palace-house
    —YHWH had given-him-rest, round-about, from all his ene-
        mies—

2 that the king said to Natan the prophet:
Now see:
I sit in a house (made) of cedars,
while the Coffer of God sits in the midst of a curtained-shrine!
Natan said to the king:
All that is in your heart, go, do (it),
for YHWH is with you.

4 But it was on that (very) night
that the word of YHWH was to Natan, saying:

5 Go and say to my servant, to David:
Thus says YHWH:
Will *you* build me a house for my staying-in?

---

21 IN THE PRESENCE OF YHWH: As in vv.
3–4, the doublet suggests a scribal mistake.
7:1 PALACE-HOUSE: The first occurrence in
the chapter of the "house" motif, leading to
focusing on David's dynastic "house."

6 Indeed, I have not stayed in a house from the day of my
    bringing-up the Children of Israel from Egypt until this
    day;
  I have been going-about in tent and in Dwelling.

7 Wherever I have been going-about among all the Children of
    Israel,
  have I (ever) spoken a word with one of the judges of Israel
  whom I commissioned to shepherd my people, Israel, saying:
  Why have you not built me a house of cedars?

8 So-now,
  thus you are to say to my servant, to David:
  Thus says YHWH of the Heavenly-Armies:
  I myself took you from the pasture, from after the flock,
  to be Prince over my people, over Israel.

9 I have been with you
  wherever you have gone,
  and have cut off all your enemies from before you;
  I will make you a great name,
  like the name of the great-ones that are on the earth,

10 and I will make a place for my people, for Israel,
  I will plant them,
  and they will dwell beneath it,
  so that they will shudder no more,
  so that malicious (men) will not continue to afflict them, as in
    former-times,

6 IN TENT AND IN DWELLING: Cf. the
second half of the book of Exodus, where
the portable Tabernacle is described.

7 JUDGES: Reading *shivtei* as *shofetei*; cf. I
Chron. 17:6 and v. 11 below.

*A*nd King David came and sat in
the presence of Yhwh

II Sam. 7 : 18

11   from the day that I commissioned judges over my people
        Israel.
       And I will give-you-rest from all your enemies.
       Yhwh has told you that Yhwh will make you a house:

12   when your days are fulfilled
       and you lie beside your fathers,
       I will raise up your seed after you,
       (one) who comes-out from your innards,
       and I will make-firm his kingdom.

13   *He* will build a house to my name,
       and I will make-firm his kingly throne for the ages;

14   *I* will be to him as a father,
       and he will be to me as a son.
       When he commits-iniquity,
       I will rebuke him with the staff of men, and with the blows of
         mortals;

15   but my loyal-love will not turn-aside from him,
       as I turned-it-aside from Sha'ul, whom I turned-aside from
         before you.

16   Secure is your house and your kingdom for the ages before
       me,
       your throne will be firm for the ages!

17   According to all these words and according to all this vision,
       thus did Natan speak to David.

18   And King David came and sat in the presence of Yhwh,
       he said:
       Who am I, my Lord Yhwh,
       and who is my household,
       that you have brought me this far?

19   And still this was too-small in your eyes, my Lord Yhwh—

you have also spoken of your servant's house far (into the
   future)!
This is the rule for a man-of-status, my Lord Yhwh!

20   And what more can David speak further to you,
   since you yourself know your servant, my Lord Yhwh?

21   For the sake of your word and according to your heart
   you have done all this greatness,
   to make-(it)-known to your servant.

22   Therefore you are great, my Lord Yhwh,
   indeed, there is none like you
   and no God beside you
   according to all that we have heard with our ears.

23   And who is like you people, like Israel,
   a singular nation on earth,
   whom God went-forth to redeem for himself as a people,
   to make for himself a name
   and to do for you great-things, and awe-inspiring-acts for your
      land,
   before your people that you redeemed for yourself from
      Egypt,
   (by driving out) nations and their gods?

24   You have made-firm for yourself your people Israel, as a
      people for yourself for the ages,
   and *you*, O Yhwh, have become God for them.

25   So-now, Yhwh God,
   as for the word that you have spoken about your servant and
      about his house—

19 THE RULE FOR A MAN-OF-STATUS:
   Following Kimhi.

O establish it for the ages,
and do as you have spoken.

26 And may your name be-great for the ages, saying:
Yнwн of the Heavenly-Armies is God over Israel,
and the house of your servant David,—may it be firm before
you!

27 For you, Yнwн of the Heavenly-Armies, God of Israel,
have revealed to your servant's ear, saying:
A house I will build for you;
therefore your servant has found his heart so as to pray to you
this prayer.

28 So-now, my Lord Yнwн,
you are God, and your words are truth;
you have spoken to your servant this good (word).

29 So now,
be-pleased, and bless the house of your servant,
to be for the ages in your presence,
for you, my Lord Yнwн, have spoken (it),
and through your blessing may the house of your servant be
blessed for the ages!

8:1 It was (some time) after this
that David struck the Philistines and subdued them,
and David took Meteg Amma from the hand of the Philistines.

2 And he struck Mo'av:
he measured them with a rope, making them lie down on the
ground:
he measured two rope-lengths for putting-to-death

8:2 HE MEASURED THEM: That is, he de-
cided which of the prisoners was to die.

and a full rope-length for letting-live.
And Mo'av became servants to David, bearers of tribute.

3 And David struck Hadad'ezer/Hadad-is-Help, son of Rehov,
   king of Tzova,
   as he was going to restore his monument at the (Euphrates)
   River.

4 David conquered from him a thousand and seven hundred
   horsemen and twenty thousand men, foot-soldiers,
   and David hamstrung all the chariot-horses, leaving of them
   (only) a hundred chariot-horses.

5 When the Arameans from Damascus came, to help
   Hadad'ezer king of Tzova,
   David struck-down from Aram twenty thousand men.

6 And David put standing-garrisons at Aram of Damascus,
   and Aram became servants to David, bearers of tribute.
   Thus YHWH granted-deliverance to David wherever he went.

7 And David took the gold shields that were upon Hadad'ezer's
   servants
   and brought them to Jerusalem,

8 while from Betah and from Berotai, Hadad'ezer's towns,
   King David took an exceedingly great (amount of) bronze.

9 When To'i king of Hamat heard that David had struck down
   Hadad'ezer's entire force,

10 To'i sent Yoram his son to King David,
   to inquire of his peace and to give-him-blessing

MO'AV . . . ARAM: The Moabites and
the Arameans.
3 HADAD: An Aramean storm god, usually
identified with Baal.

9 HAMAT: Trad. English "Hamath," the
region northeast of Tzova, itself above
Damascus.

on account of his doing-battle with Hadad'ezer, and (that) he
    had struck him-down,
—for a man of doing-battle with To'i was Hadad'ezer—
and in his hand were objects of silver and objects of gold and
    objects of bronze.

11 These too David consecrated to YHWH,
    (along) with the silver and the gold that he had hallowed from
        all the nations that he had subdued:

12 from Edom and from Mo'av, and from the Children of
    Ammon,
    from the Philistines and from Amalek,
    and from the spoil of Hadad'ezer son of Rehov, king of Tzova.

13 And David made a name (for himself) on his return from strik-
    ing Edom in the Valley of Salt, eighteen thousand (dead).

14 He put garrisons in Edom—throughout all Edom he put gar-
    risons—
    and all Edom became servants to David.
    Thus YHWH delivered David wherever he went.

15 And David reigned-as-king over all Israel,
    and David began-to-establish justice and equity for all his
        people.

16 Now Yo'av son of Tzeruya was Over the Army,
    Yehoshafat son of Ahilud was Recorder,

---

10 DOING-BATTLE WITH TO'I: Experienced in conflict with him.

12 EDOM: Following ancient versions. MT
has "Aram," which looks similar in Hebrew.

13 VALLEY OF SALT: Just south of the Dead
Sea (the biblical "Sea of Salt").

16 OVER THE ARMY: The title of the commander in chief.

17 Tzadok son of Ahituv and Avimelekh son of Evyatar were
     priests,
   Seraya was scribe,
18 and Benayahu son of Yehoyada was Over the Kereitites and
     the Peleitites,
   while the sons of David were priests.

---

17 TZADOK: Trad. English "Zadok." He becomes the ancestor of the predominant
priestly family under the Davidic dynasty.
SERAYA: "Sh'va" in 20:25, below.

18 KEREITITES AND PELEITITES: David's
personal bodyguards, recruited from foreigners (the Kereitites were probably from
Crete).

*D*AVID IN CONTROL AND
OUT OF CONTROL (II:9–12)

T*HE* *SECTION* *BEGINS* with demonstrations everywhere of David's power: he effectively limits the house of Sha'ul to one crippled individual who depends on him for his daily bread; and, amid a campaign against the neighboring Ammonites, manages to win peace from the powerful Arameans. As ruler of a small empire, as a military and political success, David seems to be the king with everything, including multiple wives and sons to succeed him.

Into this moment of triumph the Bible inserts the turning point of II Samuel and one of the greatest of all biblical tales: the story of David and Bat-Sheva. While later Jewish tradition, both in the biblical book of Chronicles (which omits this story) and in the Talmud (which whitewashes David), clearly found it difficult to reconcile the important symbolic figure of David with the way he appears in this story, the Book of Samuel features it dramatically as the root of much that is to follow, and lavishes a good deal of artistic attention and skill upon it. It is, like so many central biblical tales, constructed on a foundation of leading words—in this case, "lie" and "send." Rather than being mere signposts, these words undergo what Trible suggestively calls a "pilgrimage"; they are transformed within the story, and bring us along on the journey. From the initially neutral "lying-place," David's rooftop couch, we are taken to the crime, where he "lies" with Bat-Sheva (11:4). The verb next appears in Uriyya's righteous refusal to go back home in the midst of the war "and I, I should come into my house / to eat and to drink and to lie with my wife?" (11:11). It then becomes part of David's punishment: "I will take-away your women. . . . your fellow . . . will lie with your women" (12:11). The ending moments of the story trace David's movement back into the realm of forgiveness and resolution, with his "lying upon the ground" (12:16), pleading for his son's life, and his final, legitimate "lying" with Bat-Sheva, which results in the conception of the promised heir, Shelomo. Thus an initially neutral term becomes the vehicle for a well-trodden biblical journey of sin and repentance.

The other key word, "send," has a parallel function. Eleven times (in twenty-six verses), messages and people are sent, almost always by David, the master manipulator. The long arm of royal power reaches into the home of a private citizen and to the battle-field; the king is seemingly able to move his subjects around like chess pieces. Much, but not all, of the sending is successful, but it is in any event countered by the divine hand in 12:1 ("So YHWH sent Natan to David"). Despite David's well-thought-out plans, he can-not in the end stand up to God's sending—a phrase that is almost always connected to prophets in the Bible. Natan's mission is a clas-sic one, with prophet pitted against king. It will be structurally repeated (along with parallel circumstances) in the great encounter between Eliyyahu (Elijah) and Ah'av (Ahab) in I Kings 21. In our story, it is only when David's repentance is accepted, and his punishment doled out, that we encounter the last "sending" of the sequence, in which God approves of the new son.

One might also note the text's repetition of "eat" (a sexual metaphor?) and "dead" (with the illegitimate child's demise being seen as payback for Uriyya's), as well as the many meanings of the term "house," in an even broader spread than what we observed in chapter 7. Indeed, the story as a whole appears to be structured upon the various characters, moving from house to house—in this case the palace, Uriyya's home, the sanctuary, and the domicile of the prophet Natan; looming over all the physical movement is the fate of David's household and dynastic house.

The story finds additional uses for sound. Natan's parable in chapter 12, which some scholars feel does not fit the situation very well, is profoundly connected to its referent by the prophet's description of the lamb in 12:3: "from his morsel it would eat, from his cup it would drink, in his bosom it would lie— / it became to him like a daughter /*bat*." As literary critics have pointed out for some years (cf. Simon 1967), the "eat/drink/lie" sequence echoes Uriyya's earlier refusal of 11:11, quoted above, and the coincidence of *Bat*-Sheva's name is surely no coincidence. So while the unwitting king angrily condemns the rich man of the parable, the audience, its ears tuned aright, can feel the trap being sprung.

Also noteworthy and almost unprecedented is God's message in 12:11. It is noteworthy in its rhetoric and unprecedented in its use of rhyme (here represented by six consecutive lines ending in "your . . ."). It is as if God's words cannot be ignored simply because they echo throughout the throne room.

The David and Bat-Sheva story is an intimate look at David's many moods, and shows what he is capable of, for good and for ill, in a variety of situations. In the writer or editor's scheme of things in II Samuel, it is a point from which David, despite the happy endings of this chapter (Shelomo's birth and David's capture of Rabba), can never fully recover. From now on the misfortunes of the country will be identical with those of the House of David.

*D*avid and Bat-Sheva

9:1 David said:

Is there yet anyone that remains from the House of Sha'ul?

—that I may show him loyalty for the sake of Yehonatan.

2 Now the House of Sha'ul had a servant, his name was Tziva,

and they called him (to come) to David.

The king said to him:

Are you Tziva?

He said:

Your servant.

3 The king said:

Is there no one yet (left) from the House of Sha'ul,

that I may show him the loyalty of God?

Tziva said to the king:

There is yet a son of Yehonatan, stricken (in the) feet.

4 The king said to him:

Where is he?

Tziva said to the king:

Here, he is at the house of Makhir son of Ammiel, in Lo
     Devar.

5 King David sent and had-him-taken from the house of Makhir
     son of Ammiel, from Lo Devar.

6 When Mefiboshet son of Yehonatan son of Sha'ul came to
     David,

he flung-himself on his face and prostrated-himself.

And David said: Mefiboshet!

He said:

Here is your servant.

9:4 LO DEVAR: Northeast of Bet She'an, on
   the east bank of the Jordan.

7 David said to him:
Do not be afraid,
for I will show, yes, show you loyalty for the sake of Yehonatan
your father;
I will return to you all the lands of Sha'ul your grandfather,
and you, you will eat bread at my table regularly.
8 He prostrated-himself and said:
What is your servant,
that you have turned-your-face toward a dead dog like me?
9 The king called to Tziva, Sha'ul's servant, and said to him:
All that was Sha'ul's and all his household's, I give to your
lord's grandson;
10 you are to work the soil for him, you and your children and
your servants,
and you are to bring-in (the produce), so that it may be for
your lord's grandson as food, and he may eat it:
and Mefiboshet your lord's grandson shall eat bread regularly
at my table.
—Now Tziva had fifteen sons and twenty servants. —
11 Tziva said to the king:
According to all that my lord king commands his servant,
thus will your servant do.
And Mefiboshet was eating at David's table, like one of the
king's children.
12 Now Mefiboshet had a young son, his name was Mikha,
while all those dwelling in Tziva's house were servants to Mefiboshet.

---

7 RETURN: Or "restore."
LANDS: Lit, "fields."

11 WAS EATING AT DAVID'S TABLE: Following LXX; MT has "at my table."

13 So Mefiboshet stayed in Jerusalem,
for at the king's table he ate regularly.
Now he was lame in his two feet.

10:1 It was (some time) after this
that the king of the Children of Ammon died,
and Hanun his son became-king in his stead.
2 David said:
I will show loyalty to Hanun son of Nahash,
as his father showed loyalty with me.
So David sent to comfort him by the hand of his servants, for
his father.
But when David's servants came to the land of the Children of
Ammon,
3 the officials of the Children of Ammon said to Hanun their
lord:
Is David (really) honoring your father in your eyes,
when he sends you comforters?
Isn't it (rather) to spy out the town, and explore it and over-
throw it
(that) David has sent his servants to you?
4 So Hanun took David's servants,
he shaved off half their beards
and cut off their uniforms halfway-up, as far as their seats,
then he sent them off.
5 When they told David (about it),

10:1 AMMON: The region around today's   3 OFFICIALS: Elsewhere the Hebrew word
Amman, capital of Jordan.   is translated "commanders."

he sent (men) to meet them,

for the men were exceedingly humiliated.

The king said:

Stay at Jericho until your beards have grown,

then you may return.

6   When the Children of Ammon saw that they had made-
     themselves-reek to David,

the Children of Ammon sent and hired Arameans (from) Bet
     Rehov and Arameans (from) Tzova, twenty thousand foot-
     soldiers,

the king of Maakha, a thousand men,

and men of Tov, twelve thousand men.

7   When David heard,

he sent Yo'av and all the army, the mighty-men.

8   And the Children of Ammon went out and arranged-their-
     ranks (for) battle, at the entrance to the gate,

while the Arameans (from) Tzova and Rehov and the men of
     Tov and Maakha were alone in the open-field.

9   And when Yo'av saw that the face of battle was upon him; in
     front and in back,

he chose from all the choice-warriors in Israel

and put (them) in ranks to meet the Arameans,

10   while the rest of the fighting-people he placed in the hand of
     Avishai his brother,

and arranged-ranks to meet the Children of Ammon.

11   Then he said:

If Aram is too strong for me,

you will be my deliverance,

and if the Children of Ammon are too strong for you,

I will go to deliver you.

12 Be strong and let us be-strengthened, for the sake of our
    people and for the sake of the towns of our God,
  while Yhwh—may he do what is good in his eyes!

13 And Yo'av approached, and the fighting-people who were with
    him, for battle against Aram,
  and they fled before him.

14 Now the Children of Ammon saw that Aram had fled,
  and they (too) fled before Avishai and came-back to the town.
  And Yo'av turned from (attacking) the Children of Ammon,
    and came-back to Jerusalem.

15 When Aram saw that they were smitten before Israel,
  they gathered (their forces) together;

16 and Hadad'ezer sent and brought-out the Arameans who were
    across the River, so that they came to Heilam,
  with Shovakh commander of Hadad'ezer's army in front of
    them.

17 When (it) was told to David,
  he gathered all Israel and crossed the Jordan, coming to
    Heilam;
  and the Arameans arrayed-their-ranks to meet David, and did-
    battle with him.

18 And the Arameans fled before Israel;

---

12 BE STRONG AND LET US BE-STRENGTHENED: This phrase was later adopted by Jews in a different context: to be sung whenever a book of the Torah is completed in the cycle of weekly synagogue readings.

17 HEILAM: Well south of Damascus, due east of the Sea of Galilee.

David killed from the Arameans seven hundred charioteers
and forty thousand horsemen,
while Shovakh, the commander of Hadad'ezer's army, he
struck-down, so that he died there.

19 And when all the kings (who were) Hadad'ezer's servants saw
that they had been smitten before Israel,
they made-peace with Israel and served them;
for the Arameans were afraid to continue (trying to) deliver
the Children of Ammon.

11:1 Now it was at the turning of the year, at the time of kings'
going-forth,
that David sent Yo'av and his servants with him, and all Israel:
they wrought-ruin to the Children of Ammon and besieged
Rabba,
while David stayed in Jerusalem.

2 Now it was around the time of sunset
that David arose from his lying-place and went-for-a-walk
upon the roof of the king's house,
and he saw a woman washing herself, from on the roof,
the woman was exceedingly fair to look at.

3 David sent and asked after the woman:

11:1 KINGS: LXX; MT suggests "messengers."
Either meaning is attractive given the story;
I lean toward "kings" as an indictment of
David's being at the palace and not with the
troops.

RABBA: Rabbat-Benei-Ammon, today Am-
man.in translation.
2 HIS LYING-PLACE: More simply,
"couch," but I have sought to retain the key
verb "lie"

But Uriyya lay down at the entrance to the king's house,
     with all his lord's servants,
he did not go-down to his house.

II Sam. 11 : 9

they said: Isn't this Bat-Sheva daughter of Eli'am, wife of
    Uriyya the Hittite?

4 David sent messengers, and he had-her-brought,
    she came to him and he lay with her
    —now she had just purified-herself from her state of *tum'a*—,
    then she returned to her house.

5 The woman became pregnant,
    she sent and had-it-told to David, she said: I am pregnant!

6 So David sent (word) to Yo'av:
    Send me Uriyya the Hittite.
    And Yo'av sent Uriyya to David.

7 When Uriyya came to him,
    David inquired after the well-being of Yo'av, the well-being of
        the fighting-people, and the well-being of the battle,

8 then David said to Uriyya:
    Go-down to your house and wash your feet!
    Uriyya went out of the king's house,
    and after him went out a portion from the king,

9 but Uriyya lay down at the entrance to the king's house, with
    all his lord's servants,
    he did not go-down to his house.

---

3 BAT-SHEVA: Trad. English "Bathsheba."
URIYYA THE HITTITE: Trad. English
"Uriah." A high-ranking officer in David's
army (cf. 23:39 below). His name, ironically,
is a pious Israelite one, meaning "YHWH is
my Light."

4 PURIFIED-HERSELF: The verb *kiddesh* in
other context denotes "hallowing"; here it
is simply the non-priestly word for purification.

HER STATE OF *TUM'A*: Bat-Sheva's
washing is connected to the end of her
menstrual period, during which intercourse
would have been forbidden (cf. Lev. 18:19). It
is significant in this story because it means
that her pregnancy could not stem from her
husband, who has been at the front.

8 WASH YOUR FEET: Likely a euphemism
for intercourse.
PORTION: Of food.

10 They told David, saying:
　　Uriyya has not gone-down to his house.
　　David said to Uriyya:
　　Isn't it from a (long) journey that you have come?
　　Why haven't you gone-down to your house?

11 Uriyya said to David:
　　The Coffer and Israel and Judah are staying at Sukkot,
　　my lord Yo'av and my lord's servants are camping on the sur-
　　　　face of the open-field—
　　and I, I should come into my house
　　to eat and to drink and to lie with my wife?
　　As you live, as your (very) being lives: Were I to do this
　　　　thing . . . !

12 David said to Uriyya:
　　Stay here today as well; tomorrow I will send you back.
　　So Uriyya stayed in Jerusalem on that day.

13 Now on the morrow David had him called, and he ate and
　　　　drank in his presence, and he made him intoxicated.
　　And he went out at sunset to lie down in his lying-place with
　　　　his lord's servants;
　　but to his house he did not go-down.

14 So it was in the morning
　　that David wrote a letter to Yo'av and sent it by the hand of
　　　　Uriyya;

15 he wrote in the letter, saying;
　　Put Uriyya right at the front of the battle, the strongest-point,

---

11 SUKKOT: Another location on the east
bank of the Jordan.

and turn-back behind him, so that he is struck-down and dies.

16 So it was,

when Yo'av had observed the city,

that he placed Uriyya at the place where he knew that there
were men of valor;

17 and when the men of the city went out to do-battle with Yo'av,

there fell (some) of the fighting-people, of David's servants,

and there also died Uriyya the Hittite.

18 Then Yo'av sent and had David told all the details of the battle,

19 he charged the messenger, saying:

When you have finished reporting everything about the battle
to the king,

20 it will be:

if the king's anger starts up and he says to you:

Why did you draw-near the city to do battle?

Didn't you know that they would shoot down from on the
wall?

21 Who struck-down Avimelekh son of Yerubboshet—

wasn't it a woman, (who) threw down on him a riding
millstone from on the wall,

so that he died at Tevetz?

For-what (reason) did you approach the wall? —

Then you are to say:

21 AVIMELEKH SON OF YERUBBOSHET:
Trad. English "Abimelech son of Jerub-
besheth." The reference is to a son of
Gideon (Yerubbaal or Yerubbashet) who in
Judges 9 proclaims himself king over the
men of Shechem and, not surprisingly,
meets an untoward end. Yo'av's message, if

delivered, would be a not-so-subtle dig at
David's behavior, another royal disaster
related to a woman.
RIDING MILLSTONE: The rolling portion
of a millstone apparatus, thus a large
upright stone wheel.

Also your servant Uriyya the Hittite died.

22 The messenger went off, he came and told David all that Yo'av
   had sent him (to say),

23 the messenger said to David:
   Indeed, the men were mightier than we, they went out at us
   into the open-field;
   we were upon them, up to the entrance to the gate,

24 but the shooters shot down at your servants from on the wall,
   so that there died (some) of the king's servants,
   and also your servant Uriyya the Hittite died.

25 David said to the messenger:
   Say thus to Yo'av:
   Don't let this thing be evil in your eyes,
   for like-this and like-that the sword devours!
   Strengthen your battle against the city and destroy it!
   And (you) strengthen him!

26 When Uriyya's wife heard that her husband was dead,
   she beat (the breast) for her lord;

27 but when the mourning-period was past, David sent and had
   her brought to his house;
   she became his wife, and she bore him a son.
   But the thing that David had done was evil in the eyes of
   Yhwh,

12:1 and Yhwh sent Natan to David,
   he came to him and said to him:
   There were two men in a certain town,

---

25 DEVOURS: Lit., "eats."
   STRENGTHEN HIM!: Encourage him.
26 URIYYA'S WIFE: She is not called "Bat-

Sheva" again until David's crime has been
punished by the death of their child (12:
24).

one rich and one poor.

2 The rich-one had flocks and herds, exceedingly many,

3 while the poor-one had nothing at all except for one little lamb
which he had bought;

he kept-it-alive, and it grew up with him, together with his
children:

from his morsel it would eat, from his cup it would drink, in
his bosom it would lie—

it became to him like a daughter/*bat*.

4 And there came a journey-goer to the rich man,

but he thought-it-a-pity to take from his flocks or from his
herds, to make (something ready) for the wayfarer who had
come to him,

so he took the poor man's lamb and made-it-ready for the man
who had come to him.

5 David's anger flared up against the man exceedingly,

he said to Natan:

As YHWH lives,

indeed, a son of death is the man who does this!

6 And for the lamb he shall pay fourfold,

because he did this thing, and since he had no pity!

7 Natan said to David:

You are the man!

Thus says YHWH, the God of Israel:

I myself anointed you king over Israel,

I myself rescued you from the hand of Sha'ul,

---

5 SON OF DEATH: Deserving death.
6 FOURFOLD: In keeping with the law in Ex.
21:37. On the other hand, the LXX's "seven-
fold" fits in nicely with the other sevens in

the story, including the one suggested by
the heroine's name (one meaning of *sheva*
is "seven").

8 I gave you the house of your lord, and the women of your lord
      into your bosom,
   I gave you the House of Israel and Judah—
   and as if (that were) too little, I would have added yet this and
      that to you.
9 Why have you despised the word of YHWH, to do what is evil
      in my eyes?
   Uriyya the Hittite you have struck-down by the sword,
   his wife you have taken for yourself as a wife—
   him you have killed by the sword of the Children of Ammon.
10 So now—
   the sword shall not depart from your house for the ages,
   because you despised me and took the wife of Uriyya the Hit-
      tite to be a wife for you!
11 Thus says YHWH:
      Here, I will raise up against your (person)
      evil from your house,
      I will take-away your women
      from before your eyes,
      I will give (them) to your fellow
      and he will lie with your wives,
      under the eyes of this sun.
12 For you, you did it in secret,
   but I, I will do this thing in front of all Israel and in front of the
      sun.
13 David said to Natan:
   I have sinned against YHWH!

11 (PERSON): As mentioned above, this verse rhymes, somewhat unusually for biblical poetry, so I have sought to have each line end with "your _____."
THIS SUN: In broad daylight

204

Natan said to David:

YHWH himself has transferred your sin—

you will not die;

14 nevertheless, because you have scorned, yes, scorned "YHWH's enemies" by (doing) this thing,

the son, himself, who is born to you: he must die, yes, die.

15 Natan went back to his house.

And YHWH smote the child that Uriyya's wife had borne to David, so that he became ill.

16 And David besought God on behalf of the boy,

David fasted a fast;

whenever he came (home) he would spend-the-night lying upon the ground.

17 The elders of his house arose about him to raise him up from the ground,

but he was unwilling and would not take food with them.

18 Now it was on the seventh day that the child died.

David's servants were afraid to tell him that the child was dead, for they said:

Here, while the child was alive, we spoke to him but he did not hearken to our voice;

so how can we say to him: The child is dead? He might do evil!

19 When David saw that his servants were whispering (among themselves),

David understood that the child was dead.

David said to his servants:

Is the child dead?

13–14 HIMSELF: Following Andersen.

14 "YHWH'S ENEMIES": Later scribes were not comfortable with the phrase "scorned YHWH," so they added the "enemies" to blunt the sense.

18 EVIL: That is, to himself.

𝒯hen David arose from the ground

II Sam. 12 : 20

They said:

(He is) dead.

20 Then David arose from the ground,

he washed, anointed himself, and changed his clothes,

and he came into the house of YHWH and prostrated himself;

then he came (back) to his house, requested that they put food
before him, and ate.

21 His servants said to him:

What (kind of) thing is this that you have done?

For the sake of the living child, you fasted and wept,

but now that the child is dead, you arise and eat food!

22 He said:

As long as the child was still alive, I fasted and wept,

for I said (to myself): Who knows, perhaps YHWH will be gra-
cious to me, and the child will live!

23 But now he is dead—why should I fast?

Can I make him return again?

I may go to him,

but he will not return to me.

24 And David comforted Bat-Sheva his wife,

he came to her and lay with her;

She bore a son and called his name Shelomo / His Peace.

25 But YHWH loved him, and he had (a message) sent by the hand
of Natan the prophet:

he called his name Yedidya / Beloved of YHWH, by the grace of
YHWH.

---

24 SHELOMO: Trad. English "Solomon." The connotation of peace (or "well-being," another meaning of Heb. *shalom*), appears in the name of another son, Avshalom. Per-haps this is David's wishful thinking.

25 YEDIDYA: Trad. English "Jedediah," meaning "beloved of YHWH" (rather like "David," hinting at a resolution to the story).

26 And Yo'av waged-battle against Rabba of the
      Children of Ammon and conquered the
      royal city.

27 And Yo'av sent messengers to David,
      he said:
      I have waged-battle against Rabba,
      and I have also conquered the water city.

28 So now,
      gather the rest of the fighting-people and
         encamp against the city, and conquer it,
      lest I conquer the city myself, so that my name
         is called over it!

29 So David gathered all the fighting-people, and
      went to Rabba,
      he waged-battle against the city and
         conquered it,

30 and he took their king's crown from off his
      head
      —its weight was an ingot of gold, with a pre-
         cious stone (in it)—
      and it was (henceforth) on David's head,
      while the spoils of the city he brought-out,
         exceedingly much.

31 And the people who were in it he brought-out
      and set (to work) with the saw, and with
      picks of bronze, and with axes of bronze,

And David comforted Bat-Sheva his wife

II Sam. 12 : 24

and had them pass through the brick-kiln.

Thus he would do with all the towns of the Children of
Ammon.

Then David and all the fighting-people returned to Jerusalem.

THE GREAT REBELLION (II:13–20)

WHAT COULD NOT have been imagined about the David who slew Golyat, outmaneuvered Sha'ul, conquered Jerusalem, and received God's spirit and blessing, now comes to pass. Beginning with an episode in which sexual transgression and violence immediately make their reappearance, family ties are betrayed and destroyed, and David's once "firm" kingdom—his "house"—totters. Jerusalem becomes dangerous, and the king is forced into exile across the very Jordan by way of which, in biblical tradition, the Israelites conquered the land. Only intervention by God, and continued action by David's ruthless general Yo'av, prevents David from being overthrown or assassinated.

The cycle of stories about Avshalom's revolt concerns both David's decline—which had begun in chapter II with his nonparticipation in the Ammonite campaign and his subsequent foray into adultery and murder—and the downfall of his rebel son. Avshalom is many things, but none so much as his father's son, with his good looks, worldly wisdom, and charisma. It is as if David is forced to relive what Sha'ul had experienced of him.

The central narrative dilemma of the section is how David will deal with Avshalom's violent and rebellious actions. Justice, which Israelite kings were covenant-bound to uphold, is ill-served by David's half-hearted behavior, but, as Gros Louis (1982) notes, "he has already abandoned justice with Uriah" (Uriyya). The text unequivocally traces the king's decline to his moral lapse of chapter 11.

The vocabulary of the cycle is striking and effective. The ebb and flow of David's flight and restoration are traced through the repeated use of "cross" and "return" in chapters 15 and 19. The Amnon and Tamar story with which the cycle opens recalls some of the leading words of the David and Bat-Sheva episode ("lie," "feed," "dead"), but also introduces the central word-play of the entire sequence: variations on the word "heart" (see the Introduction to this volume). The "heart-shaped-dumplings" (13:6) which Amnon requests of his sister foreshadow a major issue: who, the king or his long-haired son, will command the affections ("heart") of the people (15:6, 19:15)? It is surely no accident that Avshalom dies "in the heart" of a tree, thrust, not through the groin as were the earlier political casualties in the book, but through the heart (18:14).

Then, too, Avshalom's name ("Father is Peace") is subject to significant word play in the narrative. The king, after their initial reconciliation, tells his son to "go in peace" (15:9); Ahitofel advises Avshalom that he will personally kill the king, and thus bring about peace (17:2–3); David's anxious question about his son, "(Is there) peace with him?" (18:29, 32, the biblical phrase for "Is he well?") plays up the irony of what we know but he does not: that his "peaceful" Avshalom is dead. The king is finally able to return to his throne "in peace" (19:25, 31), but it is only through decisive, violent acts by Yo'av and the "wise woman" of Avel (20:10, 21), cloaked in words of "peace" (20:19), that the kingdom will be made safe at last.

It is worth noting that, just as the book opened with a woman (Hanna) as a character who expressed central emotions and ideas, this section (and much that has preceded it) turns on the deeds done to and by women. The Bat-Sheva incident is followed immediately by the rape of Tamar, which in turns gives way to the "wise woman" of Tekoa as a vehicle for seeming reconciliation between David and Avshalom. It will take another such woman to bring the rebelling to a close in chapter 20; her counsel leads to the last of the book's beheadings, a symbolic comment, perhaps, on the perils of leadership (Polzin 1989).

In fact the story of the revolt is fleshed out by a large supporting cast of colorful characters: rebels, advisors, adherents, crafty men and women, and concubines. Some have names built on the word "brother" (*ahi*)—Ahitofel, Ahima'atz. Others' names betray their function (Ittai the "accompanier," Hushai the advisor who causes Avshalom to make a "hasty" and fatal decision). The words and deeds of all these secondary characters help to throw the protagonists' sometimes impulsive, sometimes agonized decisions into relief.

In the end, as Flanagan (1988) has pointed out, the rebellion stories are not primarily about who David's heir will be (although for decades scholars have referred to chapters 9-20 as the "Succession Narrative") but rather about survival. Here David resembles no other biblical character so much as Yaakov (Jacob) in Genesis. Like the patriarch, David is heavily involved with women; he is unable to put a brake on his sons' behavior, which reflects some of his own; and his passivity in dealing with them strangely echoes that of Yaakov in Gen. 37. Both men, who are themselves younger sons, find trouble as a result of "love" (Propp); they experience exile and the threat of death, and, bereaved of beloved sons in their declining years, end their lives as shadows of their former selves, so different from such paragons as Avraham and Moshe.

These parallels, and others, have led to speculation about the relationship between Genesis (and other parts of the Five Books of Moses) and Samuel. Some scholars (e. g., Rendsburg and Rosenberg 1986) see Davidic concerns retrojected back onto the age of the patriarchs. More recently, and forcefully, Friedman makes the claim that much of the material from Genesis through Samuel comes from the same authorial hand. Whatever the compositional process may have been, the links are undeniable and important. They show us a literature gripped by poignant central themes: predestination and free will, chosenness and its ramifications, and the fateful consequences of human actions—all with rich variations in the biblical text.

13:1 It was (some time) after this:

Avshalom son of David had a fair sister, her name was Tamar,

and Amnon son of David fell-in-love with her.

2 And Amnon was distressed to (the point of) making-himself-
sick because of Tamar his sister,

for she was a virgin,

and so it seemed-impossible in Amnon's eyes to do anything to
her.

3 Amnon had a friend, his name was Yonadav son of Shim'a,
David's brother;

and Yonadav was an exceedingly worldly-wise man.

4 He said to him:

Why are you so haggard, O son of the king, morning after
morning?

Shouldn't you tell me?

Amnon said to him:

(It's) Tamar, sister of Avshalom my brother—I love (her)!

5 Yonadav said to him:

Lie down on your lying-place and feign-sickness;

when your father comes to see you, say to him:

Pray let Tamar my sister come

and feed me some bread,

let her make-ready some food before my eyes, in order that I
may see,

and I will eat from her hand.

6 So Amnon lay-down and feigned-sickness,

and when the king came to see him, Amnon said to the king:

---

1 TAMAR: Pronounced Tah-*mahr*. The name
means "date-palm."

3 WORLDLY-WISE: Heb. *hakham* denotes not
only intellectual but also practical wisdom.

Pray let Tamar my sister come
and heat two heart-shaped-dumplings before my eyes,
that I may be-fed from her (own) hand.

7 David sent (word) to Tamar, in the palace-house, saying:
Pray go to the house of Amnon your brother,
and make-ready for him some food.

8 So Tamar went to the house of Amnon her brother, while he
was lying-down,
she took some dough, kneaded (it), heated (it) before his eyes,
and boiled the heart-shaped-dumplings,

9 then she took the pot and placed it before him,
but he refused to eat.
Amnon said:
Have everyone go out from me!
And everyone went out from him.

10 Amnon said to Tamar:
Bring the food into the inner-room, that I may be-fed from
your (own) hand.
So Tamar took the heart-shaped-dumplings that she had made,
and brought them to Amnon her brother, into the inner-room.

11 When she brought (them) close to him (for him) to eat,
he overpowered her and said to her:
Come, lie with me, sister!

12 She said to him:
No, brother, do *not* force me,
for such is not to be done in Israel—
don't do this vile-thing!

---

6 HEART-SHAPED-DUMPLINGS: See Introduction, p. xxiii above. Food in the shape of
organs was known elsewhere in the ancient

Near East (my thanks to Professor Chaim
Cohen).

11 OVERPOWERED: Or "took-hold-of."

13 And as for me, where would I take my disgrace?
And as for you, you would be like one of the vile-ones in Israel!
So-now, pray speak to the king—he will not withhold me from
you.

14 But he would not hearken to her voice,
he overpowered her and forced her, lying with her.

15 And (then) Amnon hated her with an exceedingly great hatred,
indeed, greater was the hatred with which he hated her
than the love with which he had loved her;
Amnon said to her:
Get-up, go-away!

16 She said to him:
About this great evil—more than the other-thing that you did
to me—sending me away . . . !
But he would not hearken to her;

17 he called to his attending lad
and said:
Pray send this-one away from me, outside,
and lock the door behind her!

18 —Now on her was an ornamented tunic,
for thus were clothed the king's virgin daughters in robes.—
So his attendant brought her outside, and locked the door
behind her.

12–13 SUCH IS NOT TO BE DONE . . . DIS-
GRACE: The same language is used in
Gen. 34, the rape of Dina narrative.
VILE-THING: for the sense of *neveila* as
"violation," and its importance in Samuel,
see Schwartz.

13 HE WILL NOT WITHHOLD ME: In order
for her plea to have any force, such a thing
must have been possible in royal society.

16 ABOUT THIS GREAT EVIL . . . : The
halting syntax here may be less a function
of a defective text, as some have main-
tained, than of Tamar's emotional state
(Michelle Kwitkin-Close, written communication).

18 ORNAMENTED TUNIC: Like Joseph's
famous one in Gen. 37:3.

217

19 And Tamar put ashes onto her head,
    while the ornamented tunic that was on her, she tore;
    she put her hands on her head
    and went-along, going-along and crying out.

20 Avshalom her brother said to her:
    Has Amnon your brother been with you?
    Now, sister, be-silent—he is your brother;
    don't take this thing to heart!
    So Tamar sat desolate in the house of Avshalom her brother.

21 Now King David heard about all these things,
    and he was exceedingly upset.

22 And Avshalom did not speak with Amnon, (anything) from
        evil to good,
    for Avshalom hated Amnon over the fact that he had forced
        Tamar his sister.

23 Now it was, after two-years' time,
    that they were shearing (sheep) for Avshalom in Baal Hatzor
        that is near Efrayim,
    and Avshalom called all the king's sons.

24 Avshalom came to the king
    and said:
    Now here, your servant is having shearing (done);
    pray let the king and his servants go with your servant.

25 The king said to Avshalom:
    No, my son, now we cannot go, all-of-us,

---

21 UPSET: Yet he apparently does not act further.
23 BAAL HATZOR: Well north of Jerusalem.

EFRAYIM: Presumably a town; McCarter
suggests an original name of Ofra.

let us not weigh-heavily on you!
However much he pressed him, he would not go,
but he gave him farewell-blessing.

26 Avshalom said:
If not, pray let Amnon my brother go with us.
The king said to him:
Why should he go with you?

27 But Avshalom pressed him (further),
so he sent Amnon with him, along with all the king's sons.

28 And Avshalom charged his serving-lads, saying:
Pray notice: when Amnon's heart is merry with wine,
and I say to you: Strike-down Amnon!
then put him to death, don't be afraid!
Haven't I myself charged you?
Be-strong, be sons of valor!

29 So Avshalom's lads did to Amnon as Avshalom had charged;
and all the king's sons arose and mounted each-one on his
mule, and they fled.

30 And it was, (when) they were on the way,
that the rumor came to David, namely:
Avshalom has struck-down all the king's sons,
not a single-one of them is left!

31 The king arose and tore his garments, and lay-down on the
ground,
while all his servants stood (over him) with torn garments.

32 But Yonadav son of Shim'a, David's brother, spoke up and said:
Let not my lord think that all the lads, the king's sons, have
died,
for Amnon alone has died;

for by Avshalom's mouth (this) has been determined since the
time of his humbling Tamar his sister.

33 So-now,
don't let the king take the word to heart, saying: All the king's
sons have died,
for Amnon alone has died,

34 and Avshalom has gotten-away.
And the serving-lad standing-watch lifted up his eyes and saw:
Here: many people were going on the road behind him, from
the side of the hill.

35 Yonadav said to the king:
Here, the king's sons have come;
according to your servant's word, so it was!

36 And it was, when he finished speaking,
that here, the king's sons came,
lifting up their voices and weeping,
and also the king and all his servants wept, an exceedingly
great weeping.

37 —Now Avshalom had gotten-away;
he had gone to Talmai son of Ammihud, king of Geshur.—
And he mourned for his son all the days.

38 Avshalom had gotten-away and gone to Geshur,
and he was there for three years.

39 And the king's spirit ceased going-out to Avshalom,
for he felt-sorrow concerning Amnon, for he was dead.

---

32 MOUTH: Or, as elsewhere, "order."
39 AND THE KING'S SPIRIT CEASED
GOING-OUT: MT has "David the King
ceased," but "David" (Heb. *d-w-d*) is proba-

bly an error for "spirit" (Heb. *r-w-h*), and
early biblical Hebrew uses "the king————"
rather than the word order here.

14:1 When Yo'av son of Tzeruya came-to-know
    that the king's heart was (again) toward Avshalom,

2 Yo'av sent to Tekoa
    and he took from there a worldly-wise woman,
    he said to her:
    Pray feign-mourning, pray clothe yourself in garments of
        mourning,
    don't pour oil (on yourself),
    but be like a woman (who) for these many days has been
        morning over someone-dead.

3 You are to come to the king
    and are to speak to him according to these words.
    And Yo'av put the words in her mouth.

4 When the Tekoite woman talked to the king,
    she flung-herself upon her brow to the ground, prostrating-
        herself,
    and said:
    Deliver (me), O king!

5 The king said to her:
    What is (the trouble) with you?
    She said:
    Truly, I am a widow woman—my husband died.

6 Now your handmaid had two sons,
    but the two of them scuffled in the open-field, with no rescuer
        (to come) between them;
    the one struck-down the other-one, and caused his death.

---

2 TEKOA: Ten miles south of Jerusalem.
POUR OIL: The application of oil was considered a part of personal hygiene in the
ancient world; to omit it was a sign of
mourning.

7 And here, the whole clan arose against your handmaid
and said:
Give-over the one (who) struck-down his brother,
that we may put-him-to-death for the life of his brother, whom
he killed,
though we destroy even the heir!
So they will extinguish my (last) ember that remains,
not providing for my husband a name or a remnant on the face
of the earth!

8 The king said to the woman:
Go (back) to your house,
and I myself will issue-a-command regarding you.

9 The Tekoite woman said to the king:
Upon me, my lord king, be the iniquity, and upon my father's
house,
but the king and his throne are clear (of blame).

10 The king said:
The one who speaks (anything amiss) to you, have-him-
brought to me,
he will not continue to harm you.

11 She said:
Pray let the king be mindful of Yhwh your God
—too-much might the blood redeemer bring-ruin—
so that they do not destroy my son!
He said:
As Yhwh lives,
if a hair of your son should fall to the ground . . . !

---

7 REMNANT: Or "survivor."
11 BLOOD REDEEMER: A member or mem-
bers of a family or clan whose duty it was
to avenge the death of a kinsman.

12 The woman said:
   Pray let your handmaid speak a word to my lord king.
   He said:
   Speak.

13 The woman said:
   Why have you planned in this (way) against God's people?
   By the king speaking this word, (he is) as one guilty,
   by the king not letting his banished-one return.

14 For we will die, yes, die,
   like water running into the ground that cannot be collected.
   But God will not bear a life away,
   he will plan plans, so as not to banish from him a banished-
      one.

15 So-now,
   I have come to speak this word to the king, my lord,
   since the people made-me-afraid.
   Your handmaid said (to herself): Let me now speak to the king;
   perhaps the king will act-upon the word of his maidservant.

16 Indeed, the king will hearken
   to rescue his maidservant from the grasp of the (avenging)
      man,
   from destroying me and my son together, (away) from the
      inheritance of God.

17 Your handmaid said (to herself):
   Pray may the word of my lord king be for (my) rest,
   for like a messenger of God, thus is my lord king,
   to hear out the good and the evil—
   may Yhwh your God be with you!

16 INHERITANCE OF GOD: Unlike the "inheritance of Yhwh" in I 26:19, II 20:19, and II 21:3, this expression appears to refer to the ancestral estate (Lewis).

18 The king answered, he said to the woman:
Don't conceal from me a thing that I ask of you!
The woman said:
Pray let my lord king speak.

19 The king said:
Is the hand of Yo'av with you in all this?
The woman answered and said:
As you live, my lord king,
there is no turning-right or turning-left from all that my lord
    king has spoken;
indeed, your servant Yo'av himself commanded me,
he himself put in the mouth of your handmaid all these words.

20 (It was) in order to change-around the face of the matter
(that) your servant Yo'av did this thing;
but my lord is wise,
like the wisdom of a messenger of God,
to know all that is on earth.

21 Then the king said to Yo'av:
Here now, I have done this thing.
So go, return the lad Avshalom!

22 Yo'av flung-himself on his face to the ground and prostrated-
    himself, and he blessed the king;
Yo'av said:
Today your servant knows that I have found favor in your eyes,
    my lord king,
(seeing) that the king has acted-upon his servant's word!

23 And Yo'av arose and went to Geshur,
and he brought Avshalom to Jerusalem.

24   The king said:

Let him turn-around to his house,

but my face he is not to see!

So Avshalom turned-around to his house,

but the king's face he did not see.

25   Now like Avshalom there was no man as fair throughout all

      Israel, (so) exceedingly to be praised;

from the sole of his foot to his crown,

there was no defect in him.

26   When he shaved his head

  —it used to be that at the end of the year, (every) year, he

      shaved (it), for it was-heavy upon him and (he had) to shave

      it—

that he would weigh the hair of his head: (it was) two hundred

      shekel-weights, by the king's (weighing-) stone.

27   And there were born to Avshalom three sons and one daugh-

      ter, whose name was Tamar,

she was a woman fair to look at.

28   And Avshalom stayed in Jerusalem for two years of days,

but the king's face he did not see.

29   Avshalom sent to Yo'av, to send him to the king,

but he would not come to him.

He sent again, a second-time,

but he would not come.

30   So he said to his servants:

25 NO DEFECT: The language used elsewhere to describe an animal fit for sacrifice,
or a priest qualified to serve in the sanctuary.

See, Yo'av's piece-of-land is near me, and he has barley there;
go, kindle it with fire!
So Avshalom's servants kindled the piece-of-land with fire.

31 And Yo'av arose and came to Avshalom at the house,
he said to him:
Why did your servants kindle the piece-of-land that I have with
fire?

32 Avshalom said to Yo'av:
Here, I sent (word) to you, saying:
Come here, that I may send you to the king, to say:
Why did I come-back from Geshur?
It would be better for me (if) I were still there!
So now,
let me see the king's face,
and if there is any iniquity in me, let him put-me-to-death!

33 So Yo'av came to the king and told him,
and he called for Avshalom;
he came to the king and prostrated-himself to him upon his
brow to the ground before the king,
and the king kissed Avshalom.

15:1 Now it was, (somewhat) after this,
that Avshalom prepared for himself a chariot and horses,
with fifty men running before him.

2 And Avshalom would start-early,
he would stand by the road of the main-gate,
and it was that every man who had a case-for-quarrel (with
which) to come before the king, for adjudication,

Avshalom would call to him, he would say:
What town are you from?
And he would say:
From a certain one of the tribes of Israel is your servant.

3 Then Avshalom would say to him:
See, your words are good and correct,
but hearer you have none on the part of the king!

4 And Avshalom said:
O that they would make me judge in the land,
(that) to me might come every man who would have a case-
for-quarrel or a matter-for-judgment
—I would declare him in-the-right!

5 So it was, when a man would come-near, to prostrate-himself
to him,
that he would stretch out his hand and take-hold-of him, and
kiss him.

6 And Avshalom did according to this manner for all Israel who
would come for adjudication to the king,
so Avshalom stole away the heart of the men of Israel.

7 It was at the end of four years, that Avshalom said to the king:
Pray let me go, that I may pay my vow that I vowed to YHWH,
in Hevron,

8 for your servant vowed a vow when I stayed at Geshur in
Aram, saying:
If YHWH will let-me-return, yes, return to Jerusalem,
I will serve YHWH!

---

7 FOUR: Following some LXX manuscripts; 10 SPY-RUNNERS: Following B-R; from Heb.
MT has "forty." *regel*, "foot" (cf. Gen. 42:9).

9   The king said to him:
Go in peace.
So he arose and went to Hevron.

10 And Avshalom sent spy-runners throughout all the tribes of
     Israel, saying:
When you hear the sound of the *shofar,* you are to say:
Avshalom reigns-as-king in Hevron!

11 Now with Avshalom went two hundred men from Jerusalem,
     invited-guests, going in their innocence,
     they did not know anything.

12 And Avshalom sent (for) Ahitofel the Gilonite, David's advisor,
     from his town, from Gilo,
     when he was to slaughter slaughter-offerings.
     And the banding-in-conspiracy was powerful;
     the people with Avshalom went-on becoming-many.

13 And a message-teller came to David, saying:
The heart of the men of Israel (has gone) after Avshalom!

14 So David said to all his servants who were with him in Jeru-
     salem:
Arise, let us get-away,
for we will have no remnant (left) before Avshalom!
Hurry to go,
lest he hurry and overtake us and thrust evil upon us

11 INVITED-GUESTS: Lit. "those called."
INNOCENCE: Or "simplicity."
12 AHITOFEL: Pronounced "Ahee-*toe*-fell," a
name meaning "my brother is beauty." He
is Bat-Sheva's grandfather.

GILO: Pronounced "Gee-*loe*," a town probably to the southwest of Hevron.
14 THRUST EVIL: The same Hebrew verb
translated by "banished" in the previous
chapter.

and strike the city with the mouth of the sword!

15 The king's servants said to the king:
According to all that my lord king chooses, here are your servants!

16 So the king and all his household went off on foot,
and the king left ten concubine women to keep watch over the
palace-house.

17 The king and all the fighting-people went off on foot,
and they stopped at the Far House.

18 Now all his servants were crossing over next to him,
that is, all the Kereitites and all the Peleitites
and all the Gittites, six hundred men who came on foot from
Gat,
were crossing over in front of the king.

19 The king said to Ittai the Gittite:
Why will you go, even you, with us?
Return and stay with the king,
for you are a foreigner, and also you are an exile from your
(own) place.

20 (Just) yesterday (was) your coming;
and today should I make you wander with us, in (our) going-
forth?
I am going wherever I am going;
return, and have your brothers return with you,
(in) loyalty and faithfulness!

---

17 THE FAR HOUSE: Presumably the edge of the city.

18 KEREITITES . . . PELEITITES . . . GIT-
TITES: Aegean/Mediterranean mercenar-
ies, David's bodyguard.

21 Ittai answered the king, he said:
   As Y<small>HWH</small> lives and as my lord king lives,
   only in the place where my lord king is, whether for death or
      for life—
   indeed, there will your servant be!

22 David said to Ittai:
   Go, cross over!
   So Ittai the Gittite and all his men and all the families that were
      with him crossed over.

23 Now the entire region was weeping in a great voice while all
      the people were crossing over,
   while the king was crossing Wadi Kidron,
   while all the fighting-people were crossing over, facing the
      road to the wilderness.

24 And here: also Tzadok and all the Levites with him were carry-
      ing the Coffer of the Covenant of God;
   they set down the Coffer of God, and Evyatar (also) went-up,
   until all the people had completed crossing through the city.

25 The king said to Tzadok:
   Return the Coffer of God to the city;
   if I find favor in Y<small>HWH</small>'s eyes,
   he will let me return and let me see it, along with his abode.

26 If thus he says: I am not pleased with you,
   here I am—
   let him do with me as is good in his eyes.

---

22 FAMILIES: Others, "children, toddlers,"
but the Heb. *taf* is often too narrowly con-
strued.

23 WADI KIDRON: The valley separating the
(old) city of Jerusalem from the Mount of
Olives.

27 And the king said (further) to Tzadok the priest:

Are you a seer?

Return to the city in peace,

along with Ahima'atz your son and Yehonatan son of Evyatar—your two sons with you (both).

28 See, I myself will tarry at the crossings in the wilderness

until word comes from you, telling me (something).

29 So Tzadok and Evyatar returned the Coffer of God to Jerusalem,

and they stayed there.

30 But David was going-up the ascent of Olives, going-up and
weeping,

(with) his head covered, and (with) him walking barefoot,

while all the people who were with him covered each-man his
head

and went-up, going-up and weeping.

31 Now David was told, saying:

Ahitofel is among those banding-together with Avshalom!

David said:

Pray make-foolish Ahitofel's advice, O Yhwh!

32 So it was, when David was coming to the peak, where (people)
would prostrate-themselves to God,

that here: (coming) to meet him was Hushai the Arkite, his
tunic torn and earth on his head.

33 David said to him:

If you cross-over with me,

---

32 ARKITE: From the southernmost territory
of Efrayim, northwest of Rama.

you will be to me a burden;

34 but if to the city you return
and say to Avshalom: Your servant will I, O king, be—
servant to your father was I formerly,
but now, I will be your servant!—
then you will annul Ahitofel's advice for me.

35 Won't there be with you there Tzadok and Evyatar, the priests?
It will be
that all the words that you hear from the king's house, tell to
Tzadok and Evyatar the priests,

36 (for) here, with them there are their two sons, Ahima'atz of
Tzadok and Yehonatan of Evyatar;
you are to send to me by their hand any words that you hear.

37 And Hushai friend of David entered the city
(just) as Avshalom was about to enter Jerusalem.

16:1 Now David had crossed a little beyond the summit
when here: Tziva, Mefiboshet's retainer, (coming) to meet
him,
along with a brace of saddled donkeys,
and on them were two hundred (loaves of) bread, a hundred
raisin-cakes, a hundred (cakes of) figs, and a skin of wine.

2 The king said to Tziva:
What do you (mean) with these?
Tziva said:
The donkeys are for the king's household, for riding,

16:1 RETAINER: Heb. *na'ar*, elsewhere "serving-lad" or "fighting-lad," but here signify-
ing someone older.

the bread and the figs are for eating (by) the lads,

and the wine is for drinking (by) those weary in the wilderness.

3 The king said:

And where is your lord's son?

Tziva said to the king:

Here, he is sitting in Jerusalem,

for he says (to himself): Today the House of Israel will return
   to me my father's kingdom!

4 The king said to Tziva:

Then here, yours is all that was Mefiboshet's!

Tziva said:

I prostrate-myself!

May I find favor in your eyes, O my lord king!

5 Now when David came to Bahurim,

here: a man was going-out from there, from the clan of the
   House of Sha'ul,

his name was Shim'i son of Gera,

going-out, going-out and cursing (him);

6 he pelted David with stones, and all of King David's servants,

along with all the fighting-people and all the mighty-men to
   his right and to his left.

7 And thus did Shim'i say when he cursed him:

Get-out, get-out, Man of Blood, Man of Worthlessness!

8 God has returned upon you all the blood of the House of
   Sha'ul, in whose place you reign-as-king,

Yhwh has given the kingdom into the hand of Avshalom your
   son,

for here, you are in your evil-fate,

for you are a man of blood!

9   Avishai son of Tzeruya said to the king:

Why should this dead dog curse my lord king?

Pray let me cross-over and take-off his head!

10   But the king said:

What is there between me and you, O sons of Tzeruya?

Let him curse (me), for if YHWH says to him: Curse David,

who is to say: Why do you do thus?

11   And David said to Avishai and to all his servants:

Here, my (own) son, who came-out of my body, is seeking my
        life;

how much more, then, the Binyaminite!

Let him be, that he may curse (me),

for YHWH told him to.

12   Perhaps YHWH will look upon my affliction

and YHWH will return me good in place of his curses on this
        day.

13   Then David and his men went on (their) way;

but Shim'i was going-along the flank of the hill, alongside him,

going-along and cursing and pelting stones alongside him

and dumping dust (on him).

14   And the king and all the people that were with him came back
        weary,

so they paused-for-breath there.

---

8 YOU ARE IN YOUR EVIL-FATE: That is,
you are experiencing misfortune.

12 AFFLICTION: Following ancient versions.

13 DUMPING DUST: Heb. "bedusting (him
with) dust."

Within the illustration:
2 SAMUEL 16, 22
TAUBES
אל בנ

*A*nd Avshalom came in to his
father's concubines
II Sam. 16 : 22

15 Now Avshalom and all the people, the men of Israel, came to
Jerusalem,

and Ahitofel with him.

16 And it was, when Hushai the Arkite, David's friend, came to
Avshalom,

that Hushai said to Avshalom:

(Long) live the king! (Long) live the king!

17 Avshalom said to Hushai:

Is this your loyalty (to) your friend?

Why didn't you go with your friend?

18 Hushai said to Avshalom:

No—

rather, the one whom YHWH and this people, all the men of
Israel, have chosen,

for him I will be, with him I will stay.

19 And second, whom should I serve, if not in the presence of his
son?

As I served in the presence of your father,

so I will be in your presence.

20 Avshalom said to Ahitofel:

Give, (both of) you, advice—

what should we do?

21 Ahitofel said to Avshalom:

Come in to your father's concubines, whom he left to watch
over the palace-house;

when all Israel hears that you have made your father reek,

they will be strengthened, the hands of all who are with you.

21 COME IN TO YOUR FATHER'S CONCU-
BINES: Fulfilling Natan's oracle of 12:11.
Usurping the sexual bed of the father
appears elsewhere as a method of symboli-
cally taking power by the son; cf. Gen. 35:22.

22 So they spread out for Avshalom a tent on the roof,
    and Avshalom came in to his father's concubines, before the
        eyes of all Israel.

23 Now the advice of Ahitofel which he advised
    was in those days like inquiring of the word of God;
    thus was all of Ahitofel's advice, so for David, so for Avshalom.

17:1 Ahitofel said to Avshalom:
    Pray let me choose twelve thousand men,
    and let me arise and pursue after David tonight.

2 And when I come upon him,
    and he is weary and slack of hands,
    I will alarm him,
    so that all the people that are with him will flee.
    Then I will strike-down the king alone,

3 and I will return all the people to you,
    so that when everything is returned
    —the man whom you seek—
    all the people will be (in) peace.

4 And the word was right in Avshalom's eyes
    and in the eyes of all the elders of Israel.

5 But Avshalom said:
    Pray call also Hushai the Arkite;
    we will hear what is in his mouth, his also.

6 When Hushai came to Avshalom, Avshalom said to him, say-
        ing:

---

23 LIKE INQUIRING OF THE WORD OF
GOD: Like an oracle.
17:2 SLACK: Cf. 4:1 above.
3 SO THAT WHEN . . . : The Hebrew is
unclear; LXX adds after "return": "to you as
a bride returns to her husband; you seek
only one man's life. . . ."
PEACE: Again playing on Avshalom's name.

According to this word did Ahitofel speak;

shall we act-upon his word?

If not, *you* speak.

7   Hushai said to Avshalom:

Not good is the advice that Ahitofel has advised this time!

8   And Hushai said (further):

You know your father and his men,

that they are mighty-ones,

and that they are bitter of feelings,

like a bear bereaved in the open-field,

and your father is a man of war—

he will not spend-the-night with the people.

9   Here now,

he is hiding in one of the pits or in one of the halting-places;

and it will be

when (soldiers) fall in them at the start (of battle),

and a hearer hears of it and says:

There has been a (serious) blow to the people that (follow)

after Avshalom—

10   even if he be a son of valor,

whose heart is like the heart of a lion,

he will melt, yes, melt-away.

For all Israel knows that a mighty-man is your father,

and sons of valor (are those) who are with him!

11   So I advise:

let there be gathered, yes, gathered to you all Israel, from Dan

to Be'er Sheva,

like the sand that is by the sea for multitude,

with your presence walking among them.

12 And when we come upon him
in one of the places where he can be found,
lighting upon him as dew falls on the ground,
there will not be left to him or to all the men that are with him
even a single one.

13 Now if he gathers-himself into a town,
then let all Israel bring ropes into that town
and we will drag it, as far as the wadi, until there cannot be
found there (even) a pebble!

14 And Avshalom and all the men of Israel said:
Good is the advice of Hushai the Arkite, (more) than the
advice of Ahitofel!
—For Yhwh had ordained to annul the good advice of
Ahitofel,
in order that Yhwh might bring evil upon Avshalom.

15 Now Hushai said to Tzadok and to Evyatar, the priests:
Like this and like that, Ahitofel advised Avshalom and the
elders of Israel,
and like this and like that I advised.

16 So-now,
send quickly and tell David, saying:
Don't lodge tonight at the crossings of the wilderness,
by-all-means cross-over, yes, cross-over,
lest they be swallowed-up, the king and all the people that are
with him!

11 AMONG THEM: So ancient versions; MT reads "in battle," i.e., leading the troops.

16 CROSSINGS: Heb. *arevot,* but some manuscripts have *avarot,* crossings, which corresponds to 15:28 above.

17 Now Yehonatan and Ahima'atz were staying at Ein
   Rogel/Fuller's Spring;
   and a handmaid would go and tell them,
   and they would go and tell King David,
   for they could not be seen coming to the town.
18 But a serving-lad saw them and told Avshalom,
   so the two of them went quickly and came to the house of a
      man in Bahurim;
   he had a well in his courtyard,
   and they went-down (into it) there.
19 And the woman took and spread a screen over the face of the
      well,
   then she scattered over it some groats,
   so that nothing was noticeable.
20 So when Avshalom's servants came to the woman in the
      house,
   and they said: Where are Ahima'atz and Yehonatan?,
   the woman said to them:
   They (already) crossed the pond of water!
   They sought but did not find (them),
   so they returned to Jerusalem.
21 And it was, after their going-away,
   that they came-up out of the well, and went and told King
      David,
   they said to David:
   Arise and quickly cross the water,
   for thus-and-so has Ahitofel advised concerning you.

---

17 EIN ROGEL: A spring south of Jerusalem's   20 POND: The Hebrew word is obscure.
main Gihon Spring.

22 So David arose, and all the people who were with him,
      they crossed the Jordan, till the light of daybreak,
      till there was no one lagging who had not crossed the Jordan.

23 Now when Ahitofel saw that his advice was not acted-upon,
      he saddled his donkey, and arose and went to his house, to his
        town,
      and when he had given-charge regarding his household, he
        strangled-himself, so that he died.
      He was buried in the burial-place of his father.

24 Now David had come to Mahanayim while Avshalom crossed
        the Jordan, he and all the fighting-men of Israel with him.

25 And Amasa, Avshalom put in place of Yo'av, Over the Army
      —Amasa was the son of a man whose name was Yitra the
        Yizre'elite,
      who had come in to Avigayil daughter of Nahash, sister of
        Tzeruya, Yo'av's mother.

26 And Israel and Avshalom encamped in the region of Gil'ad.

27 And it was, when David came to Mahanayim,
      that Shovi son of Nahash from Rabba of the Children of
        Ammon
      and Makhir son of Ammiel from Lo Devar and Barzillai the
        Gil'adite from Rogelim

---

23 STRANGLED: Hanged.

24 MAHANAYIM: Another connection with
   the patriarch Yaakov; his name was
   changed to Israel at this site (Gen. 32).

25 YIZRE'ELITE: Following Levenson and

Halpern, who postulate from this reading
that Avshalom was offering to restore to
Amasa his father's position (this Yizre'el
was near Hevron). MT has the puzzling
"Israelite."

28 brought-forward couches and basins and potter's vessels,
    wheat and barley and meal and parched-grain,
    beans and lentils,
29 honey and curds and sheep and cheese (from) cattle
    for David and for the people that were with him, to eat,
    for they had said:
    The people are hungry and weary and thirsty in the wilder-
        ness!

18:1 Then David counted (for battle) the fighting-people that were
        with him;
     he put over them commanders of thousands and commanders
        of hundreds.
2 And David sent-forth the fighting-people: a third in the hand of
        Yo'av, a third in the hand of Avishai son of Tzeruya, Yo'av's
        brother, and a third in the hand of Ittai the Gittite.
    And the king said to the fighting-people:
    I will go-out, yes, go-out, even I myself, with you!
3 But the people said:
    You are not to go-out,
    for if we have to flee, yes, flee,
    they won't take us to heart,
    and even if half of us die,
    they won't take us to heart;
    but *you* are like us ten thousandfold,
    so-now, it is better if you are (there) for us in the town, to
        provide-help.

---

28 BEANS AND LENTILS: MT repeats   3 TAKE US TO HEART: Pay any attention to
"parched-grain" at the end of this sequence.   us.

His is head became held-fast in the oak,
so that he was left-hanging between heaven and earth
II Sam. 18 : 9

4 The king said to them:
Whatever is good in your eyes, I will do.
So the king stayed by the gate,
while all the fighting-people went-out by the hundreds and by
the thousands.

5 And the king charged Yo'av and Avishai and Ittai, saying:
Go-gently for me on the lad, on Avshalom!
—Now all the people heard the charge of the king to all the
commanders on the matter of Avshalom.

6 And the fighting-people went-out into the open-field to meet
Israel,
the battle occurred in the forest of Efrayim.

7 And the fighting-people of Israel were smitten there, before
David's servants;
there occurred there a great smiting on that day—twenty
thousand (dead).

8 And the battle there was scattered over the face of all the
ground;
more did the forest devour among the fighting-people than the
sword devoured on that day.

9 And Avshalom happened upon David's servants:
Avshalom was riding on a mule,
and when the mule came under the thick-boughs of a great
oak,
his head became held-fast in the oak,
so that he was left-hanging between heaven and earth,

6 THE FOREST OF EFRAYIM: Northwest
of Mahanayim and on the east side of the
Jordan.
8 MORE DID THE FOREST DEVOUR: Ultimately the victory is attributable to God,
not to David's army.
9 OAK: In Genesis and Judges, a tree often
connected to revelation.
LEFT-HANGING: Following ancient versions, 4QS^a. MT has "put."

while the mule that was under him crossed-on.

10 A certain man saw (him) and told Yo'av,
he said:
Here, I saw Avshalom hanging from an oak!

11 Yo'av said to the man, the one telling him:
Now here, you saw (him)—
so why didn't you strike him down there to the ground?
I would have to (have) given you ten pieces-of-silver and a belt!

12 The man said to Yo'av:
(Even) if I were feeling-the-weight in my palms of a thousand
pieces-of-silver,
I would not stretch out my hand against the king's son,
for (it was) in our hearing that the king charged you and
Avishai and Ittai, saying:
Guard for me the lad Avshalom!

13 Or if I had wrought against his life some falsehood
—and nothing is concealed from the king—
then *you* would have stood aloof!

14 Yo'av said:
I won't wait-around thus before you!
So he took three darts in his palm
and pierced Avshalom's heart (with) them
—he was still alive in the heart of the oak.

15 There surrounded (him) ten fighting-lads, Yo'av's weapons
bearers;
they struck Avshalom and put-him-to-death.

16 Then Yo'av sounded-a-(piercing) blast on the *shofar,*

12 FOR ME: Reading *li* with ancient versions
and some manuscripts; MT has *mi,* "whoever (you may be)."

14–16 PIERCED: Lit., "drove," but the Hebrew
verb here and in v. 16, for blowing the *shofar,*
is the same (my thanks to Michelle Kwitkin-
Close for the suggestion).

so that the fighting-people turned-back from pursuing after
    Israel,
for Yo'av held-back the people.

17 They took Avshalom
and threw him in the forest, into a great pit,
and set up over him a heap of stones, exceedingly large,
while all Israel fled, each-man to his tent.

18 Now Avshalom had undertaken to set up for himself, during
    his lifetime, the standing-pillar that is in the Valley of the
    King,
for he had said (to himself): I have no son through whom to
    have my name recalled.
So he called the standing-pillar by his name;
it is called Avshalom's Monument to this day.

19 Now Ahima'atz son of Tzadok said:
Pray let me run and bring-the-news to the king that Yhwh has
    adjudicated-favorably for him from the hand of his enemies!

20 Yo'av said to him:
You are not to be a man of news on this day;
you may bring-news on another day,
but on this day, you are not to bring-news,
since the king's son is dead.

---

17 A HEAP OF STONES: Alluding to another executed lawbreaker, Akhan (Achan) in Josh. 7.

18 I HAVE NO SON: This seems to contradict 14:27; perhaps it is an indication that no male heirs survived Avshalom.

AVSHALOM'S MONUMENT: This should not be confused with "Absalom's Monument" east of the current Old City walls of Jerusalem; the latter is a Hasmonean (second–first century B.C.E.) structure.

21 Then Yo'av said to a Cushite:
  Go, tell the king what you have seen.
  The Cushite prostrated-himself to Yo'av and ran off.

22 But Ahima'atz son of Tzadok once again said to Yo'av:
  Come what may, pray let me run, me too, after the Cushite.
  But Yo'av said:
  Why should you run, my son,
  when you have no news (that) will find (you favor)?

23 —Come what may, I want to run.
  So he said to him: Run!
  And Ahima'atz ran by the way of the Oval, and passed the
      Cushite.

24 Now David was sitting between the two gateways,
  and the watchman on the roof of the gate went over to the
      city-wall;
  he lifted up his eyes and saw: here, a man was running alone!

25 The watchman called out and told the king,
  and the king said:
  If he is alone, (there is) news in his mouth.
  And as he went, going-along and coming-nearer,

26 the watchman saw another man running;
  the watchman called out to the gatekeeper
  and said:
  Here, (another) man is running alone!
  The king said:
  This-one too is bringing-news.

---

21 CUSHITE: An Ethiopian or Nubian.
23 THE OVAL: The lower Jordan Valley.
24 TWO GATEWAYS: Likewise, there are two
  messengers and "two camps" (the meaning
  of "Mahanayim"—reflecting David's con-
  flicting emotions about Avshalom (Fokkelman 1981).

27 The watchman said:

I see (that) the running-manner of the first-one is like the
running-manner of Ahima'atz son of Tzadok.

The king said:

He is a good man, and with good news he comes!

28 Ahima'atz called out and said to the king: Peace!

And he prostrated-himself to the king, his brow to the ground,
and said:

Blessed is YHWH your God,

who has turned over the men who lifted their hand against my
lord king!

29 The king said:

Is there peace with the lad, with Avshalom?

Ahima'atz said:

I saw a great commotion when Yo'av sent off the king's servant and your servant,

but I don't know what (it was about).

30 The king said:

Turn-around and station-yourself here.

He turned-around and stopped.

31 And here, the Cushite came,

and the Cushite said:

Let my lord king receive-the-news

that YHWH has vindicated you today from the hand of all those
rising against you!

32 The king said to the Cushite:

Is there peace (with him), the lad Avshalom?

The Cushite said:

28 TURNED OVER: A word associated with
David's flight from Sha'ul (cf. I. Sam.).

> May they be like that lad, my lord king's enemies and all those
> who have risen against you for evil!

19:1 The king was shaken;
> as he went-up to the upper-part of the gate, he wept,
> and thus he said as he went:
> O my son Avshalom,
> my son, my son Avshalom!
> Who would give
> my dying, my (own) in your place!
> O Avshalom, my son, my son!

2 And it was told to Yo'av:
> Here, the king is weeping and mourning over Avshalom.

3 Now the deliverance became mourning on that day for all the
> people,
> for the people heard on that day, namely:
> The king is in pain over his son.

4 So the people stole away on that day, while coming into the
> city,
> like people stealing away humiliated when they flee in battle.

5 Now the king wrapped his face,
> and the king cried out in a loud voice:
> O my son Avshalom,
> Avshalom, my son, my son!

6 When Yo'av came to the king in the palace-house,
> he said:
> Today you have shamed the face of all your servants
> who helped your life escape today

19:1 WHO WOULD GIVE: That is, "if only."

O *my son Avshalom,*
my son, my son Avshalom!
II Sam. 19 : 1

and the life of your sons and daughters, and the life of your
    wives, and the life of your concubines—

7 by loving those-who-hate-you, and by hating those-who-love-
    you!

For you have declared today that you have no commanders or
    servants;

for I know today that if Avshalom were alive, and all of us
    today were dead,

that then it would be right in your eyes!

8 So-now, arise, go-out

and speak to the heart of your servants,

for by Yhwh I swear, that if you do not go-out,

no man will lodge with you tonight,

and this will be evil for you

more than all the evils that have come upon you from your
    youth until now!

9 So the king arose and sat at the gate,

while to all the people they declared, saying:

Here, the king is sitting at the gate!

And all the people came before the king.

Now all Israel had fled, each-man to his tent;

10 and it was that all the people were in strife throughout all the
    tribes of Israel, saying:

The king has rescued us from the grasp of our enemies,

he himself helped us escape from the grasp of the Philistines;

but-now he had to run-away from the land, from Avshalom,

---

9 SAT: The action seems to be a kind of re-
enthronement; cf. McCarter.

11 while Avshalom, whom we anointed over us, has died in battle.
So-now,
why are you keeping-silent (about) having the king return?

12 Now King David (himself) sent to Tzadok and Evyatar the
priests, saying:
Speak to the elders of Judah, saying:
Why should you be the last to return the king to his house?
—For the word of all Israel came to the king, to his house.—

13 You are my brothers, you are my bone and my flesh;
so why should you be the last to return the king?

14 And to Amasa, say:
Are you not my bone and my flesh?
Thus may God do to me, and thus may he add,
if you do not become commander of the army before me all
the days (to come), in place of Yo'av.

15 Thus he inclined the heart of all the men of Judah, as one
man;
they sent (word) to the king:
Return, you and all your servants!

16 So the king returned, coming to the Jordan,
while Judah came to Gilgal to go and meet the king,
to conduct the king across the Jordan.

17 And there hurried-out Shim'i son of Gera, the Binyaminite
who was from Bahurim,
he went-down with the men of Judah to meet King David,

18 and a thousand men with him from Binyamin,
along with Tziva, the retainer from the House of Sha'ul,
and his fifteen sons and his twenty servants with him;
they sped to the Jordan ahead of the king,

19 while the river-crossing was being-crossed, in order to conduct
  the king's household across,
 to do what was good in his eyes.
 Now Shim'i son of Gera flung-himself before the king, as he
  was crossing the Jordan,

20 he said to the king:
 Don't impute iniquity to me, my lord,
 don't call-to-mind what your servant iniquitously-did on the
  day that my lord king went-out from Jerusalem,
 that the king should take (it) to heart!

21 For your servant knows that I have sinned,
 but here: I have come today, as the first of the entire house of
  Yosef,
 going-down to meet my lord king.

22 Avishai son of Tzeruya spoke up and said:
 For that, shouldn't Shim'i be put-to-death?
 Indeed, he cursed the Y<small>HWH</small>'s anointed!

23 David said:
 What is there between me and you, O sons of Tzeruya,
 that you have become an adversary to me today?
 Today should a man be put-to-death in Israel?
 Indeed, don't I know that today I am (again) king over Israel?

24 And the king said to Shim'i:
 You will not die.
 And the king swore-an-oath to him.

25 Now Mefiboshet (grand)son of Sha'ul went-down to meet the
  king
 —he had not done his toenails, nor had he done his mustache,
 and his garments he had not scrubbed,

from the day of the king's going-away until the day that he
    came-back in peace—

26 and it was, when he came from Jerusalem to meet the king
    that the king said to him:
    Why didn't you go with me, Mefiboshet?

27 He said:
    My lord king, my (own) servant deceived me;
    for your servant said (to himself): I will have my donkey sad-
      dled and ride it, and go to the king—though your servant is
      lame.

28 But he has slandered your servant to my lord king;
    yet my lord king is like a messenger of God—
    so do as is good in your eyes.

29 For all my father's household were nothing but men (deserv-
      ing) death from my lord king;
    yet you set your servant among those eating at your table!
    So what more right do I have to cry out any more to the king?

30 The king said to him:
    Why speak your words any more?
    I have decided:
    You and Tziva are to divide (between you) the fielded-property.

31 Mefiboshet said to the king:
    Let him even take all of it,
    seeing that my lord king has come back in peace to his house!

32 Now Barzillai the Gil'adite had come-down from Rogelim

---

28 SLANDERED: Heb. *regel*, related to "foot" (as in "to run around spreading rumors"). This is ironic coming after a description of lameness. See also references to a place called Rogelim.

and had crossed the Jordan with the king, to send him off at
the Jordan.

33 Now Barzillai was exceedingly old, (at) eighty years;
he had sustained the king when he had stayed at Mahanayim,
for he was a man of exceedingly great-wealth.

34 The king said to Barzillai:
You cross over with me, and I will sustain you beside me in Jerusalem.

35 But Barzillai said to the king:
How many (more) are the days and years of my life,
that I should go-up with the king to Jerusalem?

36 I am eighty years old today;
do I know (to distinguish) between good and evil?
Or does your servant taste what I eat or what I drink?
Or do I hearken any more to the voice of singing-men or
singing-women?
So why should your servant be any more a burden to my lord
king?

37 Scarcely could your servant cross the Jordan with the king;
why does the king reward me with this reward?

38 Pray let your servant return, that I may die in my (own) town,
beside the burial-place of my father and my mother.
But here is your servant Kimham—
let him cross over with my lord king,
and then do for him what is good in your eyes.

39 The king said:
With me let Kimham cross,
and I myself will do for him what is good in your eyes,

---

38 KIMHAM: Perhaps Barzillai's son.

and whatever you choose (to lay) upon me, I will do for you.

40 All the fighting-people crossed the Jordan,
and when the king was about to cross over,
the king kissed Barzillai and gave-him-farewell-blessing,
and he returned to his place.

41 Then the king crossed over to Gilgal, while Kimham crossed
over with him.
Now all the fighting-people of Judah conducted the king
across,
and also half the fighting-people of Israel.

42 And here, all the men of Israel were coming to the king;
they said to the king:
Why have our brothers, the men of Judah, stolen you away
and conducted the king and his household across the Jordan
and all of David's men with him?

43 All the men of Judah answered the men of Israel:
Because the king is closely-related to me!
Why are you so upset about this matter?
Have we consumed, yes, consumed any of the king('s food)?
Or has any been carried, yes, carried to us?

44 The men of Israel answered the men of Judah, they said:
I have ten shares in the king,
yes, in David, I more than you;
why (then) do you insult me?
Wasn't my word, mine, the first for returning my king?
But the words of Judah's men were rougher than the words of
Israel's men.

20:1 Now there happened-to-be there a worthless man, his name
was Sheva son of Bikhri, a Binyaminite man;
he sounded-a-blast on the *shofar* and said:
We have no portion in David,
no inheritance for us in the son of Yishai;
every-man to his tents, O Israel!
2 So all the men of Israel went-up from (following) after David
(to following) after Sheva son of Bikhri,
while the men of Judah clung to their king, from the Jordan to
Jerusalem.
3 When David came to his palace-house in Jerusalem,
the king took the ten concubine women whom he had left to
watch over the house
and put them in a house under-guard and sustained them,
but in to them he did not come,
for they were tied-off until the day of their death to living widowhood.
4 Then the king said to Amasa:
Summon to me the men of Judah for three days,
while you—stay here.
5 Amasa went to summon Judah,
but he delayed from the appointed-time that he had appointed.
6 And David said to Avishai:
Now,
Sheva son of Bikhri will be more evil for us than Avshalom!

20:1 SHEVA: The name recalls an earlier trouble-
ridden story, that of David and Bat-Sheva.
3 TIED-OFF . . . LIVING WIDOWHOOD:
Some see this as a reminder of Avshalom's
usurpation, but it may also be another indication that David is not the man he once was.
5 DELAYED: Heb. *va-yoher* echoes *ahar,*
aharei, "after," a theme word in this chapter,
which concerns the pursuit of the rebel
Sheva.

So you, take your lord's servants and pursue after him,
lest he find himself fortified towns, and escape (before) our
   eyes.
7 So Yo'av's men went-out after him,
with the Kereitites and the Peleitites and all the mighty-men;
they went-out of Jerusalem to pursue after Sheva son of
   Bikhri.
8 They were beside the great rock that is in Giv'on,
when Amasa came up in front of them.
Now Yo'av was girded (with) his uniform, his (military) dress,
and on him was a girded sword bound on his loins, in its
   sheath;
when he went-out, it fell down.
9 And Yo'av said to Amasa:
Are you (in) peace, my brother?
And Yo'av's right hand took-hold of Amasa's beard, to kiss
   him,
10 but Amasa did not guard-himself from the sword that was in
   Yo'av's (other) hand,
and he struck him with it in the fifth (rib), so that his innards
   poured out on the ground;
he did not (have to do it) to him a second-time—and he died.
Now Yo'av and Avishai his brother pursued after Sheva son of
   Bikhri,
11 while a man was standing over him, from the serving-lads of
   Yo'av,

8 GIV'ON: The rebellion stories end where the conflict between the house of David and the house of Sha'ul had its bloody beginning (see 2:13) (Exum).

9 TOOK-HOLD . . . TO KISS HIM: Parallel to Avshalom's approach to his legal supplicants in 15:5.

he said:
Whoever desires Yo'av, and whoever is for David—(follow)
    after Yo'av!

12 Now Amasa was rolling in blood in the middle of the road;
when the man saw that all the people were stopping,
he turned over Amasa from the road into the open-field, and
    threw over him a garment,
—when anyone who came by saw (him), he would stop—.

13 When he had pushed him out of the road,
all the men who were (following) after Yo'av crossed-over
to pursue after Sheva son of Bikhri.

14 They crossed throughout all the tribes of Israel to Avel (of) Bet
    Ma'akha, to all the Bikhrites,
they assembled and came just after him.

15 When they came, they besieged it, at Avel of Bet Ma'akha,
they cast up a mound against the town, and stopped at the
    bulwark,
while all the fighting-people that were with Yo'av were
    wreaking-ruin, to cause the wall to fall.

16 Now a wise woman called out from the town:
Hearken! Hearken! Pray say to Yo'av:
Come-near to here, I would speak with you!

17 He came-near to her.
The woman said:
Are you Yo'av?
He said:
I am.
She said to him:

---

15 WREAKING-RUIN: Others, "battering."

Hearken to the words of your maidservant.

He said:

I am hearkening.

18 She said, saying:

They used to speak, yes, speak in former-days, saying:

When they inquire, yes, inquire in Avel,

then they end (the matter)!

19 It is I (who) am (among those) most-at-peace, most-trusted in Israel,

(but) it is you (who) seek to deal-death to a town, a mother-city in Israel!

Why would you swallow-up the inheritance of Yhwh?

20 Yo'av answered and said:

(Heaven) forbid, forbid for me, if I cause it to be swallowed up, if I bring-ruin!

21 Not thus is the matter;

but a man from the hill-country of Efrayim, Sheva son of Bikhri his name,

lifted his hand against the king, against David.

Give up him alone, and I will go from the town!

The woman said to Yo'av:

Here, his head will be thrown to you by the way of the wall!

22 The woman came to all the people with her wisdom;

they cut off the head of Sheva son of Bikhri and threw it to Yo'av;

then he sounded-a-blast on the *shofar,*

and they scattered from the town, each-man to his tents,

while Yo'av returned to Jerusalem, to the king.

19:1 IT IS I: The woman appears to be speaking for the whole town.

23 Now Yo'av was Over all the Army of Israel,
    while Benayahu son of Yehoyada was Over the Kereitites and
        Over the Peleitites,
24 and Adoram was Over the Labor-Gangs,
    and Yehoshafat son of Ahilud was the Recorder,
25 and Sh'va was Scribe,
    and Tzadok and Evyatar were priests,
26 while also Ira the Ya'irite was priest to David.

26 IRA: Pronounced "ee-ra."

Closing the Circle (II:21–24)

The book of Samuel does not end with David's death. That, and the complex and again violent machinations which accompany the accession of his son Shelomo (Solomon) to the throne, have been placed in the two opening chapters of the book of Kings, perhaps as the first succession story in a long sequence to follow. Nevertheless, the final section of our book has its own integrity and sense. As has long been noted, chapters 21–24 are chiastic (inverted) in structure: David's two last poems (22:1–23:7) are surrounded, first by accounts of his heroes' exploits, and then by two stories of disaster (famine and plague) and relief, in which God ultimately "lets-himself-be-entreated" (21:14, 24:25). Chapter 21 begins the process of resolving some of the book's issues. Sha'ul's sons, of whom we have heard little since David's assuming power, are here resurrected by the text, only to meet a grisly end. But with their execution, the throne is basically secure. A poignant note is sounded by the figure of Sha'ul's concubine Ritzpa, the Bible's Antigone; her care for the corpses of the house of Sha'ul leads David to mercifully bury them, along with the conflict-ridden past that has marked the path of Israelite kingship so far.

The long poem in chapter 22, of which a parallel text exists as Psalm 18, is one of the older pieces in the Bible, as attested by its spelling and grammatical forms. It also uses ideas found both in other early Israelite poems (Ex. 15 and Deut. 32–33) and in the literature of Ugarit, a city north of (and flourishing earlier than) Israel: a god's impressive appearance and a king's victory song (cf. Cross and Freedman for an extended treatment of the poem). Like the end of Deuteronomy, the book of Samuel thus moves toward its conclusion on a note of heightened rhetoric. It is David as he might have been before the Bat-Sheva incident (Baldwin).

Similarly, David's "last words" at the beginning of chapter 23 present the picture of a king, not in decline, but supremely confident in his God and in himself. The short poem counterbalances the increasingly weakening figure of David, who as the next book (Kings) opens, will be impotent and largely overshadowed by others in the palace.

The final narrative moments of Samuel (chapter 24) bring some moral resolution—David accepts responsibility for his people's suffering—and portend a glorious future: like Avraham acquiring the cave of Makhpela (and hence a legal foothold in the land) in Genesis 23, David acquires the site of the future Temple, which he had so fervently desired to build in II Sam. 7. The journey that began in the northern town of Shilo, home of the Coffer of YHWH, with a priest-leader whose eyesight was failing, ends in the royal city of Jerusalem, permanent home of the Coffer, presided over by a chosen king whose eyes are certainly open. The kingship, whose initially rocky road the narratives of the Book of Samuel have traced, seems to be accepted as part of the landscape, however grudgingly.

21:1 There was a famine in David's days, for three years,
year after year,
and David besought the face of YHWH.
YHWH said:
Upon Sha'ul and upon (his) house is blood-guilt,
because he caused-the-death of the Giv'onites!

2 The king called for the Giv'onites and said to them:
—now the Giv'onites were not from the Children of Israel,
but rather from the remnant of the Amorites,
yet the Children of Israel had sworn (an oath) to them;
but Sha'ul had sought to strike them, in his zeal for the Children of Israel and Judah—

3 David said to the Giv'onites:
What shall I do for you?
By what may I effect-atonement,
So that they will bless the inheritance of YHWH?

4 The Giv'onites said to him:
We have no (desire for) silver or gold with Sha'ul and with his house,
and we have no (desire to) put any man to death in Israel!
He said:
Whatever you say, I will do for you.

5 They said to the king:
The man that wanted-to-destroy us,
who intended for us that we should be annihilated from remaining-standing throughout all the territory of Israel:

21:1 THE DEATH OF THE GIV'ONITES: This refers to an event not cited in the Bible. Apparently Sha'ul, in contravention of the treaty between Israel and the Giv'onites recorded in Josh. 9:15, had killed some of the latter. The incident is used here as a background, to once again absolve David of direct blame for his rivals' deaths.

6 let there be given to us seven men of his descendants,
   and we will impale them to Yhwh at Giv'a of Sha'ul, the
      chosen-one of Yhwh!
   The king said:
   I will give (them) over.
7 But the king spared Mefiboshet son of Yehonatan son of
      Sha'ul,
   because of the sworn-oath of Yhwh that was between them,
      between David and Yehonatan son of Sha'ul.
8 So the king took the two sons of Ritzpa daughter of Ayya,
      whom she had borne to Sha'ul, Armoni and Mefiboshet,
   and the five sons of Meirav daughter of Sha'ul, whom she had
      borne to Adriel son of Barzillai the Meholatite,
9 and gave them into the hand of the Giv'onites;
   they impaled them on the hill, in the presence of Yhwh,
   and the seven of them fell together.
   —Now they were-put-to-death at the time of the harvest, the
      first-days, at the start of the barley harvest.—
10 Then Ritzpa daughter of Ayya took sackcloth
   and spread it out for herself on a rock
   from the start of the harvest until water poured out on them
      from the heavens;
   she did not permit the fowl of the heavens to alight on them
      by day

---

8 AYYA: A bird of prey (perhaps a kind of fal-
con) mentioned in Lev. 11:14 (and Deut.
14:13); appropriate to the action here (Garsiel 1991).
MEIRAV: Following ancient manuscripts;
MT has "Mikhal."

9 THE START OF THE BARLEY HAR-
VEST: The beginning of spring.
10 ON THEM: The bodies of Sha'ul's sons.

or the wildlife of the open-field by night.

11   When David was told what Ritzpa daughter of Ayya, Sha'ul's
concubine, had done,

12   David went
and took the bones of Sha'ul and the bones of Yehonatan his
son from the inhabitants of Yavesh Gil'ad,
who had stealthily-taken them from the square of Bet Shan,
where the Philistines had hung them up at the time that the
Philistines struck-down Sha'ul at Gilbo'a,

13   and he brought-up from there the bones of Sha'ul and the
bones of Yehonatan his son,
and they gathered the bones of those-impaled.

14   And they buried the bones of Sha'ul and of Yehonatan his son
in the land of Binyamin, in the side-chamber of the burial-
place of Kish his father.
And when they had done all that the king had commanded
them,
God let-himself-be-entreated for the land after that.

15   And there was battle again by the Philistines with Israel;
David went-down, his servants with him,
and they did-battle with the Philistines.

16   And David was weary,
and he was taken-captive by Benov, who was of the descendants of the Shades,

---

16   TAKEN-CAPTIVE: Following B-R.
BENOV: McCarter and others suggest that
this difficult text has lost the correct name
of the hero, Dodo.

SHADES: A race of primordial heroes, the
Refa'ites or Rafites, whose name may originally refer to the spirits of the dead.

—the weight of his lance was three hundred *shekel*-weights of
    bronze,
while he was girt in new-armor—
he intended to strike David down;

17 but Avishai son of Tzeruya helped him,
he struck-down the Philistine and put him to death.
Then David's men swore-an-oath to him, saying:
You must not go-out with us again into battle—
that you not extinguish the lamp of Israel!

18 It was (sometime) after this
that there was battle again, in Gov, with the Philistines.
And Sibbekhai the Hushatite struck-down Saf, who was of the
    descendants of the Shades.

19 And there was battle again, in Gov, with the Philistines,
and Elhanan20 son of Yaarei Oregim the Betlehemite struck-
    down Golyat the Gittite
—now the shaft of his spear was like a weavers' beam.

20 And there was battle again in Gat,
and there was an immense man,
the fingers of his hands and the toes of his feet were six and six
    (apiece)—twenty-four in number;
he too was descended from the Shades.

21 He mocked Israel,

---

18 GOV: I Chron. 20:4 has "Gezer"; perhaps "Gov" was anticipating the next verse. In any event, its location is unknown.

19 ELHANAN . . . : Either a separate tradition regarding Golyat's death, or, in the traditional view, an alternative name for David.

WEAVERS': Earlier in the verse, "Oregim" is a homonym (perhaps the result of a scribal error).

but Yehonatan son of Shim'a, David's brother, struck him
down.

22 These four were descended from the Shades, in Gat;
they fell by the hand of David and by the hand of his servants.

22:1 And David spoke to YHWH the words of this song
at the time that YHWH rescued him from the grasp of all his
enemies and from the grasp of Sha'ul;

2 he said:
YHWH is my crag and my fortress, one helping me escape!

3 My God is my rock, in whom I seek-refuge,
my shield, the horn of my deliverance,
my secure-height, my place-of-retreat,
my deliverer—from treachery you deliver me!

4 Praised-One I call YHWH,
from my enemies I am delivered.

5 For they encompassed me, the breakers of Death,
torrents of Belial tormented me;

6 the ropes of Sheol surrounded me,
there greeted me the snares of Death.

7 In my distress I called YHWH!
to my God I called.
He heard my voice from his palace,
my cry-for-deliverance (reached) his ears.

8 The earth did quake and shake,

CHAPTER 22: In this difficult chapter I have been
guided by the work of Cross and Freedman
with advice from Greenstein (written communication).

3 PLACE-OF-RETREAT: Following Goldman.

5 BELIAL: Another term for the underworld.

the foundations of the heavens shuddered,
they quaked, because he was upset;

9   smoke rose-up from his nostrils;
fire from his mouth, devouring,
coals burned-forth from him.

10   He spread apart the heavens and came-down,
a heavy-cloud beneath his feet,

11   he mounted a winged-sphinx and flew,
he glided upon the wings of the wind.

12   He set darkness round-about him as his hut,
the (heavenly) sieve of water, in masses of clouds;

13   from the brightness in front of him
burned-forth coals of fire.

14   He thundered from the heavens, did YHWH,
the Most-High gave forth his voice.

15   He sent forth arrows and scattered them,
lightning and panicked them.

16   Then were seen the sources of the sea,
revealed, the foundations of the land,
at your rebuke, O YHWH,
at the rush of his nostrils' breath.

17   He stretched out (his hand) from on high and took me,
he drew me out of mighty waters.

18   He rescued me from my enemies (so) fierce,

---

11 GLIDED: Reading, as is customary, *yid'eh* for *va-yeira*.

13 FROM THE BRIGHTNESS . . . COALS: The text is quite problematic here; perhaps "coals" has dropped down from v. 9.

14 HIS VOICE: Often in the Bible, thunder is imaged as "YHWH's voice."

16 YOUR: The possessive suffix is missing in MT, but exists in Psalm 18:16.

from those hating me, for they were mightier than I.

19 They met me on the day of my calamity,
but Yhwh became support for me.

20 He brought-me-out to a wide-place,
he saved me because he was pleased with me.

21 Yhwh rewarded me according to my innocence,
according to the purity of my hands, he paid-me-back.

22 For I have kept the ways of Yhwh,
and have never been wicked before my God.

23 For all his regulations are before me,
his laws I have not turned-aside from me;

24 I have been wholehearted with him,
I have kept myself from iniquity.

25 Yhwh has paid-me-back according to my innocence,
according to my purity before his eyes.

26 With the loyal-ones you-are-loyal,
with the wholehearted mighty-man you are whole,

27 with the pure (of heart) you are pure,
but with the crooked you are twisted.

28 An afflicted people you will deliver,
but the haughty-eyed, you bring-low.

29 Yes, you are my lamp, O Yhwh,
my God brightens my darkness.

30 Yes, with you I assault a troop,
with my God I can leap over a wall.

---

28 THE HAUGHTY-EYED . . . : Cross and
Freedman's reading, taken from combining
this verse and Psalm 18 .

29 MY GOD: Suggested by manuscripts; MT
has "Yhwh."

30 TROOP: JPS, on the basis of later Hebrew,
reads "barrier," paralleling "wall."

31 This God, whole is his way,
    the word of YHWH is tested,
    a shield is he for all who take-refuge in him.

32 For who is God besides YHWH?
    Or who is a rock besides our God?

33 God encompasses me with might,
    he makes wholeness his way.

34 Setting his feet like does,
    on his back he makes me stand.

35 Training my hands for battle,
    (enabling) my arms (to) stretch a bow of bronze.

36 You have given me your shield of deliverance,
    your battle-cry makes-me-great.

37 You have widened my steps under me,
    my ankles do not slip.

38 I pursue my enemies, I annihilate them,
    I turn not back until their destruction.

39 I batter them, I shatter them, so that they rise no more,
    they fall beneath my feet.

40 You have armed me with might for battle,
    bowed my adversaries beneath me.

41 My enemies, you have given me (the backs of) their necks,
    those-hating-me, I exterminate them.

42 They cried-for-help, but there was no deliverer,
    to YHWH, but he did not answer them.

---

33 HE MAKES: Heb. *va-yitten*, from Psalm 18:33, as opposed to MT *va-yatter*.

35 (ENABLING) MY ARMS (TO) STRETCH A BOW: Cross and Freedman emend to "together with the javelin and the bow of bronze."

39 BATTER . . . SHATTER: Heb. *vaak-halleim . . . va-emhazteim*.

43 I crush-them-fine like the dust of the ground,
 like the dirt of the streets I pulverize them and pound
  them.

44 You have saved me from my people's strife,
 you have guarded me as the head of nations;
 a people unknown to me serves me,

45 foreigners come-cringing to me,
 hearing by the ear, they hearken to me.

46 Foreigners wilt,
 they gird-themselves from their fortresses.

47 As Yhwh lives, blessed is my rock,
 exalted is my God, the rock of my deliverance.

48 (He is the) God giving me vengeance,
 bringing-down peoples beneath me,

49 taking-me-out from my enemies.
 Over my adversaries you have exalted me,
 from the man of treachery you have rescued me.

50 Therefore I praise you, O Yhwh, among the nations,
 and to your name I sing-melodies,

51 who increases the deliverance of his king,
 who shows loyalty to his anointed-one,
 to David and to his seed,
 for the ages!

---

43 PULVERIZE THEM AND POUND THEM: Heb. *adikkeim erka'eim.*
44 MY PEOPLE'S: LXX has "peoples'."
45 HEARKEN: With the connotation of obedience.
49 FROM THE MAN OF VIOLENCE: Cross and Freedman, and others, find this line strange and out of place.
51 WHO INCREASES: Heb. *magdil,* following the written text of MT and Psalm 18:51.
FOR THE AGES!: repeating the important refrain from II 7:13ff.

23:1 Now these are David's last words:

Utterance of David son of Yishai,

utterance of the man raised-on-high,

anointed-one of Yaakov's God,

the favored-one of Israel's Strength:

2   The spirit of YHWH speaks through me,

his discourse is on my tongue.

3   The God of Israel talks,

to me the Rock of Israel speaks:

A ruler over humans, a righteous-one,

a ruler with the awe of God,

4   is like the light of daybreak (as) the sun rises,

a daybreak without clouds,

by dint of brightness,

by dint of rain, the herbage of earth.

5   —Yes, is not so my house before God?

For a covenant for the ages he has made for me,

arranged in all and (placed) under guard

Yes, all my deliverance, all my desire,

yes, will he not cause it to sprout?

6   But the worthless—

like a thorn tossed-away are they all,

for by no hand (alone) can they be picked-up,

7   the man who touches them must fill (his hand) with iron or

the shaft of a spear,

23:1 FAVORED-ONE OF ISRAEL'S STRENGTH: Understanding *zimra* (here in the plural) as in Ex. 15:2, the Song at the Sea. Others, "the sweet singer of Israel."

4 IS LIKE: MT has "and" before these words; ancient versions omit.

but with fire they will burn, yes, burn (them) where (they)
stay!

8   These are the names of the mighty-men that David had:
Yashav'am the Tahkemonite, head of the officers;
he swung his axe over eight hundred slain at one time.

9   Now after him was Elazar son of Dodo son of Ahohi
—among the three mighty-men with David when they
mocked the Philistines gathered there for battle,
when the men of Israel went-up.
10 (Now) he arose and struck-down the Philistines, until his hand
became-weary,
so that his hand stuck to the sword.
YHWH wrought a great deliverance on that day;
the people returned after him only to strip (the slain).
11 Now after him was Shamma son of Agei the Hararite;
(once,) when the Philistines gathered at Lehi,
there was a piece of open-field there full of lentils,
and when the people fled before the Philistines,
12 he took-a-stand in the middle of the piece-of-land and rescued
it, striking down the Philistines.
Thus YHWH wrought a great deliverance.

13 (Once) three of the Thirty chiefs went-down, and they came
at harvest-time to David at the Cave of Adullam,

8 YASHAV'AM THE TAHKEMONITE: The
text is in difficult shape; I Chron. 11:11 reads
the name as "Yashov'am son of Hakhmoni."

while a group of Philistines was encamped in the Valley of the
    Shades.

14 Now David was then at the fortress,
while a garrison of Philistines was then at Bet Lehem.

15 And David had a craving, he said:
Who will give me water to drink from the cistern of Bet
    Lehem that is at the gate?

16 The three mighty-men broke through into the camp of the
    Philistines,
they drew water from the cistern of Bet Lehem that is at the
    gate,
they carried it away and brought it to David.
But he would not drink it, pouring it out (instead) to YHWH;

17 he said:
(Heaven) forbid for me, by YHWH, doing this;
is it the blood of men who were going forth (at risk) of their
    lives?!
So he would not drink it.
These (deeds) did the three mighty-men.

18 Now Avishai brother of Yo'av son of Tzeruya was the head of
    the Thirty
—he swung his spear over three hundred slain,
so he had a name among the Thirty.

19 Among the Thirty he was honored, so that he became a com-
    mander for them,
but to the (status of the) Three he did not come.

---

17 IS IT THE BLOOD . . . : The Hebrew text seems to be missing a few words.

18 THIRTY: According to manuscripts; MT has "Three."

20 Now Benayahu son of Yehoyada, the son of a valiant man, was
abundant in brave-deeds, from Kavtze'el;
(it was) he who struck down the two (sons of) Ariel of Mo'av,
he went-down and struck a lion in the midst of a cistern, on a
day of snow;

21 and (it was) he (who) struck an Egyptian man, a man of (giant)
appearance,
—now in the Egyptian's hand was a spear;
he went-down at him with (only) a staff,
he snatched the spear from the Egyptian's hand, and killed him
with his (own) spear.—

22 These-things did Benayahu son of Yehoyada;
he had a name among the Thirty mighty-men.

23 Among the Thirty he was honored,
but to the (status of the) Three he did not come,
and David put him over his bodyguard.

24 Asa'el brother of Yo'av was among the Thirty,
(with) Elhanan son of Dodo of Bet Lehem,

25 Shamma the Harodite,
Elika the Harodite,

26 Heletz the Paltite,
Ira son of Ikkesh the Tekoite,

27 Avi'ezer the Annatotite,
Mevunnai the Hushite,

28 Tzalmon the Ahohite,
Mah'rai the Netofatite,

29 Heilev son of Ba'ana the Netofatite,

20 (SONS OF): Supplied by LXX.

Ittai son of Rivai from Giv'a of the Children of Binyamin,

30 Benayahu (the) Pir'atonite,
Hiddai from the wadis of Ga'ash,

31 Avi-Almon the Arvatite,
Azmavet the Barhumite,

32 Elyahba the Sha'alvonite,
the Children of Yashen,

33 Yehonatan (son of) Shamma the Hararite,
Ahi'am son of Sharar the Ararite,

34 Elifelet son of Ahasbai the Bet Ma'akhatite,
Eli'am son of Ahitofel the Gilonite,

35 Hetzrai the Carmelite,
Pa'arai the Arbite,

36 Yig'al son of Natan of Tzova,
Bani the Gadite,

37 Tzeleg the Ammonite,
Nah'rai the Be'erotite, weapons bearer of Yo'av son of
Tzeruya,

38 Ira the Yitrite,
Garev the Yitrite,

39 Uriyya the Hittite—
altogether, thirty-seven.

24:1 And Yhwh's anger again flared up against Israel,
so he incited David against them, saying:
Go, take-a-census of Israel and Judah.

24:1 TAKE-A-CENSUS: In order for there to be resolution at the end of the chapter and the book, there has to be a problem—and here it appears to be the presumptuousness of power in numbering the population (there may also be here an ancient reluctance, rooted in a belief in magic, to count). The impulse is planted by God, perhaps to end the book with a lesson to kings on the limits of their control.

2 So the king said to Yo'av, commander of the forces that were
    with him:
  Pray roam throughout all the tribes of Israel, from Dan to
    Be'er Sheva,
  and count the fighting-people,
  that I may know the number of the people.
3 Yo'av said to the king:
  May Yʜwʜ your God add to the people, (as many) as they are,
    (as many) as they are, a hundred fold!
  My lord king's eyes can see (for themselves);
  so my lord king—why does he desire this matter?
4 But the king's word was strong upon Yo'av and upon the com-
    manders of the forces,
  so Yo'av and the commanders of the forces went out from the
    king's presence to count the people, Israel;
5 they crossed the Jordan and encamped in Aro'er, south of the
    town that is in the midst of the Wadi of Gad, toward
    Ya'zer,
6 then they came to Gil'ad and to the region of Tahtim Hodshi,
  then they came to Dan Ya'an and around to Tzidon,
7 then they came to the fortress of Tzor / Tyre and all the
    Hivvite and Canaanite towns,
  and (finally) went-out into the Negev of Judah, (toward) Be'er
    Sheva.
8 They roamed throughout the entire land,

---

2 ꜰɪɢʜᴛɪɴɢ-ᴘᴇᴏᴘʟᴇ: As indicated in verse   5 ᴇɴᴄᴀᴍᴘᴇᴅ: LXX reads "began."
9 below.

coming (back) at the end of nine months and twenty days to
    Jerusalem.

9 And Yo'av gave the number of the people thus-accounted to
    the king;

and Israel was: eight hundred thousand mighty-men of valor,
    unsheathing the sword,

and the men of Judah: five hundred thousand men.

10 But David's heart struck him (with remorse) after he had num-
    bered the people;

David said to YHWH:

I have sinned exceedingly in what I have done!

So-now, O YHWH, pray transfer the iniquity of your servant,

for I have been exceedingly foolish!

11 David arose at daybreak,

and the word of YHWH was to Gad the prophet, David's vision-
    ary, saying:

12 Go, you are to speak to David:

Thus says YHWH:

I will hold three (things) over you;

choose yourself one of them, and I will do it to you.

13 Gad came to David and told him,

he said to him:

Shall there come upon you seven years of famine in your land,

or three months of your fleeing before your foe, while he pur-
    sues you,

12 HOLD THREE (THINGS) OVER YOU:
That is, give you a choice of three different
punishments.

or shall there be three days of plague in your land?

So-now, learn and see: what kind of word shall I answer to (the
one) who-sent-me?

14 David said to Gad:

I am in extreme distress;

pray let us fall into Yhwh's hand,

for great is his compassion;

but into human hands may I never fall!

15 And Yhwh gave-forth a plague among Israel, from morning
until the appointed-time,

and there died of the people, from Dan to Be'er-Sheva, seven
and seventy thousand men.

16 But when the (divine) messenger stretched forth his hand
(against) Jerusalem, to bring-it-to-ruin,

Yhwh felt-sorry concerning the evil,

and he said to the messenger, the one bringing-ruin among the
people:

Enough now, let your hand slack-off!

Now Yhwh's messenger was (then) beside the threshing-floor
of Aravna the Yevusite.

17 David said to Yhwh, when he saw the messenger, the one striking-down the people,

he said:

Here, (it is) I who have sinned,

(it is) I who have done-iniquity,

---

13 RETURN: Answer.
14 MAY I NEVER FALL: Contrasting with
the "fall" of Sha'ul at the end of I Samuel.
16 ARAVNA: Trad. English "Arauna," whose
threshing-floor lay higher than David's
palace. It was the future site of Shelomo's
Temple.

but these sheep, what have they done?

Pray let your hand be against me and against my father's
house!

18 And Gad came to David on that day

and said to him:

Go-up, erect to YHWH a slaughter-site

at the threshing-floor of Aravna the Yevusite.

19 So David went-up, according to the word of Gad, as YHWH had
commanded him.

20 Aravna looked out

and saw the king and his servants crossing-over to him,

and Aravna went out and prostrated-himself to the king, his
brow to the ground,

21 and Aravna said:

Why does my lord come to his servant?

David said:

To acquire from you the threshing-floor, to build a slaughter-
site to YHWH,

so that the plague may be restrained from upon the people!

22 Aravna said to David:

May my lord king take and offer-up whatever is good in his
eyes!

See, an ox is for the offering-up

and the sledges and the gear of the oxen are for (use as) wood;

23 all (this) does Aravna give, O king, to the king!

And Aravna said (further) to the king:

May YHWH your God show you good-will!

24 The king said to Aravna:

No,

rather I will acquire, yes, acquire (it) from you at fair-price;

I will not offer-up to Yhwh my God offerings-up (gotten) for
   nothing!

So David acquired the threshing-floor and the ox for silver, fifty
   weights;

25 and David built (there) a slaughter-site to Yhwh,

he offered-up offerings-up and *shalom*-offerings.

And Yhwh let-himself-be-entreated for the land,

so that the plague was restrained from upon Israel.

*O*ld David

Suggestions for Further Reading

The following is a partial list which is intended to be suggestive and thought-provoking rather than comprehensive. It also includes items referred to in the introductions and notes. The reader who wishes a brief but thoughtful and articulate introduction to Samuel would do well to check out Rosenberg (1987); from here, works such as Exum's will provide a stimulating entry into the riches of the text. For those seeking to engage the philological and critical aspects of Samuel, as well as to review previous scholarsip, McCarter's two volumes remain the standard treatment.

Ackerman, James S. "Knowing Good and Evil: A Literary Analysis of the Court History in 2 Samuel 9–20 and I Kings 1–2." *Journal of Biblical Literature* 109:1 (Spring 1990): 41–60.

———. "Who Can Stand before YHWH, The Holy God? A Reading of I Sam. 1–15." *Prooftexts* 11:1 (January 1991), 1–25.

Adar, Zvi. *The Biblical Narrative.* Jerusalem: World Zionist Organization, 1959.

Alter, Robert. *The Art of Biblical Narrative.* New York: Basic Books, 1981.

———. *The World of Biblical Literature.* New York: Basic Books, 1992.

Andersen, Francis. *The Sentence in Biblical Hebrew.* The Hague: Mouton, 1974.

Arnold, Patrick. "Migron." *Anchor Bible Dictionary.* New York: Doubleday & Co., 1992.

Baldwin, Joyce G. *1 & 2 Samuel* (Tyndale Old Testament Commentaries). Leicester, England: Inter-Varsity Press, 1988.

Bar-Efrat, Shimon. *Narrative Art in the Bible.* Sheffield, Eng.: The Almond Press, 1989.

Bellefontaine, Elizabeth. "Customary Law and Chieftainship: Judicial Aspects of 2 Samuel 14:4–21." *Journal for the Study of the Old Testament [JSOT* hereafter*]* 38 (1987): 47–72.

Brettler, Marc. "The Composition of I Samuel 1–2." *Journal of Biblical Literature* 116:4 (Winter 1997): 601–12.

———. *The Creation of History in Ancient Israel.* London: Routledge, 1995.

Buber, Martin. "Biblical Leadership." *On the Bible.* New York: Schocken Books, 1982: 137–150.

Buber, Martin, and Franz Rosenzweig. *Buecher der Geschichte.* Cologne: Jakob Hegner Verlag, 1956.

———. *Scripture and Translation.* Lawrence Rosenwald and Everett Fox, eds. Bloomington IN: Indiana University Press, 1994.

Campbell, Anthony F. *Of Prophets and Kings.* Catholic Biblical Quarterly Monograph Series 17. Washington, D.C.: The Catholic Bible Association of America, 1986.

Conroy, Charles C. *Absalom Absalom! Narrative and Language in 2 Sam. 13–20.* Analecta Biblica 81. Rome: Pontifical Biblical Institute, 1978.

Coote, Robert B., and Keith W. Whitelam. "The Emergence of Israel: Social Transformation and State Formation Following the Decline in Late Bronze Age Trade." *Semeia* 37 (1986): 107–47.

Cross, Frank Moore, Jr. "Traditional Narrative and the Reconstruction of Early Israelite Institutions." In *From Epic to Canon*. Baltimore: Johns Hopkins University Press, 1998.

———, and David Noel Freedman. *Studies in Ancient Yahwistic Poetry.* Grand Rapids: Wm. B. Eerdmans Publishing Co., 1975.

Damrosch, David. *The Narrative Covenant.* San Francisco: Harper & Row, 1987.

Dotan, Trude and Moshe. *People of the Sea.* New York: Macmillan Publishing Co., 1992.

Driver, Samuel Rolles. *Notes on the Hebrew Text of the Books of Samuel.* Oxford: Clarendon Press, 1890.

Eslinger, Lyle. "Viewpoints and Point of View in I Samuel 8–12." *JSOT* 26 (1983): 61–76.

Exum, J. Cheryl. *Tragedy and Biblical Narrative.* Cambridge: Cambridge University Press, 1996.

Feliks, Yehuda. *Nature and Man in the Bible.* London: Soncino, 1981.

Finkelstein, Israel, and Nadav Na'aman, eds. *From Nomadism to Monarchy: Archaeological and Historical Aspects of Early Israel.* Jerusalem: Yad Yitzhak Ben-Zvi/Israel Exploration Society; Washington D.C.: Biblical Archaeology Society, 1994.

Fishbane, Michael. "1 Samuel 3: Historical Narrative and Narrative Poetics." In Kenneth R. R. Gros Louis with James S. Ackerman, eds. *Literary Interpretations of Biblical Narratives*, Vol. 2. Nashville: Abingdon Press, 1982, 191–203.

Flanagan, James W. *David's Social Drama*. Sheffield, Eng.: Almond Press, 1988.

———. "Samuel, Book of 1–2: Text, Composition, and Content." In *Anchor Bible Dictionary*. New York: Doubleday & Co., 1992.

Fokkelman, Jan. *Narrative Art and Poetry in the Books of Samuel*.

Vol. 1: *King David*. Assen: Van Gorcum, 1981

Vol. 2: *The Crossing Fates*. Assen: Van Gorcum, 1986.

Vol. 3: *Throne and City*. Assen: Van Gorcum, 1990.

Vol. 4: *Vow and Desire*. Assen: Van Gorcum, 1993.

Fox, Everett. *The Five Books of Moses* (The Schocken Bible, Vol. 1.). New York: Schocken Books, 1995.

Friedman, Richard L. *The Hidden Book in the Bible*. San Fransisco: HarperSanFrancisco, 1998.

Garsiel, Moshe. *Biblical Names: A Literary Study of Midrashic Derivations and Puns*. Ramat Gan, Is.: Bar-Ilan University Press, 1991.

———. *The First Book of Samuel*. Jerusalem: Rubin Mass Ltd., 1990.

Gaster, Theodor H. *Myth, Legend, and Custom in the Old Testament*. Vol. 2. New York: Harper & Row, 1975.

Geller, Stephen. "The Struggle at the Jabbok," in *Sacred Enigmas*. London: Routledge, 1996, 9–29.

Gitay, Yehoshua. "Reflections on the Poetics of the Samuel Narrative: The Question of the Ark Narrative." *Catholic Biblical Quarterly* 54 (1992), 220–30.

Goldman, S. *Samuel,* The Soncino Books of the Bible. London: Soncino Press, 1949.

Gordon, R. P. *1 & 2 Samuel*. Sheffield, Eng.: JSOT Press, 1993.

Gros Louis, Kenneth R. R. "The Difficulty of Ruling Well: King David of Israel." *Semeia* 8 (1977): 15–33.

———. "King David of Israel." In *Literary Interpretations of Biblical Narratives,* Vol. II. Nashville: Abingdon Press, 1982, 204–19.

Gunn, David M. "In Security: The David of Biblical Narrative." In J. Cheryl Exum, ed., *Signs and Wonders: Biblical Texts in Literary Focus*. Atlanta: Scholars Press, 1989, 133–51.

———. *The Fate of King Saul*. Sheffield: Almond Press, 1980.

———. *The Story of King David*. Sheffield, Eng.: JSOT Press, 1982.

Hackett, Jo Ann. "1 and 2 Samuel." In Carol A. Newsom and Sharon H. Ringe, eds., *The Women's Bible Commentary*. Louisville: Westminster/John Knox Press, 1992.

Jeffrey, David Lyle, ed. *A Dictionary of Biblical Tradition in English Literature*. Grand Rapids: Wm. B. Eerdmans Pub. Co., 1992.

Jobling, David. *1 Samuel*. Collegeville, Minn.: The Liturgical Press, 1998.

———. *The Sense of Biblical Narrative I*. Sheffield, Eng.: JSOT Press, 1987.

Klein, Ralph W. *I Samuel*. Word Biblical Commentary 10. Waco, Tex.: Word Books, 1983.

Levenson, Jon D. "I Samuel 25 as Literature and History." *Catholic Biblical Quarterly* 40 (1978): 11–28.

———, and Baruch Halpern. "The Political Import of David's Marriages." *Journal of Biblical Literature* 99:4 (December 1980): 507–18.

Lewis, Theodore J. "The Ancestral Estate (*nahalat elohim*) in 2 Sam. 14:26." *Journal of Biblical Literature* 110:4 (Winter 1991): 597–612.

Long, Burke O. *Images of Man and God*. (Sheffield, Eng.: The Almond Press, 1981).

McCarter, P. Kyle. *I Samuel*. Anchor Bible 8. Garden City, N.Y.: Doubleday & Co., 1980.

———. *II Samuel*. Anchor Bible 9. Garden City: Doubleday & Co., 1984.

Marcus, David. "David the Deceiver and David the Dupe." *Prooftexts* 6:2 (May 1986), 163–71.

Miles, Jack. *God: A Biography*. New York: Alfred A. Knopf, 1995.

Miscall, Peter D. "For David's Sake: A Response to David M. Gunn." In Exum, *Signs and Wonders*, 153–63.

———. *1 Samuel: A Literary Reading*. Bloomington: Indiana University Press, 1986.

Mullen, E. Theodore, Jr. *Narrative History and Ethnic Boundaries*. Atlanta: Scholars Press, 1993.

Polzin, Robert. *Samuel and the Deuteronomist*. San Francisco: Harper & Row, 1989.

———. "On Taking Renewal Seriously: I Sam. 11:1–15." In Lyle Eslinger and Glen Taylor, eds., *Ascribe to the Lord: Biblical and other Studies in Memory of Peter C. Craigie* (JSOT 67). Sheffield, Eng.: Academic Press, 1988.

———. *David and the Deuteronomist*. Bloomington: Indiana University Press, 1993.

Propp, William H. "Kinship in 2 Samuel 13." *Catholic Bible Quarterly* 55 (1993), 39–53.

Rendsburg, Gary. *The Redaction of Genesis*. Winona Lake, Ind.: Eisenbrauns, 1986.

Rosenberg, Joel. *King and Kin*. Bloomington: Indiana University Press, 1986.

———"1 and 2 Samuel." In Robert Alter and Frank Kermode, eds., *The Literary Guide to the Bible*, pp. 122–45. Cambridge: Harvard University Press, 1987.

Sakenfeld, Katherine Doob. "Loyalty and Love: The Language of Human Interconnections in the Hebrew Bible." In Michael Patrick O'Connor and David Noel Freedman, eds., *Backgrounds for the Bible*. Winona Lake, Ind.: Eisenbrauns, 1987.

Schneidau, Herbert N. *Sacred Discontent*. Berkeley: University of California Press, 1977.

Schwartz, Regina M. "Adultery in the House of David: The Meta-narratives of Biblical Scholarship and the Narratives of the Bible." In Alice Bach, ed., *Women in the Hebrew Bible*. London: Routledge, 1999, 335–50.

Simon, Uriel. "The Poor Man's Ewe-Lamb: An Example of a Juridical Parable." *Biblica* 48 (1967): 207–42.

———. *Reading Prophetic Narratives*. Bloomington: Indiana University Press, 1997.

Smith, Morton. "The So-Called 'Biography of David.'" *Harvard Theological Review* 44 (1951), 167–69.

Soggin, J. Alberto. *An Introduction to the History of Israel and Judah*. Valley Forge: Trinity Press International, 1993.

Spina, Frank Anthony. "Eli's Seat: The Transition from Priest to Prophet in I Samuel 1–4." *Journal for the Study of the Old Testament* 62 (1994): 67–75.

Sternberg, Meir. *The Poetics of Biblical Narrative*. Bloomington: Indiana University Press, 1985.

———. "The Bible's Art of Persuasion: Ideology, Rhetoric, and Poetics in Saul's Fall." In Paul R. House, ed., *Beyond Form Criticism*. Winona Lake, Ind.: Eisenbrauns, 1992, 234–271.

Steussy, Marti J. *David: Biblical Portraits of Power*. Columbia, S.C.: University of South Carolina Press, 1999.

Trible, Phyllis. *Texts of Terror*. Philadelphia: Fortress Press, 1984.

Ulrich, Eugene Charles, Jr. *The Qumran Text of Samuel and Josephus*. Harvard Semitic Monographs 19. Chico, Calif.: Scholars Press, 1978.

Waltke, Bruce K., and Michael P. O'Connor. *An Introduction to Biblical Hebrew Syntax*. Winona Lake, Ind.: Eisenbrauns, 1990.

Weinfeld, Moshe. *Social Justice in Ancient Israel and in the Ancient Near East*. Minneapolis: Fortress Press, 1995.

LIST OF ILLUSTRATIONS

$\mathcal{A}$BOUT THE TRANSLATOR

Everett Fox holds the Allen M. Glick Chair in Judaic and Biblical Studies at Clark University in Worcester, Massachusetts. He is the translator of *The Five Books of Moses*: The Schocken Bible, Vol. 1; the author of studies on biblical narrative and its translation; and co-editor, with Lawrence Rosenwald, of *Scripture and Translation,* a collection of essays by Martin Buber and Franz Rosenzweig. He lives in Massachusetts.